Inside
High
School

The Student's World

Inside High School

The Student's World

Philip A. Cusick
Michigan State University

HOLT, RINEHART AND WINSTON, INC.
New York Chicago San Francisco Atlanta
Dallas Montreal Toronto London Sydney

Preface

This book is my attempt to describe the way a number of students behave in high school and to explain the way their behavior affects themselves, the teachers, administrators, and the entire school organization. It was undertaken with the hope of developing a clearer understanding of the way these students see and act in high school, and subsequently to develop a better understanding of why they do what they do. The information-gathering procedure was based on the assumption that any group of individuals will develop a reasonable way of behaving in their environment, and if one wishes to understand that behavior, he can do so by joining them, submitting himself to the routine, rules, and regulations that structure their world, and recording everything that goes on.

I gathered the descriptions during a six-month period in which I attended a high school daily, associated myself with some students, went to class, ate in the cafeteria, and took part in the informal classroom and corridor activity. After becoming accepted, I even joined in their out-of-school social life for the purpose of comparing what they did in school with what they did out of school. That I was thirty-two years old and had been a teacher and administrator for a number of years made little difference to the students. They were willing to accept me on the basis of my actions, and cared little for what I had done or said I had done before I knew them. That is the way with most of us. We know and trust people by the way they behave, not by their list of past accomplishments.

Although there may be no such thing as a single "representative high school," I tried to choose one that contained a number of characteristics common to many other secondary schools. It is moderately large, draws its lower- to middle-class students from small towns and rural and suburban areas, offers a comprehensive list of courses, and is organized so that teachers teach preplanned classes to groups of students during a set number of periods each day. A reader who knows anything at all about secondary schools will recognize the school and the descriptions of student activities in classes, cafeteria, and corridors, and will, I believe, be able to see similarities between the students in this school and the students he teaches or plans to teach.

The book is intended for a dual audience. First, it is written for those who plan to begin careers in public schools and who need to have some realistic appraisal of that environment and those students if they are to become successful. Secondly, it is written for those like myself, teachers and administrators, who make the business of public education their professional career. We are always in danger of becoming so immersed in our own roles in the educational world that we forget that students may see and act toward school differently from the way we do. Hopefully, this book will contribute to our understanding of the school from the students' point of view. I hope that after reading the book both groups will be encouraged to spend more time observing and interacting with students before instructing them.

In order to facilitate the narrative, I have attempted to exclude personal opinions and editorializing from the main body of the chapters. Rather, I have presented the descriptive data as I saw it, and saved the discussion questions for the summaries. I chose this approach in the hope that the data would stand by itself and that a reader, if he wished to draw his own conclusions, would be free to do so without getting confused in my personal opinions.

There are a number of individuals that I would like to thank for their assistance in this project, but to name them might endanger the anonymity of the school in which the data was gathered. I think they know who they are.

P. A. C.

Contents

CHAPTER 1

Introduction:
The Nature
of the Question

What is it like to be a high school student? . . . to enter a large building of corridors and classrooms every morning, where one is expected to be in homeroom at 8:05, English class at 9:00, then on to gym or history or perhaps home economics, math, or mechanical drawing, finally to the cafeteria where one eats his lunch with noisy and excited friends before rushing off to another class with another teacher? Or perhaps, since there is no such thing as a representative "high school student," we could ask what it is like to be any particular student. What was Horatio Gates Senior High to Jack, the captain of the football team, the most popular senior, an all-county defensive end, one who, by his own choosing, could be vice-president rather than president of the student council? Was his experience similar to that of Nick's, a small, shy boy who would volunteer to a total stranger, "You probably noticed I'm not too popular around here. I don't have many friends." Or consider Jean, the highest achieving student in the school, number one in her class for three years, one who, in her junior year, was awarded a national merit scholarship and accepted at a prestigious college. Was the school in which she spent her time the same school from which her classmate Ken skipped fifty-eight days in one year because he had no friends? Or Tony, the personable and accomplished senior class president, did he see the school as did Bill, who spent his days hanging around the halls and his evenings stealing from cars?

Do any of us who presume to understand, work in, and make decisions about high schools have any basic understanding or any feeling for what students see or think about when they look at their school and their relationship to that school? Despite the vast body of literature on high school students, the answer to the question is probably "No." There is actually very little that gives us any feeling for the way high school students actually deal with their classes, teachers, desks, assignments, books, papers, rules, and regulations. Nor do we have satisfactory answers to a host of related questions: How do students regard their role of "student"? What parts of the school are important to them? Why do they choose to ignore other parts? What accommodation do they work out with the rules and regulations which confront them? What, after all, are they really learning?

While the complexity of the total school situation makes such questions difficult to answer, all students must, in a sense, think something of school and their relation to school. Most attend class, fulfill requirements, take part in some school-sponsored events or activities, and, in general, deal with the school in a fairly reasonable and orderly fashion. Even those few who are less compliant with the organization's demands, who consistently skip classes, ignore assignments, and become familiar sights in the vice-principal's office, must have developed some ordered understanding of their relationship to the school which they consistently defy. After all, if one is to make any sense of his daily routine, he cannot behave in a completely random fashion, but must develop a patterned, and fairly consistent way of dealing with his situation.

What we are actually looking for is more complicated then simply an attitude or description of behavior. Essentially, what we want is an explanation of the students' "perspective" which Tamotsu Shibutani defines as "an ordered view of one's world; what is taken for granted about the attributes of various objects, events and human nature. It is an order of things remembered and expected as well as actually perceived, an organized conception of what is plausible and what is possible."[1] The term "per-

---

[1] Tamotsu Shibutani, "Reference Groups as Perspectives," in Jerome Manis and Bernard Meltzer, eds., *Symbolic Interaction* (Boston: Allyn and Bacon, 1967), p. 161.

spective" includes both actions and beliefs about those actions. It assumes that a human being is an active agent, constantly engaged in the process of constructing his social self, and that what he does depends on how he perceives himself in relation to various features of his environment. In turn, his beliefs reflect an evaluation of his actions in terms of their success or failure. It is this dynamic process of interaction between self and environment and the resulting combination of an individual's beliefs and actions in relation to that environment that the term "perspective" attempts to explain.

Implied in this concept is the assumption that a school, or indeed any social situation, may not be taken as a single, plainly discernable entity, commonly perceived and understood by all those related to it. Rather, we accept a school—or any organization—as a dynamic and multi-faceted process, the perceived nature of which varies according to both individual and collective perspectives. Certainly we may expect teachers to think of and react to school in a fashion different from students, administrators from teachers, and students from both teachers and administrators.

Therefore, this book represents an attempt to understand a single high school from the viewpoint of some of its students. More specifically, it seeks to develop a statement of the "perspective" used by those students to deal with their school. This will involve a number of elements. Since it was demonstrated that the students develop perspective in relation to their environment, Chapter 2 begins by describing as closely as possible that total school environment. Chapter 3 deals with a general description of the behavior of all students, and since the intent of this book is to detail specific student behaviors, Chapters 4, and 5 deal with students and, in general, with the way most of their activity and involvement seems to be centered around their friendship patterns. Chapter 6 then describes the actions of four isolated students who had no friends and who therefore behaved differently from the majority. In all the chapters there are many passages which raise questions for people who are interested in, or plan careers in, public schools. For the most part I have saved questions, suggested answers, and my editorializing for the chapter summaries, rather than incorporate them into the descriptive passages. I preferred to keep the narrative as unembellished and objective as possible. Chapter 7 proposes an explanation of the relationship between student perspectives and the school environment. Finally, in Chapter 8 there is some attempt to discuss all these issues as they effect the learning process in that particular secondary school.

The justification for this effort can be stated quite simply. If we are to have any understanding of what individuals make of their lives, then we have to make a genuine attempt to see and understand their world as they see and understand it. Therefore, those of us who plan to teach in or administer, understand, and make decisions about the powerful and extensive system of secondary education in America should make some rudimentary attempt to see that system as do the individual students and their friends who confront it every day. If we fail to see it as they see it, we will not understand what they do, nor ultimately, what we do.

The Method of Inquiry

A further implication of the term "perspective" is that if one is to gain a reasonable understanding of a social environment, he should study it from the viewpoint of the groups which create it. The best method with which to carry on such a study is the field method used by anthropologists, that of participant observation. The method is conceptually simple. A participant observer begins by locating himself by and making himself acceptable to those he wishes to study. While it may not be absolutely necessary for him to adopt their dress and customs, he has to begin by respecting their behavior and accepting them as reasonable human beings. Then, over an extended period of time, he makes himself familiar with their day to day lives, keeps extensive notes and records of their comments and behavioral patterns, and eventually, through reworking and studying his notes, attempts an accurate description and explanation of their behavior. He can easily check his perceptions by asking them to describe and explain a particular event or asking them to verify his perceptions for accuracy. Having consciously placed himself in that situation, he will become socialized, will become a participant in the subject group, and will to some degree take on the perspective which he is studying; that is, he will begin to develop patterns of belief and behavior similar to those of his subjects.

If this process is done consciously and explained carefully, it can add insight into a social situation. It can give the writer an awareness of what it means to gradually become one of the subjects, and thus he can more clearly explain that group's perspective against this own at various stages of his assimilation into that society. By being continually conscious of his own development, the researcher will avoid the problem of becoming so entangled in the process that he loses his objectivity. His concluding conceptual scheme must, therefore, be the one developed by the subjects, not by himself.

A general criticism of the participant observation method is that since the subjects are usually limited in number and selected by chance, the resulting data, while interesting, is not transferable to other situations. On a superficial level that might appear true. However, those of us who undertake such studies feel that men are more alike than they are different, and what is reasonable behavior for one human being in a given situation will, at least in some way, be reasonable behavior for others given the same situation. Furthermore, a good description of the behavior of individuals in any situation can be intelligible to an individual regardless of the differences between that individual and the subjects.

It is true that in this case only one school was selected and only a small number of students comprised the sample. Yet in addition to the understanding the reader can gain of the students who actually comprise the sample, it is hoped that because of this school's similarity to other schools, he can also gain a better understanding of the behavior of secondary school students in general.

Selection of the School

Having phrased the questions and selected the methodology, the problems of where to begin—which school to study and why, how to gain permission from administrators, teachers, and students, and perhaps most importantly, which students to study—all had to be dealt with in order.

The problem of access to a school was really quite simple. It is unnecessary to describe the steps taken; it is enough to say that if one presents himself as serious, genuinely interested, and neutral, there are many schools to which he would be granted access as a participant observer in the student subculture. A number of superintendents agreed that the project was basically worthwhile and said they would recommend it to their building principals and in turn to their teachers. A school was selected and the necessary permissions were granted.

The most serious question concerned the selection of students. This particular school has 1100 tenth-, eleventh-, and twelfth-grade students who were partially separated into academic, vocational, and business sequences. Of course, it would be impossible to meet, observe, and participate with all these individuals under those circumstances. However, a number of studies on school and on adolescent behavior has indicated that students subdivide themselves into small groups, and therefore it was decided to attempt entrance into a small, informal group of students and begin the study from there.[2] It was hoped that acceptance into a group would lead not only to acceptance by other students, but would provide an important experience in itself.

I then presented myself to the school and after a num-

[2] See August B. Hollingshead, *Elmtown's Youth* (New York: Wiley, 1949); C. W. Gordon, *The Social System of the High School* (New York: Free Press, 1957); and James Coleman, *The Adolescent Society* (New York: Free Press, 1962).

ber of brief introductions and explanations, met three senior boys chosen because both the vice-principal and the English chairman agreed, "He had to start somewhere." I was introduced to the three, explained that I was from the university, and that I wanted to see what school was like from the students' side. While appearing amused, they were quite friendly and agreed to guide me around for as long as I liked. And so began a six month period during which I attended school each day, went to classes, ate in the cafeteria, hung around the halls, and took part in gym and other activities. I also attended athletic events, club and council meetings, and, by the end of the second month, was regularly attending weekend activities and social events.

The issue of my acceptability to the group members and other students was much easier to accomplish than to plan. It was, after all, not my intent to become an adolescent but only to become a member of an adolescent group in school. While a youthful appearance probably helped, a firm belief that distances between people are caused more by specific role differentiation than by nature probably helped more. Taking off a former role of teacher-administrator and the suit, tie, official manner, and didactic communication pattern that went with it, and putting on and accepting the group norms, behavior, and dress, combined with an unthreatening manner, was really all that was needed. Of course acceptance by and rapport with students took time. It was not until the end of the second month that an invitation came to share an evening over some beer, but it was only a matter of a few weeks before my presence in the places where students gathered in school was viewed as natural. Throughout the study I found like W. F. Whyte in *Street Corner Society* that acceptance by the people I was studying "depended on the personal relationship I developed far more than upon any explanation I might give."[3]

[3] William F. Whyte, Street Corner Society (Chicago: University of Chicago Press, 1967), p. 300.

CHAPTER 2

Understanding
the School Environment

Most of us think of schools as places where the young go to learn how to work out their lives in a particular society. As such they are not thought of as settings for action and life, but as settings for preparation and training. However, for the students who inhabit them every day, schools are more than just training grounds. They are places where the business of life is actually being carried out, and the normal things students do there are probably done more in the name of immediate needs, expectations, and desires than in the name of unspecified future events. Of course, preparation and training do take place, but probably more as a result of what actually occurs than of what might be intended as long-range educational goals.

If one accepts this, he can best begin a study of schools and students by examining those students' daily activities. Since they, like all individuals, carry out their actions not in a vacuum but in relation to some definite situation, the logical place to begin is with an examination of the school environment. Of course, these adolescents also carry on activities in other places, and throughout the book references will be made to out-of-school activities, but this book concerns students and their high school and will, therefore, begin with the school.

The School District

Horatio Gates is the central high school of the Hillsborough-Cowpens[1] School District. Encompassing an area

[1] The proper names of people and places have been altered to insure anonymity.

of 105 square miles, the district is located near a medium-sized metropolitan area, and its 14,000 inhabitants are regarded as an integral part of that area. Within the district are three distinct towns: Hillsborough, which has a population of 6000; Cowpens, with a population of 2500; and Winnsboro, with 800 inhabitants. Hillsborough is adjacent to the metropolitan area's industrial complex; in fact, a traffic sign is the only indication that one has even left the central city. Immediately past Hillsborough the two-lane country roads begin and one must travel a number of miles before reaching either Winnsboro to the east or Cowpens to the north. Cowpens is an attractive rural town with its own churches, lodge halls, and coffee shops, while Winnsboro consists only of a cluster of houses around a few streets off a secondary road. A former canal port, Winnsboro has probably changed very little in the past one hundred years.

Generally the inhabitants of all the towns are employed in the factories, offices, and businesses of the metropolitan areas. Some are professionals, some semi-professionals or skilled craftsmen, many are laborers, a few are self-employed, and a number still run the family farm, though most of these work a night shift in one of the factories. Both Hillsborough and Cowpens were once regarded as "railroad" towns, but railroading has declined and today provides only a small percentage of the available employment.

As a legal entity the school district was formed in 1963 when the schools of Hillsborough and Cowpens consolidated. Winnsboro, which formerly had its own elementary school, was already sending its high school students to Hillsborough. Presently the district has five elementary schools, grades K–5 with a total of 3000 pupils; one middle school, grades 6–9 with a total of 1800 pupils; and one consolidated high school, grades 10–12 with an enrollment of 1100. Following the practice of other districts which were encouraged by the state to consolidate, the elementary schools remained in the same neighborhood and served the same families, while the middle school and the high school were planned and constructed in centralized areas with students bussed to them from the entire district.

The budget for the district is $7,257,000, which means that approximately $1230 is spent per year per child, an expenditure which compares favorably with similar districts throughout the state. Of this amount, 50 percent is collected in property taxes while the remainder comes from state support. The district is administered by a superintendent, business manager, personnel manager, assistant superintendent for curriculum, and a director of secondary education, all of whom share a central office complex in Hillsborough. Governing the operation of the entire school district are the eleven members of the popularly elected Board of Education.

The School

Horatio Gates Senior High School is located on a large tract of land between Hillsborough and Cowpens. It is a modern, well-equipped building completed in 1965 at a cost of $4,500,000. In front of the school is a large well-kept lawn; to the south, the teachers' parking lot; to the north, the students' parking lot; to the rear, the athletic area dominated by the bleachers on either side of the football field. The area immediately surrounding the property is taken up by farm land, some of which is presently being transformed into building lots.

Figure 1 shows a floor plan of the school which is a single story structure planned to house various interest areas and academic disciplines in different wings. Administrative and guidance offices are in the A wing, English and social studies in the B wing, industrial arts in the C wing, sciences in the D wing, and physical education in the F wing. At the center is the library which includes a main reading room which is 30 $\times$ 85 feet and carpeted, one conference and three listening rooms, an office, special workroom, 10,000 volumes, and a collection of periodicals. In addition to the walls of bookcases, the furnishings include a check-out counter, card catalog file, a number of tables and chairs, and two metal bookracks containing a small paperback collection.

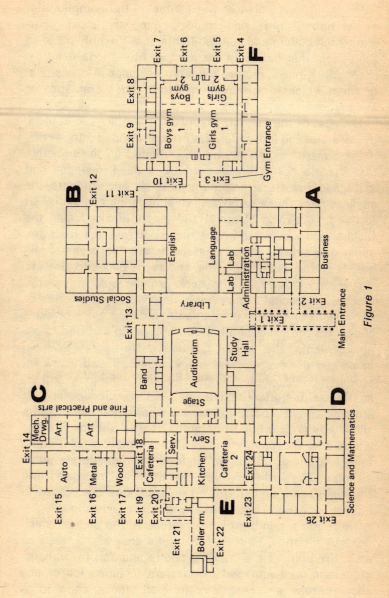

Figure 1

The auditorium, also at the center of the complex, deserves note. With its padded seats, expensive looking curtains, high ceiling and colored lights, it is the only place in the school that indicates extra expenditure. It is used for assemblies, plays, picture taking, other special occasions, or when a class or group wishes to practice dramatics or singing.

The rest of the school, except for the offices, cafeteria, gymnasium, and industrial arts area, is divided into rectangular classrooms. These are all arranged on the principle that the teacher is the one who has the knowledge and skills and, therefore, has the front desk; and students, the seekers after these same sets of knowledge and skills, sit in five or six rows of metal and plastic desks facing the teacher and waiting to be instructed. Across the front and along one side of these classrooms are the green chalkboards and/or bulletin boards, and at the opposite side are a row of windows. In the back are the closets for the teacher's personal things and a simply designed series of book cases or shelves used to store old magazines or extra books. On the walls and bulletin boards, in addition to announcements, the school calendar advertising the local bank, and the ever-present clock, may be found a few instructional aid posters, one showing a famous author, another a historical event, or in the science lab, an atomic weight chart. Otherwise the cinderblock walls show only their green or beige paint. The tile paved halls, which take up roughly one-fifth of the plant's total cubic feet, are clean, broad, well-lighted and completely unobstructed. The lockers which line them are recessed into the walls, and even the drinking fountains are placed in niches to avoid breaking the long, clean even lines.

There are a number of other areas in the school which deserve mention. First is the athletic area which takes up an entire wing of the building and in addition to its handsome and well-equipped gymnasium includes locker and shower areas, an exercise room, staff offices, and a large storage area. In another wing are the shops, one for auto mechanics, one for woodworking, and a third used for both ceramics and printing. In addition to the workshops, there are classrooms where the industrial arts teachers may take the students for study and book work to support their more practical experiences. The school's other important feature is the large group instruction room. It is theatre-shaped, complete with a small stage and projection booth, and designed to hold about one hundred students. All of the school's separate areas reflect the same air of functional, well-maintained, unpretentious severity, and there is little danger of mistaking the building for anything but the modern American high school built to serve good, sensible education to many people at a moderate cost.

The Organization of the School

In order to understand a social institution, one must consider the assumptions upon which it is based, and in the case of a school this will involve a brief consideration of the goals of education. Many attempts have been made to isolate these goals, but those presented by the National Education Association seem to encompass most of them. That organization's Educational Policies Committee suggested that the basic goals of education are: (1) self-realization, (2) human relationship, (3) economic efficiency, and (4) civic responsibility.[2] These are obviously interrelated; that is, one achieves self-realization by developing satisfying human relationships, contributing economically to his own and society's welfare, and becoming a responsible member of the nation. The school's justification for existence is that it can continually identify and articulate a specific body of knowledge, skills, and behavioral patterns, and as students learn these in the prescribed manner, so they will become able to fulfill the stated goals.

There may be a number of ways to transmit knowledge, but generally public schools are organized vertically. That is, it is assumed that those staff members who possess the needed knowledge, skills, and behavioral patterns are the

[2] National Education Association, Educational Policies Commission, *Policies for Education in American Democracy*, 1946, pp. 185–253, quoted in Chris A. Deyoung, *Introduction to American Public Education*, 3d ed. (New York: McGraw Hill, 1955), p. 411.

superordinates; the students, seekers after these items, are the subordinates. The learning takes place as the knowledge, skills, and behavioral patterns are transmitted vertically from above to below, teacher to student. The implied assumption, of course, is that the passing on is best done by the teacher as he actually directs or tells the students what to do and what to know. As the students listen and do, so they presumably learn; the correlation between listening and doing on one hand and learning on the other is assumed to be practically perfect.

At Horatio Gates, as in most other secondary schools, this vertical organization takes the following form. At the top is the principal who is responsible for the entire building and all the activities therein. He is answerable to the superintendent of schools, but visits by the superintendent are few and most school business is carried on inside the building. The principal is directly assisted by a vice-principal who is primarily concerned with student affairs. This vice-principal handles discipline, students' personal problems, and student functions, such as dances, school sponsored events, and other extracurricular activities. In addition, he assumes some responsibility for supervising teachers.

The teaching staff of the school is divided among a series of subject matter departments, that is, English, social studies, language, mathematics, shop, physical education, and so forth. Each speciality has a number of assigned teachers ranging from one in speech to fourteen in social studies. Nine of these departments are large enough to warrant the appointment of a teaching-chairman who is generally responsible for assisting the principal in hiring, assigning, and supervising teachers, coordinating the testing program, and maintaining continuity between the various levels of instruction in his area. Because of their additional responsibility, teaching-chairmen are given a slightly reduced teaching load and slightly more money. Beyond that, teachers are regarded as equal and each is assigned to teach a specific number of students during prearranged periods each day.

Equal to the teachers in the organization are the professionals who work in pupil personnel services. These include one full-time vocational counselor who assists students in their college and job placements, four full-time guidance counselors, and a number of staff members who share their time with the other district schools. These include nurses, school psychologists, and a social worker.

Additional school personnel should be mentioned because it will give one an appreciation of the complexity of the organization. To maintain the building and support the organization, there are a total of seventeen full- and part-time people on the janitorial staff, nineteen on the cafeteria staff, and six clerical workers. Thus, in addition to those engaged directly or indirectly in the transmission of subject matter, there are an additional forty-two school employees. And, if course, a number of people assist while seldom setting foot in the building; such as, the bus drivers and mechanics, and the central office staff.

Directly subordinate to the administrative and professional staff are the students, 1100 tenth, eleventh, and twelfth graders, all engaged in taking a series of courses leading to high school graduation. These students are undifferentiated within the formal organization. There are class designations, sophomore, junior, and senior, but the highest level senior for instance, the valedictorian of the class, is still subject to any teacher and any administrator and officially has only the rights or privileges given to a first year student. Thus, during the three years they are progressing toward graduation, all are regarded by the formal organization as being equally at the bottom of the vertically arranged hierarchy and virtually without the content knowledge of the curriculum which is deemed necessary to achieve the stated educational goals.

The Curriculum

The physical plant and the organization provide the setting within which the school program or curriculum is carried out. As in most public secondary schools, the curriculum at Horatio Gates is divided into subject areas and these are further fragmented into courses. Every student then is required to complete a specified number of courses within predetermined areas for each of his years in the institution.

Of course, diversity among students is recognized and the program provides for variety. Students select courses among three loosely defined study sequences. Those who will presumably go on to college choose the "general college" or "academic" sequence, those who wish to train as secretaries, bookkeepers, or clerks choose the "business" sequence, and those who upon graduation hope to enter the factories, crafts, or trades may choose "industrial arts." Thus, within the curriculum, students are expected to select courses which fit into some pattern and which are presumed reasonable given his future plans.

It is important to note that while students are sometimes grouped according to their sequence, because of the courses which all are required to take and of the elective system whereby a student may fill out his program by taking courses outside his sequence, there is a great deal of crossing over and mixing of students throughout the day. Students from all sequences are together in the English and social studies classes, and many students in the college sequence choose industrial arts or home economics for their electives. Therefore, students are not strictly designated as being academic or vocational, advanced or remedial, fast or slow.

All students earn five or six of the state-required eighteen units in their ninth year at the middle school. During their three years at Horatio Gates they must complete the remaining units of credit to earn a diploma. As the separate courses are combined into sequences, it is assumed that the student will internalize and assimilate these subjects into an integrated whole and will become capable of fulfilling the personal and social goals of education.

In order to determine whether a student has successfully completed the course requirements, the teachers depend on a system of numerical grades which represent student achievement in each class. The grade is a composite mark, two-thirds of which is based upon classwork and one-third upon tests. The classwork includes homework, consisting of written assignments and preparation for oral participation and actual class participation; the tests include weekly or monthly quizzes and final exams. The lowest passing grade is sixty-five percent and report cards are graded and distributed to students six times a year.

While this standard program is generally accepted, there is some effort at Horatio Gates to alter it. The most recent innovation is the humanities program. A product of the English and social studies departments, it was designed to encourage seniors to pursue independent study with a minimum of teacher direction. The program is offered for twelve periods a week and students may substitute it for English, social studies, and one elective. Open to all seniors, the program has four teachers, one each for English, social studies, music, and speech. Three days a week, the entire class of 112 meet in the large group instruction room and then, depending on the planned activity, either stay together or break into smaller interest groups with a teacher being assigned to each group.

As the school program is fragmented into a series of courses and separate activities, so the school day is fragmented into a set number of periods. There are seven of these, each lasting forty minutes. In addition there is a brief homeroom period in the morning and another following lunch, during which teachers take attendance and make announcements. Between each period there is a five minute interval for the students to get to their next area, so every forty minutes the entire population of the school picks up and moves somewhere else to begin a different activity. No one finds this odd. Since the school is divided into rectangular rooms and the curriculum into clearly delineated fragments, it is only logical that the day should be similarly divided to create an integrated whole. In sum, the building, the organizational structure, and the day are all carefully structured to facilitate the process of the teacher passing on his particular speciality to batches of students.

The extensive activity-athletic program is also regarded as an integral part of the school's curriculum. Included among these activities are: Student Council, Honor Society, Yearbook, Drama Club, Chess Club, Future Teachers, Business Club, Ski Club, Library Club, Bowling Club, and a large number of musical groups: large band, small band, marching band, drum and bugle corp, boys' chorus, senior chorus, girls' chorus, glee club, and so on. These organizations are active to varying degrees. Some seem to exist only in name, while others, the yearbook for instance, demand a great deal of time and commitment from those involved. And, of course, there is the very important athletic program. The school competes extramurally in football, soccer, basketball, wrestling, and baseball on the varsity, junior varsity, and freshman level. It also fields competing teams in gymnastics and lacrosse; has an extensive program for girls in the areas of field hockey, volleyball, gymnastics, and basketball; and in addition has a large on-going intramural sports program. In competition with a number of other suburban schools in the county, Horatio Gates usually does well in wrestling and lacrosse, poorly in basketball, track, and football. Recently, however, the new coach has been able to develop a better football team and the prospects for the county championship are improving.

The Organization and Its Subsystems

A complex organization like Horatio Gates High has within it a number of separate subsystems, two of which, production and maintenance, will be discussed here. The distinctions between the two will be helpful in later chapters when the different behavioral patterns carried on by students are explained.

We may think of an organizational subsystem as simply an integrated pattern of organization behaviors. For instance, under the heading of "production subsystem" we might include everything that is directly designed to assist in the transmission of knowledge, skills, and behavioral patterns; the specialized teaching tasks of the instructors, the set timed periods, the division of the curriculum into specialized areas, the further division of areas into courses, the testing and evaluating that constantly take place, and, of course, the actual learning. Combined and integrated these patterns of activity constitute the school's productive subsystem.

Secondary to the production subsystem is the "maintenance subsystem" which is primarily designed to support and reinforce various productive activities. This subsystem is generally administered by the vice-principal and includes the bodies of rules and regulations concerning attendance, tardiness, driving, smoking, the pass system, cafeteria, bus, and study hall conduct, use of lockers and telephones, and the care of school property. These are listed in the student handbook where there are eighteen pages devoted to do's and don't's, the majority of which admonish students to be in attendance, be on time, be orderly, obey the administrators, teachers, cafeteria workers, bus drivers, keep themselves and their school neat, and not to violate the rules of the pass system.

The single most important element of this maintenance activity is the pass system which is based on the premise that a student should be supervised at all times during the day. When he is in the classroom or cafeteria he is obviously under proper supervision, but if he leaves the room at any other than the five minute class changing times, he is supposed to have a pass stating where he is going, at what time he left, and signed by the teacher. Distributing, checking, and collecting passes takes an enormous amount of time and effort by both teachers and administrators.

While the production and maintenance subsystems are conceptually easy to identify, the former concerned with the transmission of knowledge and skills and the latter with the preservation and smooth running of the organization, in an actual situation they may be difficult to separate. For instance, the vice-principal lecturing on promptness is exercising a maintenance function in support of the school's production process. He is also teaching socially desirable behavioral patterns and is, therefore, engaged in productive activities.

Administrators and Teachers

In addition to the physical plant and organization, there are other important elements in the school. First among these is the manner in which the administrators and teachers perform their daily tasks. The principal's job is extremely complex, far more so than his previous position as football coach. Mr. Vincent is not only in charge of Horatio Gates, but is directly responsible for the ninth grade of the middle school in Cowpens. He spends at least one day a week in that school and once remarked that his problems there were equal to his problems at Horatio Gates. Because he is responsible for these schools means some of his time is spent with the superintendent and central office staff, so he is frequently absent from the school. Mr. Vincent is a practical administrator who seemed to genuinely like adolescents. Once I told him that the school seemed to be relatively trouble-free. "You don't seem to have any discipline problems."

"Oh, yeah, we have problems like skipping classes and smoking. They're discipline problems."

"But, you don't see any kids giving teachers a hard time like in many schools."

"Oh, that. Well, one thing we won't tolerate in this place is lip. We've worked hard on that for three or four years and now it's pretty good. All in all they're pretty good kids. But like smoking, one day soon we'll crack down on that. We know that there is a lot of smoking in the john. I and the vice-principal have both talked to thirty or forty of those who smoke and they know that soon we'll be suspending them. We suspend them for a while, just seven or eight, and the word filters down."

"How long do you suspend them for?"

"Oh, just till their parents come in. You'd be surprised how soon their parents come when their boy has been thrown out of school. As soon as they do, we talk and the kid comes back. Also, a lot of these parents don't know their kids smoke and are really glad we notified them."

Except for particular occasions such as suspension, Mr. Vincent actually had limited contact with students. When they were in the office, it was the vice-principal or the guidance counselors they came to see. When they were in classes, they were with teachers. From the contact he had with them, however, he seemed to have little trouble accepting their behavior and, in turn, the few remarks made by students indicated they were favorably disposed toward him. However, he frequently expressed concern that many merely come to school and "hang around with each other," admitted that school never touched many of them, "Especially the nonacademic kids," and worried about how much they actually learned in school.

Also, he strongly believed that the school had to adjust the structure to allow for the increased demand for student freedom. At this time (his third year in the office) he was working hard to change from the strict authoritarian role he had previously taken to one which was more relaxed and open. An important innovation which he encouraged was the senior lounge, a classroom set aside for seniors who wished to go there at noon or from study hall. The room was furnished with couches, soft chairs, card tables, a coke machine, and, after the middle of the year, a ping-pong table and television set were added. He believed in giving students more personal responsibility and hoped that the lounge and a more relaxed atmosphere would encourage them to be more positive about school.

Administrative actions aimed at increasing the students' interest in school may or may not have been successful with students, but they definitely compounded Mr. Vincent's problems with teachers. While careful to select a few teachers for praise, he frequently complained about the general lack of interest they showed in students. "They all want to be subject matter specialists, they're not concerned about whether the kids are getting the lecture, it's just the lecture that counts." And he cited, "inability to relate to the kids," as the reason for firing a teacher the previous year. "She knew her field, but that's not enough."

Other times he would speak of the teachers' unwillingness to involve themselves with students or to give them the personal consideration and attention he thought was necessary. Citing instances of teachers who would walk by trouble in the halls only to complain about the lack of discipline in the school, he said, "Then they complain to me, but they don't want to do anything. They're always complaining about all the freedom the kids have. They want freedom, but just you give some to the kids and watch those teachers bitch. They're not ready for giving the kids any freedom at all." He was also bitter toward a number of teachers, among them the teacher association representatives, who constantly sent students to the office for petty infractions that, according to him, should have been handled in the classroom. He particularly resented what he considered the teachers' inability or unwillingness to deal effectively with nonacademic students. "That's what I worry about—the nonacademic kids . . . How do we get to them? The teachers don't even want to try."

Hoping that things would improve if he included teachers in the school's decision making process, he set up a teachers' advisory council to deal with everything that went on in the school. But his attempt to involve them, apparently at their own request, was also frustrating. "Now that they're involved, they're finding out that it's a lot of work. They don't want the trouble of making decisions, they want someone to do it for 'em. I have been having trouble getting them to work on their committees. Like the library committee."

"What do the committees do?" I asked.

"Oh, it's part of the democratic process," he smiled. "Teachers get a big voice in running the school."

But his enthusiasm for the change was low. When he finished talking about the teachers' unwillingness to take responsibility, he seemed to relish the possibility of taking the burden back on himself. "Pretty soon, I'm going to do it for them."

These changes did not come easily for Mr. Vincent. He admitted that he was having trouble giving teachers more responsibility and freedom. "This is hard for me. I've been an administrator for eight years. Now I've got to change and get more democratic. Maybe I'm too far behind."

And his comments frequently reflected his concern over the school's public relations. He purposively encouraged activities that would "bring the kids together," and hoped that the people would more strongly support what the school was trying to do. This was certainly an important administrative issue in a district that served three distinct villages.

The vice-principal, Mr. Rossi, was very proud of his success as a former classroom music teacher in that district. He was reputed to have started the whole series of successful musical groups in the high school that had earned the school a county-wide reputation. He now has two roles: first, dealing directly with students, and secondly, supervising teachers. He shared the principal's views of teachers.

They got a new toy now, collective negotiations, that's their new toy. When that thing first came out I was teaching music and they came to me and told me I would have to stop all the extra activities I had going. You know why? Because I wasn't getting paid for it. I told them, "Bullshit." Now they want and get five periods, planning time, meetings, everything, but they don't pay any attention to the kids.

Citing an instance in the Cowpens school where teachers asked their administrators to stay out of their teachers' room, Mr. Rossi said, "Oh, you wait till they do that to me. You know what I do since that happened? I go in there every period. Just let one of them say to me that I should stay out. I'll lock the place; I'll give 'em the broom closet for their teachers' room." Rossi's animosity toward the teachers' organization was reputed to be a source of trouble among the staff. The district personnel manager reported that on one occasion, "Rossi was arguing with the head of that organization and he mentioned the teachers' contract. 'Contract? Contract? What contract?' said Rossi, holding the document up. 'You mean this piece of shit?' And he threw it in the basket."

Rossi frequently accused a number of teachers of being overly interested in their subject and of regarding students as "pleasant dummies." "We got one guy, you know what he told me when I asked him to do something one day? He said, 'I'm here to be a *scholar in residence*, not to supervise the cafeteria.' Honest to God. That's what he said, 'A scholar in residence!' "

He accused them of being too intellectual, too aloof, poor disciplinarians, and unwilling to take responsibility for students outside the class. Rossi knew that teachers wanted him to be tougher on the students. "Four-fifths of the teachers hate me because I'm too tough on them and too lenient on the kids. But the kids are in school to learn, not to be thrown out. You don't have a problem until you try to solve it. Any dummy can throw kids out, but I try to solve their problem." While Vincent shared Rossi's view of many teachers, the animosity between Rossi and the teachers did not make running the school easy. Of Rossi, Mr. Vincent remarked, "That bird's real good with the kids, but I wish he'd stop aggravating the teachers."

Rossi saw himself as the students' advocate. He was proud of his efforts toward bringing about the senior lounge and did not allow the additional conflict between him and the teachers, who said the students spent too much time there, to force its closing. When at student meetings he exorted students to keep the lounge clean, his reason was not that the lounge was really dirty. Privately he admitted, "It's not really that bad, but the teachers are always after me. They blame the lounge for the kids being in the halls."

When a dance was being planned, Mr. Rossi would be sure that a good band was hired at a reasonable cost. When the bonfire rally was being planned, he borrowed a payloader from a local contractor. When a group of students wanted to go somewhere, he made the arrangements. When it was time to buy class rings, he obtained reasonable rates. He regarded himself as a fair person primarily interested in the students and saw no conflict between these actions and his disciplinarian role. He seemed to be well-liked by students. When, as frequently happened, he went into a class or the lounge to get some one who, although in the building, had been absent from the previous class, the malfactor always went with "the man." Indeed, there was little reason not to. A talking to, an implied threat of suspension, and an appeal to one's sense of justice were the outcome. Occasionally a student would be placed on detention for two or three days, but only once in six months did an actual suspension come about. Never was there any physical violence.

While acting as their advocate, Rossi also took pains to shield students from conflict with teachers or other administrators. A constant bother in the school was lavatory smoking, and the student council was working for a separate student smoking area. Mr. Rossi suggested they drop their demand, since the Board of Education would never approve it, and he would unofficially tell the staff to avoid checking two lavatories (one for the boys and one for the girls) where students could then smoke. While the council leaders refused and took the matter to the board, they agreed that Rossi's proposal was fair and was made in their interest.

While publicly Rossi frequently berated students for not being enthused about school, he privately admitted that they were "work minded." "High School's only two years long, after that it's a car, a girl, a job, that takes up their life."

In general, both administrators shared the concern over a lack of rapport between the teachers and the students, and accused the teachers' organization of adding to the division. Both men expressed strong opinions that most teachers were more interested in their "subject" rather than the students, that they were too "intellectual," and both expressed preference for those few teachers whom they described as "oriented to the kids." Neither man had any negative comments to make about the students.

The Teachers

Teachers are hired on the basis of their subject matter speciality and presumed ability to teach. Their primary duty is to pass on to students the knowledge, skills, and behavioral patterns considered important. The breakdown into departments, the progression from English I to English IV, or general science to physics, the day with its seven time periods, and the program with its sequences, all support and reinforce the idea of subject matter speciality. Even the physical setting, which keeps the science teachers in one wing and the industrial arts teachers in another, and places one seat at the front for the teacher and twenty-five facing it for the students, all contribute to subject matter speciality and a vertically arranged organization.

The teachers' behavior in class is largely in keeping with their role as experts. They set up their class as dyadic interactions, they on one side and the students on the other. They then lecture, question, call on students to answer, pass out assignments, ask the students to read a passage or paragraph, and then criticize and discuss their responses. Point by point, line by line, page by page, they pass on those pieces of knowledge that they consider important to that particular speciality. In the structure there is little room for either speculation or reflection. If a student fails to answer within a few seconds, another student will be called on. If he gives an incorrect answer, the right one will be quickly pointed out by the teacher or someone designated by the teacher. Occasionally a "discussion" will take place, but these are more often cases of the teacher manipulating students' remarks and responses to illustrate his planned conclusion. For instance, an English teacher discussing a story by Hawthorne:

"Now class, what does the name Young Goodman Brown tell us? That he was young, right? Correct? Well, say something. Also that he was apparently good, right? Of course, didn't you read the story? How many read the story? Honestly!"

Or a social studies teacher doing an exercise from the psychology book. "Now then, how did you feel during the first exercise when you couldn't ask questions? Mr. N., did you feel . . . well, how did you feel?"

"Confused."

"Sure, confused, he felt confused. Did you also feel frustrated?"

The teacher seemed to want the boy to say frustrated and when he did not, the teacher said it for him.

Or another teacher trying to teach a point about motivation.

"You work, right? Sure you do. I know. I had a job when I was in school. Now, why do you work? So you can have money, right? Sure, if that blouse cost $1.95, at least you can say that although you didn't pay much, at least you bought it with your own money, right? Sure. It gives you a sense of . . . I mean, buying your own clothes gives you a sense of . . . What's it give you a sense of? A sense of inde . . ."

A volunteer says, "pendence."

"Right! It gives you a sense of indePENDENCE, and that is one source of motivation. RIGHT?"

There were many classes in which discussions were carried out with some skill, but even there this technique of manipulating each student's response to fit into a pre-arranged pattern was used. The problem is that often responses that do not fit into the teacher's framework are ignored. In psychology class during a discussion of rewards and punishments, the teacher asked, "What do you do when you're babysitting and the kid won't drink his milk? Do you reward him or punish him?"

"Neither, I try to reason with him," replied a girl. The remark was passed over.

Students are, of course, aware of this and on occasion express their awareness. On a discussion of law enforcement a teacher asked, "Why don't you speed down Winnsboro Road?"

"Because I'll get caught," said the student.

"Why do you say that?"

"Because it's the answer you want." That reply, too, was ignored.

Students' personal remarks, even when they fit into the general prearranged pattern, also are ignored. The teacher was trying to begin a discussion of a story by Willa Cather when Robert spoke up loudly: "Hey, I read the story."

"Please, Robert."

"But this is the first story I read in two years."

"Well, welcome to the club," replied the teacher and went on.

Exceptions do occur, especially in classes where the students are divided into work units and carry out some prearranged experiment or project in cooperation with one another. There the teacher carries on his instruction by walking around, interacting with the encouraging one group at a time. But these are classes such as physics or chemistry labs where the lab manuals and texts lay out the step by step process to be followed, and there too the methods are structured and the answers set. It is not enough just to say simply that there were good and bad classes, good and bad teachers. The fact was that the teaching in all classes, science, math, English, language, was remarkably similar. The teacher would take care of his basic maintenance activity: take attendance, close the door, accept late slips, take out his book, and call the page number; then he would structure the activity by acting out the part of questioner, encourager, teller, and explicator, doing, of course, most of what there was to do while the students watched, waited, and responded to his cues. This was the way classes were conducted day in and day out.

Subject matter speciality also enabled teachers to withhold their personal involvement from the class. For instance, when in a class debate on religion the teacher was asked to state his views, his response was that he did not think either side had a good command of the facts and recommended that they spend more time in the library. Or another teacher, when asked about his political views, referred the questioner to a particular American history teacher who "knows more about it." Of course, not allowing the structured material to get sidetracked by questions or responses of a more personal nature prevented the teacher from commiting himself to classroom interactions. For instance, while they would encourage discussions of the Vietnam conflict, one seldom heard a teacher say whether he approved or disapproved of any particular aspect of the war.

There were exceptions, and it is only fair to cite them. One teacher in particular consistently made reference to his war record, his political experience, and his own boyhood. While to the author he seemed to be doing little actual instructing, the students liked him because he brought himself into the class. But, in general, the behavior of teachers was that of subject-matter-specialists, and student-teacher interactions in and out of class were made on a didactic, seldom on a personal basis. Even the teacher cited as an exception would eventually lead his personal stories to the texts.

Since they are also responsible for the general student behavior, teachers spend a great deal of time checking excuses and passes, asking students where they are going or why, telling them to sit up and pay attention, open their books, hand in their homework, or stop talking. This type of activity seems to take up a tremendous amount of the teacher's classroom time, frequently as much as ten or fifteen minutes out of a single period. This is probably the way the teachers interpreted the admonitions of both administrators to be more concerned with discipline and behavior and, of course, the administrators wanted teachers to take responsibility for them.

While, as indicated, most of the teachers avoided student contact in class unless it was subject matter oriented, they did seem to like the students and the students seemed to like and respect them. A very few even made a point of spending their free time with students rather than in the teachers' lounge or the faculty workroom. These could be seen with the same few each day and from all appearances, those interactions seemed friendly and personal. Most, however, maintained the distance between themselves and students both in and out of class. While in the halls, teachers had a way of looking as though they were going somewhere; that is, they walked with purpose and gave little attention to the students who were literally swarming around. Following lunch there would always be a large crowd of seniors in front of the lounge. When teachers passed on the way to their faculty room, they stayed against the wall and never initiated any contact with the students. Presumably some of these were the same ones who pressed to have the lounge closed, but they never voiced objections there. The seriousness of their expressions indicated that they had no time to stop and talk. This probably reinforced their subject-matter-expert role and helped to maintain the distance between them and the students, which they probably felt was essential given the role they had to take in the classroom.

The teachers seemed to feel that the backgrounds of the students were generally poor. A number reported that the kids came from "working class homes" where there was no appreciation of learning. Mr. W. reported, "Many of the kids come from homes where both the mother and the father work, and maybe they work at the discount house until 12:00; then they deserve a couple of hours off so they head for the local gin mill, and they come home at 2:00; and in the morning, the kids get up early and go and the parents seldom get to see them."

Also, many seemed to think little of the intellectual ability of the students. They were quick to tell of the students' low reading scores, reputed to be an average of two years behind grade level: "And we don't have a reading teacher. Can you believe that?" Many cited the students' poor academic performance, preference for "jungle music," and firmly believed that the local community college was the limit of most students' ambition. Even in class a teacher, within earshot of students, would remark, "These aren't my best students, you know. Now, if you come in fifth period, you'll see better work." Some teachers openly wished for the more peaceful past when students were presumably more orderly. One remarked disparagingly, "We don't teach behavior, we should . . . but we don't anymore."

Frequently they would compare their district, rather unfavorably, to an adjoining district where seventy-five percent of the students attend college as opposed to forty percent in Hillsborough-Cowpens. One teacher recalled with disgust the football rally at which, "The whole student body stood up and cheered the captain of the football team for *five minutes!* And I know that *Kid*! He can't even *Read*! But that's the way this place is."

But there is a danger of over-generalizing about the teachers' attitude toward students. A former vice-principal,

presently the personnel manager of the district, pointed
out what most teachers thought of kids,

> That they're stupid. Haven't you seen that? No, let me
> take that back. Some of them treat the kids that way, but
> then I notice less of it as the years go on. Today you
> would hear a teacher in a faculty meeting say something
> like, "Let's face it, these kids we have aren't that good.
> Let's prepare them for something they're capable of."
> And then you would hear another teacher say that that
> attitude was wrong. "That the kids are capable of just
> about anything."

When asked which view prevailed, he replied, "That's
hard to say. I guess it depends on the conviction that the
teacher has when he or she comes in. If they've got the
attitude that the kids are essentially good and capable of
learning, then they will probably be the teachers who fight
the attitude of kids being essentially stupid!" Rossi and
Vincent, however, did not see the split. They agreed,
"Teachers think the kids are stupid," or "Teachers regard
the kids as pleasant dummies."

The issue of the teachers' attitude toware students was
further confused by tension within the teachers' ranks concerning teacher-administrator relations. On one hand,
there were those teachers referred to as the "mafia," who
side with the administrators, on the other hand, were those
whose interests center on their organization, termed by
Rossi the "airdales," presumably because they "sniff out"
issues for contract disputes. The association teachers were
unhappy about the cuts in the previous year's budget
which had eliminated a number of positions. They also
felt that the administrators were largely unsympathetic to
their demands and stated that it was a difficult school in
which to teach. The head of the humanities program, an
association representative, reported:

> But when we try to do something it doesn't go any-
> where. Like the humanities program, they don't support
> it. The other day we went to the superintendent and he
> told us to spend money. But today we find out that the
> books we ordered for the musical have to be sent back.

Why? Because the purchase order wasn't signed by his office. So he's telling us one thing and telling the administrators something else.

There is $2500 to be spent on curriculum this year. I put in two proposals, one in September and I never heard anything about it. And about a month ago someone says, "Why aren't the department chairmen doing anything in line of proposals?" So, I reapply and Vincent sends it back because he doesn't like it.

He added that the administrators "hated the humanities program because it upsets their schedule." It was said that this contributed to low morale among teachers, one of whom reported, "This school is in sad shape." All four teachers in the humanities program reported that the administration was hostile to their efforts. They were right. Both the principal and the vice-principal said that they thought it was "unstructured" and "ill-planned" and said that it "would change" in the future. Privately Vincent said he was looking outside the school for a teacher who could come in and set up a "real humanities program."

Other teachers frequently complained because they felt that the office was not backing their efforts and cited as proof instances in which they were not supported in their efforts to discipline students. Rossi's attitude toward this type of complaint was clear. "This one teacher, he brings in a kid to the office and says, 'He's late for class.' But when I looked into it I found that the kid had been late for the previous fourteen days in a row! Now I ask you, why didn't that teacher take care of the kid the first time?"

While this split between some teachers and administrators certainly existed and could have acted as a strong force somewhere in the organization, it should not be overplayed in this book about students. After all, the information about it was not gathered systematically or intentionally by participation, observation, or interviewing. It was picked up in unstructured conversations with staff members which, while undertaken to discuss the students, often wound up in discussions of other staff members. The primary insight may be that a number of staff members were more willing to discuss the internal politics of the institution than they were to talk about students.

These controversies rarely showed up in the classrooms or corridors in front of students. In fact, only once or twice in humanities class was any reference made to the fact that the administrators were hostile toward the program, and if the students had any awareness of what the teacher was even talking about, they made no mention of it there or anywhere else. Those things just never seemed to be part of the students' consciousness.

Indeed, there is little reason that they should have been. As previously explained, the teachers consistently present themselves to the students as subject matter specialists; the English teacher spoke only of English, the coach of competition, the physics teacher of experiments, the French teacher of France and verbs, the vice-principal of the virtues of promptness and order. Teachers' personal problems, conflicts, and emotional issues of any sort were thus sublimated and never displayed for the students' scrutiny. In fact, the outward appearance and demeanor of the teachers could best be described as bland.

An issue which could have been responsible for both the rather conservative climate in the school and the divisions among teachers may have been the general perceptions held by the teachers of the community. Many teachers, although they were long-time residents of the district, openly said that the inhabitants did not really support the idea of education, that the students' working-class parents were at best high school graduates who did not really think their children should go much beyond that, and further that parents would not be willing to support anything remotely "innovative" in their school. No measure was taken of the community to see if these perceptions were based on fact, but they were certainly shared by staff members at all levels. Even the new superintendent who was Jewish expressed surprise that he had even been hired in Hillsborough-Cowpens, a school district he considered "tough" and "blue-collared." He, however, was most dismayed that the staff was not attempting to raise the students' level of aspiration. He wanted the teachers to spend more time on intellectual issues, to get the students to read more, to score higher on competitive tests, and to move students toward applying to better colleges.

But efforts toward these ends were not common and were somewhat discouraged. One incident occurred the previous year in which a teacher, Mrs. J., who sponsored the publication of a student literary magazine, was asked to resign. While the magazine was not cited as the main reason, it certainly did not help her. According to the vice-principal she was too interested in the bright kids and inconsiderate of the average kids:

> A little girl came to me. This kid is a Seventh Day Adventist. I had this kid in band and she came in one day. And she was smart, real smart, but she was uptight because of the religious thing. She had this paper from J.'s class. It was an essay; it was marked 70. Now, I'm no literary scholar, but I can read. The sentences were right, the paragraphs were right, the thing made sense, and the words were spelled okay, and she had a 70. So, I went to Mrs. J. and asked her about the grade. "It lacks depth," she says. Now, I'm no literary scholar, but the thing was okay and the paragraphs were okay, the sentences made sense, and the words were spelled all right. What the hell did she want?"

Upon observing Mrs. J., he found her talking over the heads of the kids, the "less sharp kids" as he referred to them, and he "Found her forcing her sophisticated views on the kids." As he explained in his evaluation which cited these things as poor teaching, this was exactly in line with the evaluation given her by the former principal, and as a result, she was asked to resign. A teacher whose position was eliminated the previous year, but who regained employment by moving into Mrs. J.'s slot reported, "She was here for only a year. She was weird, a real raving liberal, started a paper and encouraged the kids to say all sorts of good little things, encouraged complete freedom. She didn't use her head." She was the one of whom Vincent said, "She knew her material but couldn't relate to the kids."

In general, it may be said of the staff members at Horatio Gates, just as was said earlier of the students, that they developed reasonable ways of thinking and behaving in their situation. They, too, were bound by definite physical, organizational, and conceptual constraints which combined to structure their behavior in the classroom. For instance, the classroom with its physical setting and furniture arrangement practically demanded that the teacher take the front desk. And since groups of students come in regularly and with the expectation that they will be told certain things, there is little that the teacher can do but use that front desk as a base and tell the students whatever it is that he thinks they should know. It is assumed that the teacher considers the material important and will not allow either his own or the students' personal experiences or other extraneous material to disrupt the lesson as he planned it. Therefore, if in the process of classroom interaction, the student responses do not fit into the teacher's prearranged plan, then there is little that he can do but pass it over, turn it around so that it fits his scheme, or supply the proper response himself. There are few differences in the way teachers plan their classes and present the material. The only difference was in the degree of finesse with which the teacher appeared to elicit a certain level of interest, obtain the proper response, and discourage non-task-oriented behavior on the part of the students. Of course, some teachers did make jokes and respond to jokes made by students, but these asides were not part of the lesson and were seldom allowed to go on for more than a few seconds. Even in the humanities class where there was a stated goal to "get the kids to expand themselves in different directions," and even "let them structure their own experiences," by means of nondirected individual study, the reactions of both the principal and vice-principal showed that they thought this was a waste of time.

An additional constraint on the teachers was the details of the maintenance subsystem. The business of accounting for, disciplining, and keeping records on students in class took an enormous amount of the teachers' time and effort.

Outside class they were expected to assist in keeping the halls orderly, watching the cafeteria, checking the lavatories for smokers, checking for passes, and in general supervising students wherever they happened to be. This, not their teaching, appeared to be the main point of contention between them and the administrators who apparently felt that the responsibility for the conduct of the students was being left to them, while the majority of teachers were concerning themselves only with subject matter. It appeared that most teachers regarded supervision of students as an odious burden which interferred with their teaching.

It should be remembered that the administrators were also closely bound in their responsibilities. They were obligated to see that the schedule and the curriculum ran smoothly and that it did not become disrupted by "deviant" behavior. That is, behavior which did not fit into the overall plan. When Vincent and Rossi spoke of teachers who were "not interested in the kids," they were referring to those teachers who allowed and even encouraged students to exhibit any behavior which could have disrupted the smooth running of the organization.

Summary and Discussion of Chapter 2

Student behavior does not take place in a vacuum but in a definite, organizational setting which has a number of complex forces. If one is to have any understanding of that behavior, he must make an attempt to have a corresponding understanding of that setting and some of those forces. That is why it was so important in this first chapter to give some attention to the community, the school, and the behavior of teachers and administrators.

This brief description has raised questions which might be relevant for one who either teaches or is preparing to teach in public schools. For instance, such an individual might ask: "Why do all the teachers, regardless of their subject-matter speciality, use the same instructional pattern?" Or perhaps, "Why did the administrators blame the teachers for ignoring the poorer students, when at the same time those administrators headed an organization which did not encourage student-teacher interaction on an other-than-instructional level?" Or, one might wonder if it were even possible for teachers to take the initiative and seek out more informal student contact. Would such behavior be rewarded by the administrators? Or might these teachers be fired, as was Mrs. J., because they appeared to have been overly selective in their choice of students?

To begin with, the whole issue of Mrs. J. might have been a study in itself. Why was she fired? I should mention at this point a latter conversation I had with Rossi. He was talking about Mrs. J.'s literary magazine:

> Ah, it wasn't very good, it could have been better. I threw them all out, I was happy to be rid of them . . . You know what, she [Mrs. J.] wanted to put that magazine out so I told her I'd help; I gave her a month; I gave her the rights to the print shop where we publish the paper, but come time to sell them, I says to her, "Do you have anyone to sell them?" and she says, "No." So I sold them in the cafeteria. Then I put the money in a special fund for the use by the magazine. The next issue comes out, same thing. I ask her if she had someone to sell them; "No," so I sell them in the cafeteria again, and not once did anyone on the staff, or Mrs. J., thank me for what I did, not the first time I sold them, not the second time, not once.

So, was she fired because she encouraged the kids to "say all kinds of good little things," as the teacher said, because she "talked over the heads of the less sharp kids," as the principal said, or because she failed to thank the vice-principal when he did her a favor. It appeared that she had been fired for a combination of these reasons, all of which have to do with an over concern with student ideas and intellectualizing, and a lesser concern with organizational maintenance and good administrator relations. Teachers in other schools have been fired for encouraging sharper students to intellectualize while ignoring the basic maintenance matters that administrators consider important. The grounds for firing may be justified simply as "inability to relate to students."

The student publication by itself may not have been the reason she was fired, but it certainly didn't help her. Any teacher who wishes to encourage "independent thinking" on the part of his students should be aware that such thinking will be difficult to manipulate and control once it begins. And a "student run" publication, if it is to really be student run, is bound to become critical of the present organizational structure at some point. At that point, the teacher who initiated such a project can find himself in trouble. Does that mean that idealistic, beginning teachers should be careful lest they appear to give too much attention to student intellectualizing and not enough to the maintenance of the organization? Perhaps not, but one who wishes to stimulate student thought and activity has to be aware of these things.

Attempting to make sense of the behavior of teachers and administrators at Horatio Gates, it appears that there are certain realities to which they and teachers in other similar schools pay attention. First, the school organization places at least as many constraints on teachers as it does upon students. Deviant behavior among students may be smiled upon, tolerated, or punished, but it is usually, except in extreme cases, forgiven and forgotten. Not so for teachers. The untenured teacher can be quite easily fired and one who presents himself as a potential threat to maintaining the organization had better be prepared to either hunt for a new position or conform to accepted norms. Public schools demand that organizational boundaries be respected. They have little use for "scholars in residence" or "criticial thinkers."

A second reality is that it is extremely difficult for a teacher to deviate from some rather narrow boundaries. Hypothetically, consider a teacher in Horatio Gates who might have wished to somehow "radically change" his instructional pattern. What would he do? First, remember that he still has to work within the school schedule, and therefore he has his students, just as does everyone else, in classes of 20–30 for five forty-minute periods. Then remember he has to take care of the maintenance details as does everyone else. Then, of course, his room is set; that is, with thirty chairs for students and one for him. If he wanted to begin by sitting on the floor in a circle, chairs would have to be moved, and then be moved back at the end of the period because the next teacher to use the room might not like it that way. That additional maintenance activity of chair moving would probably consume ten more of the forty minutes. One simply cannot expect the janitor to take care of such things. In fact, that janitor, if bothered by abnormal seating arrangements, might choose to let the principal know that "so and so is doing something funny in his room." I don't need to go on to make the point. If a teacher wants to be different, there are a large number of barriers to obstruct him. And even those that begin their teaching careers by wanting to become different may become discouraged, accept the organizational constraints as unavoidable, even necessary, and let those demands define their behavior. They, too, will wind up doing seventy-five percent of the talking, avoid students' personal lives, and walk down the hall in a businesslike fashion. Simultaneously, this will mean they may have to ignore the poorer students because to do otherwise would be to bypass the constraints. I don't mean to say these things to be critical of teachers and their behavior. My intent, rather, is to try to get beneath the rhetoric about "changing behavior," and be realistic about the complexity of the school organization and admit the difficulties of implementing change given the organizational structure.

There is a third reality. Mr. Vincent and Mr. Rossi were responsible for the school in the eyes of the community. Despite what they said about lack of community support and commitment, I think they were actually getting a great deal of both. What the community wanted was an orderly, well-run, clean school, one that was free of controversy, student unrest, or anything that could be called "trouble." As long as the administrators maintained that kind of school, they were secure, and the lack of parent participation in the P.T.A. was actually a vote of confidence. Had the parents perceived some kind of trouble, there would have been hundreds at the board meeting, and the two administrators might have been fired.

Admittedly, these issues are being raised more for the purpose of asking questions than of seeking answers. The main purpose of this book is still to describe students and their school behavior. The original questions remain: What does a student do in Horatio Gates? How does he make sense of his life there? How does he develop a reasonable and consistent pattern of thinking and acting so that he can fulfill his personal needs and at the same time deal effectively with institutional demands? To answer these questions we have to move beyond the description of environment, teachers, and administrators, and start to describe the students.

CHAPTER 3

The Students

General Student Behavior

A visitor to the corridors and classrooms of Horatio Gates would probably be impressed by the general appearance of the students. All but a very few are clean, neat, and moderately well-dressed. The boys wear the slim-lined or belled wash pants and button-down shirts or sweaters. The girls wear fresh blouses or sweaters, skirts of the fashionable length, stockings or knee socks, and some variation of flat heeled shoes. While a few boys keep their hair shoulder length, only a few of the entire senior class affect the hippie garb. In previous years there had been a staff-enforced dress code, but in keeping with Mr. Vincent's attempts to give the students more freedom, that had been dropped and according to both students and teachers, it did not make any difference. The students still dressed the same way.

Like their dress, their overall behavior was orderly. Having been told to expect a "tough" school, I was genuinely surprised by the apparent lack of conflict between the expectations of the staff and the desires of the students. When the bell sounded and the students were expected to go somewhere, they went. When an administrator asked for some compliance or quiet, or a teacher for attention and order, he received it. The students did not seem to find the atmosphere at all oppressive or even distasteful, and they went about their daily activities with apparent willingness. They seemed to accept, almost without question, their place at the bottom of the organizational hierarchy. At a time when the spectre of student revolt was frightening many school people, the students at Horatio Gates, even when unsupervised, would automatically stop what they were doing and stand at attention when the Pledge of Allegiance came over the PA system in the morning. Problems such as violence and drugs, that bedeviled so many schools, seemed nonexistent there. Only twice in the period when the study was being conducted were there any fights, and these were between a few boys and lasted only seconds. And while there were some who regularly took drugs, it was not generally known to other students either who they were or where they got them. According to both users and nonusers, most Gates students who wished to experience illegal thrills were content with weekend drinking parties. Only in formal classes did I hear any general discussions of drugs, and it was the teacher who initiated these discussions, not the students.

A School Day

If one is to understand the students' life in school, he could best begin by examining their day. Between 7:40 and 7:50 each morning the yellow school busses come into the circular drive and release the students at the front door. Others are entering from the side adjacent to the student parking lot. On entering the building, most students go immediately to their lockers where they remove their coats and get their books. Then many go see a guidance counselor, a teacher, the nurse, the librarian, or an administrator. Having taken care of these details, they report to their homeroom at 7:55. This homeroom period lasts ten minutes, during which the teacher takes attendance, and sends the names of those absent to the office where they are typed up for distribution to all rooms so that throughout the day teachers will know which students will be absent from their classes. Also during this time, the vice-principal or an appointed teacher recites the pledge over the PA system and makes various announcements of special events, athletic contests, or anything else that may be important. He also calls those whom he wishes to see for various reasons, the most common of them being that while the student was present the previous day he was reported absent from a particular class.

Following the homeroom period, the bell rings and at 8:05 the students depart for their first class. The halls are then jammed with the entire student body and staff going one place or another, but this lasts only a few minutes until all are in their classrooms. At Gates the students always seemed to take their seats immediately upon entering. When the teacher arrives, his first few minutes are taken up with the usual maintenance details, then the class is expected to settle down and do whatever he had planned. After forty minutes of teacher-directed, instructional activity, the bell rings, the students again fill the halls going to the next class, activity, or study hall, and so on throughout the day with classes changing and the entire student body moving around every forty minutes to begin some different activity under the direction of some other teacher. There are also two lunch periods during which the students, who are forbidden to leave the building, may go to the cafeteria to purchase a standard, state-approved school lunch. This routine may frequently be upset by special assemblies, meetings, athletic events, or fire drills, and classes are cut, shortened, or lengthened accordingly. Following the seven periods, most depart on the same bus they rode that morning, and the rest leave in their private cars.

At first glance, that is how the school day appears. But minimal consideration should convince one that there must be more to school than that. After all, adolescents are not robots or automatons, and Horatio Gates was not some manner of prison, but a public school where 1100 adolescents spent approximately seven hours a day, five days a week, for forty weeks a year. The questions asked earlier remain. What did they actually do within this routine? How did they create some sort of meaningful pattern of activity which, given their situation, seemed logical? What characteristics of the institution most strongly affected their day-to-day behavior, and how did they fulfill their basic human needs while massed together at the bottom of the school's hierarchy? These can probably best be explored by going back and beginning with the students as they enter the building.

The first thing one sees, even as the students leave the bus, is that they all appear to be going somewhere in a great hurry. Only a very few, not more than six or seven, go to the library to study. The rest are in the hall where there is a great deal of movement and where, at the same time, most, if not all, seem to be engaged in animated conversation with one another. In dyads, tryads, or larger groups, they then go on to their lockers or to the lavatory where many smoke and others simply socialize. The most common topic of conversation is cars, their own, their parents, the ones they saw or had or plan to buy someday. Following this many walk somewhere, and others simply stand around. However, one notices that it is only those who are with others who stand around. Those who are alone are seldom standing still but always seem to be going somewhere in a hurry, perhaps to their locker or to the office to get a pass or to the guidance counselor to make an appointment. Even at the beginning of the day, there is one fact of student life that starts to emerge; that is, that students are never physically alone, but are always in the company of many more individuals who for all organizational intents are identical with themselves.

It is, of course, natural that they should talk to one another before school, but when they get to their homerooms this should presumably cease, and the work of the day begin. This is, however, not the case. When they arrive at homeroom, the assigned teacher is usually busy with his own class preparations and with the maintenance details of the homeroom unit. He has to talk to a series of students asking them, "Where were you yesterday?", "The vice-principal wants to see you," "Where's your excuse?" "Here's the pass," and so on. While he is thus engaged with one or another, the rest are, within fairly broad limits, free to carry on as they wish. They may talk to one another, continue what was happening in the halls, watch others interact, or do some class work. Most, however, choose the former, that is, they talk quietly with one another, and since Horatio Gates is not repressive and teachers are not whining martinets, this talking does not bother the teacher or prevent him from carrying on the business at hand. If a boy is talking to his friend, and the teacher interrupts, the boy turns, acknowledges the teacher, and does as the teacher wishes; when that is finished, he goes back to his friend. For the first few minutes of the homeroom period, then, the students are usually continuing their private interactions.

However, this ceases and all pay attention when the vice-principal's voice comes over the PA system and he makes his announcements:

"Bus 73 is late, homeroom teachers please take note. Last night we lost a soccer game to Williamsville. The Future Teachers of America will meet in room 108 eighth period. Will the seniors and juniors please mark the ballots that are being passed out and return them to your homeroom teacher? The votes will be counted by the class officers who are to report to the vice-principal's office during eighth period. There will be a Drama Club meeting eighth period. The sale of tickets for the Friday night football game will be held on Thursday. Will the following students please report to the office, following the next bell? . . . Please stand for the Pledge of Allegiance."

At that, the students rise, stand at orderly attention, and together with the vice principal recite the Pledge. As the Pledge ends, the bell rings and out into the halls they swarm, again walking with and talking to their friends. It does not matter that they might be attending different first period classes. There is time to walk along and greet one another, or talk about whatever it is that they and their friends consider important. When they arrive at their rooms, they enter the class and sit down.

Now it is presumed that they will begin the real business of the day, that of cognitive interaction with the teacher over some academic matter, but not yet. First the teacher has to arrive, take attendance, ask for one or more late slips, ask this or that student where he was yesterday, or the day before, ask another why he did not hand in yesterday's homework, or tell him he has to go take a make-up test somewhere. And then some student will have to explain that he has to go somewhere and the teacher will have to sign a pass. These are important matters and are taken seriously by both teachers and students. A fairly representative class might be drama where Mr. Lilley was, in the first few minutes, taking care of his classroom maintenance details. "Now we're going to talk about propaganda. First the tests."

"Read our marks," says one girl.

"Your, ahem, marks, ah yes," says Mr. Lilley. "There were two failures in the class. That's because both of them forgot or just didn't bother to do something."

"Who, who?" a couple of kids in the back were saying. "Was I one of them?"

"Yes," says Mr. Lilley, "and the thing for you to do is make up the test. You can do it today or tomorrow. When are you free?"

"I'm not," says the kid. "I get out of school early on the release program."

"Well," says Mr. Lilley, "What do you do first period?"

"I don't get here first period, just second period because I don't get the car till then."

"Well, what time do you get here, is it half an hour before second period?"

"No," says the kid, "Only about five minutes."

"You're taking it second period tomorrow," says Mr. Lilley. "Be here."

Another student asks when he could take the test and Mr. Lilley says "Third period tomorrow."

"When do we get our report cards?" a kid asks.

"Well, I don't know."

"Maybe next April," says a girl.

Some teachers seem to take up the first ten minutes of the class with this type of activity, while others seem to be able to go right through it. Generally in harder classes, such as physics, calculus, or literature, the teachers were able to go through these things faster because there were fewer deviations; that is, fewer students who miss class, miss tests, fail to hand in work, come late, and so forth, but all teachers and students have to spend at least some minutes at the beginning of each period on these things. While these things are going on between the teacher and one student, the others are either watching or are again interacting quietly with their friends. In those few minutes taken up with more maintenance details, one begins to see a second important fact of student life. That is, that a tremendous amount of school time is taken up with procedural and maintenance details. Although they have been in the school for approximately forty minutes, from 7:40 until 8:20, they have spent the entire time either waiting, engaging in some sort of spectatorship, interacting with their friends, or dealing with some maintenance matter, such as with lockers, passes, coming, or going; but they have not been engaged to any significant degree in anything that could even remotely be called academic activity. This is not to imply that they were in a state of disorder or even that they were restless and bored. During this time, some seemed perfectly content to simply watch the action of other students or teachers, or continue to be actively engaged with their friends, either leaning over or back, or turning around in their desks to talk in a quiet and interested manner. Of course, this did not in any way upset the teacher nor did it prevent him from doing what he had to do.

But then it is finally time to begin. "Take out your books" or "Look at the board" or "Here are some handouts" or a lab experiment is set up and then there is some bustle as papers, pencils, and books get opened, closed, or shifted around and the students get ready to undertake the day's lesson. In Horatio Gates when the teacher begins to show signs of seriousness and wants to begin something, the students comply. Even in the classes with "tougher" students, I was always impressed by the compliance given the teacher when he finally asked for it. However, one can still expect one or more students to be unable to find the page, while another did not get a work sheet, forgot his book, or is just coming in from a dentist appointment, or from talking to the guidance counselor, or is leaving because the vice-principal wants to see him. This takes another minute or so before the class and the teacher have their attention focused on the matter at hand and learning is ready to begin. As stated, the skill with which a teacher gets a class ready depends on his personal style, class content, and the students. By the time the teacher and class are finally ready, it is pushing 8:14 in some classes. In other cases it might be 8:20 or even 8:25 before class and teacher finally settle down. It is important to remember that the maintenance and procedural activities are not limited to those first forty minutes of the morning. The bell will ring at 8:50 and both students and staff will have to go somewhere else to begin some other class and there, too, the teacher will have to call roll, take attendance, collect slips and passes, send students to the office for various appointments with counselors, nurses, college admissions recruiters, administrators, and so forth. In fact, it seems that the first period of the morning is the one in which the least amount of this kind of activity goes on. And all of these things go on between one teacher and one student, but there are twenty-five or so students in the class, and while the teacher is thus engaged with one, the rest are for all practical purposes not engaged in any cognitive interaction with the subject matter; they are instead watching and waiting. The assumption mentioned previously, concerning the teacher's subject matter expertise, demands that the teacher initiate and direct the learning activity. If his attention is diverted, the students are left to wait and they do. When the teacher finishes, they once again begin their interactions with the subject matter.

It does not seem necessary to go through the entire day to make the point that a large part of the students' day may be spent in a state of spectatorship in which he simply watches and waits. Consider just the first thirty-five or forty minutes of the morning that have already been mentioned, add the thirty-five for the total day devoted to passing in the halls, the additional forty minutes devoted to lunch, the time spent in getting ready in each of the classes, a conservative estimate of which would be at least five minutes; add five minutes more for the time taken out of class for more passing of papers, books, worksheets, or directions. Add at least half of the study hall period in which something other than academic activity is taking place and judging from the observed study halls, that too is a conservative estimate. Add an additional period when a student is engaged in something other than academic activity, that is, time spent with administrators, counselors, nurses, activities, looking for someone or going somewhere. The total is 200 minutes a day, or over three hours of the total time spent in school in which any single student can be expected to either spend his own time on procedural and maintenance details or wait while others tie up the class with their own. And that, according to my timed estimates, is conservative. There are many days when much more time is devoted to these things. It assumes that only ten minutes of the class time will be lost, that there will be no major interruptions, that the teacher will be well prepared, that there will be no discipline problems, no assemblies, no fire drills, no special events or activities, and no one interrupting the class once it begins. It also assumes that the students will be reasonably attentive, awake, willing to undertake the matter at hand, and that they and the teacher will be on the same wave-length for the other four hours.

Some Particulars of Classroom Interaction

It is not to be readily concluded that all of this time is merely wasted. If, indeed, it is a background and support for the other four hours, then one can reasonably say that there is adequate time left to spend on learning, enough for anyone, and that Horatio Gates, as such, is doing a good job. For that reason it is imperative to look more closely at the class time in which the teacher is presumably free to instruct without interruptions. The previous discussion of the usual classroom organization becomes important and relevant here. Since the teacher is a subject-matter expert, and because it is assumed, and rightly so, that he will use his time to pass on some knowledge to the twenty or thirty students, most teachers at Horatio Gates treat the class as if it were a dyadic interaction—the teacher on one side and the class on the other. Both parties, then, actively engage in the business of studying a common issue. In practice, however, this unanimity of purpose is difficult to achieve, even for good teachers. Some students will simply not be engaged in the matter, and therefore, a question directed toward them may throw off the entire class.

For instance, a teacher was trying to initiate a discussion of the origin of language:

"Where do we learn to talk? Consider for a minute. Com'on, how do we learn?"

He called on one particular boy, Red, who, watching the teacher with disdain, replied, "In school, you have to go and listen to all these stupid people talk all day long and that's where you learn."

The teacher, of course, ignored the remark, the feeling behind it, and called on another student. He could do little else. If not left alone, these remarks can lead to a distraction from the subject by both the teacher and students.

In another class a teacher was trying to discuss the novel, *Lord of the Flies*, and she was beginning to talk about the novel's symbolism: Simon's love of beauty, his death, Jack's nature and how he was beginning to prevail over Piggy's plea for reason and a civilized attitude. At this point she tried to involve the class by questioning them about the problem of evil. "It wasn't any one individual's fault for Simon's death, or was it? Are you responsible for the evil in this world? Are you responsible for the fact that many individuals in this city went to bed hungry last night?" She wanted them to talk a little about social responsibility, but then Joe spoke out, "Put 'em in concentration camps, those people on welfare, those niggers."

"What, Joe?" said the teacher.

"I said, those niggers who won't work and go on welfare—I pay $30.00 a week in taxes—should be put in concentration camps."

She couldn't ignore it, so she asked, "Why, Joe, why?"

"I know this nigger, he's got an apartment up by the university. This guy was telling me what he has for breakfast, he's reading from a menu, he says like 'What shall I have.' And on the menu it says . . . uuh . . . wine and uuhh . . . eggs and uuh uuh . . . milk. And I'm supporting him. Put 'em in concentration camps."

Then Chris spoke up, "Yeah, why won't they work? They just sit around all day and we have to support them." Immediately, of course, the teacher was on the defensive and tried to deal with the issue in a logical manner. She could not, after all, ignore that kind of comment.

"Do you have facts to prove that people on welfare are cheating? Most of them, you know, can't work, or have little children and these are mostly women." Others in the class were beginning to respond.

"There's a lot of whites on welfare, too," said a girl.

And a boy added, "He's right." And another boy on the other side of the room agreed.

"Aw, those niggers, shoot 'em or put 'em in concentration camps."

Mrs. G. knew better than to continue the issue, and saying "All right, that's enough of that," went back to the *Lord of the Flies*. As she resumed talking, there were no further comments on welfare or shooting people, but Joe and a few other boys were nodding to one another in vigorous agreement.

Mrs. G., like most teachers, took one side of the dyad and assumed that the students were with her and would respond with appropriate comments. But as Joe's behavior indicates, one simply cannot depend on that assumption. Joe wanted to express his resentments and used a fairly innocuous question to make his point. The kind of behavior that Joe exhibited is potentially present in any class and can easily emerge to destroy the subject matter planned by the teacher. After that, the students were not about to be immediately tempted back into thinking about literary symbolism.

Another type of behavior the writer repeatedly watched was that exhibited by Darlene. When she came to class, Darlene had her homework done; when the class was asked to read, she read; she came on time, left on time, and paid ostensible attention, but she would never respond to a question or say a word to the teacher. When called on for an answer in any class, she just stared straight ahead, and if the teacher, in the most gentle manner, tried to prod her a little, she just sat and stared. It really made sense for Darlene, who, for reasons of her own, just does not want to respond. She knew that the teacher could not stop the class and make a big issue of it; there are twenty-four other students in there who need attention and who, if the teacher spends her time with Darlene, will find something with which to occupy themselves. The teacher cannot let that happen. She has to deal with Darlene the way she deals with Joe. She just ignores the personal issue and goes on with the subject matter which, after all, she was hired to impart.

Red, Joe, and Darlene all exhibited some variation of that student behavior which can disrupt the class time presumably devoted to subject matter. The teacher's defense, of course, was to stick to the subject matter and interact only with those students who were paying close attention. But there are two dangers associated with this means of defense. The first is that the teacher may be forced to avoid the student's personal responses and in effect will actually be discouraging student involvement. The teachers cited in Chapter One who answer their own questions or who, in asking their questions, leave only a very narrow range of possible responses seem to do this. The second danger is that the teacher will avoid the marginal students and will concentrate his attention on a small group upon whom he can depend for a reasonable response. The others, of course, are left as spectators. Both of these often occur in classes. It is a very difficult position for the teacher to be in, but considering the setting, it is virtually unavoidable.

A closely related and very common occurrence was that of a thoughtful remark by some student going unnoticed because of the teacher's attention being taken by someone else. For instance, in one class the teacher asked them to consider the differences between the 1920s and the present. Roger, a fairly thoughtful boy, replied that as opposed to the twenties, "Today people are in tune with lone individuals like Natalie, Easy Rider, and Bronson. Those people that ride along and don't get entangled, those are our present heroes."

Unfortunately, at that moment Jim was playing around and the teacher turned and told him to "Stop it or get out," and by the time the attention was turned again to the subject matter, Roger's remark was forgotten. I told him later that I thought it was a good remark and that it was too bad no one was paying attention. "Yeah, I know," said Roger. "That's why I sit and jack off all day."

Even Joe, on one occasion when the teacher was continuing her discussion of Simon and asked why Simon's tongue was so swollen, replied, "He had a fever." The teacher, who by that time may have had enough of Joe, smiled condescendingly, completely ignored Joe's remark, and went on to explain the swollen tongue in terms of literary symbolism. It was another case of a student making an input into the class and getting no return, because the teacher with everything else on her mind could not give the needed response.

There are two important points about classroom interaction. The first is that even when all procedural and maintenance details are put aside and the teacher and students are presumably tuned in to the subject matter, there is simply no assurance that Red, Joe, or Darlene or, for that matter, any other single student is getting the points made by the teacher. The second is that when the teacher's attention is turned to a student who is exhibiting some sort of individualistic behavior, the rest of the students are, for that moment, reduced to a state of spectatorship. There is really little that they can do but sit and watch and wait. Roger's comment to me indicates many may even hesitate to feed thoughtful comments into the class because they simply go unnoticed and unrewarded.

It has to be restressed here that Horatio Gates is not some blackboard jungle, staffed with poor, unsympathetic teachers and racist, nonattentive students. It is an orderly, well-run, middle-class American school which, given a cursory inspection, would appear to be doing a fine job. But if one watches the classroom interaction process very closely, he can see the real difficulty of carrying on meaningful dialogue under certain conditions. It is not simply the teacher's fault. She does not need two more courses in methods, literature, or clinical psychology. If she attempts to explore Darlene's problem, the rest are left out. If she tries to reason with Joe and show him the error of his thinking, it will be a long, difficult, perhaps unsuccessful process and that was not what she was hired to do. If she responds to Roger's thoughtfulness, what will Jim do next? And what, after all, can a teacher say to an eighteen year old student like Red who obviously despises the whole institution.

The teacher's solution to these things is to talk, talk, and keep talking. In fact, a rough and perhaps even conservative estimate is that teachers there did seventy-five percent of the talking that went on in the class. Verbal communication is what is going on. In most classes it is the only thing that is going on, and that is partly because of the earlier stated assumption that verbal communication and learning are closely related, if not identical. But if talking is all there is and the teacher does seventy-five percent of it, what is left for the students? Twenty-five percent, of course, but divided among twenty or thirty students, this means that any single student will be allowed only a very small percentage of the active classroom participation. The two dangers mentioned earlier become very real here. The talking may be on a superficial level, and only a few may get to participate. For instance, when the vocational education teacher asked Andy a question, he replied, "I don't know. I never know what you're talking about." The teacher quickly explained the brief answer and went on. He did not even try to deal with Andy's lasting problem, but just talked right over and past Andy, who probably did not understand any more at the end of the class than he did at the beginning.

Of course, a possible answer is that the students can listen as much as they want. They are, after all, supposed to be paying attention. Yet if one takes the time to watch the listeners closely, he can see that there is a great deal of yawning, looking about, playing with papers and pencils, doodling, sleeping, looking at pictures, wallets, and whatever. It is very difficult to be an active and attentive listener for five periods a day.

Of course, there were teachers and classes which apparently interested most of the students most of the time. A good example was physics class where Mr. F. handled his maintenance issues in about one minute. He did not have to tell them to break into groups and go to their tables. They were already there by the time he said, "Now today we're going to talk about something that many consider the most difficult thing in physics. That is motion . . ."

And when it was time for the lab experiment they gathered their equipment and went about the matter in a quick, quiet, and interested manner. The teacher was free to go around the room and interact with those who asked him individual questions. There was no necessity of talking to everyone about the same thing, others had their own concerns. But this was an exception. He was cited repeatedly as being the best teacher in the school, and the fact is he had a situation where the organizational characteristics worked for, not against him: highly motivated students—no Jims, Reds, Darlenes or even Rogers in his class; a subject that demanded the physical involvement of handling equipment; a small class of sixteen students; and a subject area with built-in, logical sequence of events where the activity one engaged in on Tuesday was factually integrated with the material one learned on Monday.

It is not fair to say that this occurred only in the more academic classes. In ceramics class where the teacher had everyone actively engaged in a project the same kind of attention was present. There the teacher did not care if the students interacted quietly about their private concerns as long as they continued their work. The music teacher, too, who was reputed by many students to be "really great" was able, by engaging them all in singing, to keep just about every student involved and interested. In all three of these classes the nature of the subject was such that good order and common participation did not depend entirely on the teacher, but on the active physical and mental involvement of the students.

However, even those students who took music, physics, or ceramics did so for only one or two periods a day and for the rest of the time, they were in classes that put them in the situation described earlier. Thus, for any single Gates senior, the time spent actively engaged with some teacher over a matter of cognitive importance may not exceed twenty minutes a period for five periods a day. That is a high estimate. I would say that if an average student spent an hour to one and a half hours a day in school involved in subject matter, that was a good day.

In sum, it seems that there are a number of important points about the students and their daily routine. The organization of the school is based on certain characteristics (1) compartmentalization of knowledge, (2) teacher subject specialization, and (3) batch processing of students. These assumptions are operationalized when the students in groups of twenty to thirty are placed in classes where it is expected they will be instructed by the teacher-expert for a certain number of minutes. In practice, however, there are a number of immediate problems in this sytem. First, it requires a tremendous amount of maintenance activity which detracts from instruction time. Secondly, it forces the teacher to do most of what there is to do in the class and simultaneously limits the students' active involvement, and thirdly, it forces the teacher to purposely exclude vast ranges of possible student behavior because they can serve to disrupt the process of passing on his subject-matter speciality. The unintended consequences of these organizational characteristics seem to be that the students spend very little actual time involved in academic interaction with the teachers.

Individual Students: What Are They Doing?

Having demonstrated that there are a number of difficulties inherent in teacher-student interaction in the classroom, it remains now to look more closely at some of the behaviors of individual students. The question becomes, if these students were spending only a limited amount of time actively engaged with the teacher what were they doing the rest of the day? An incident which occurred during my first month stands out. Ed, a pleasant boy whose ambition was to become a policeman, met me in the halls and proceeded to tell me about a hunting incident in which he was fined for having one shell above the legal limit in his shotgun. As we walked to the first class, he included Vince in the conversation and as the two entered, sat down and waited for the teacher to start, they were talking about hunting. The teacher finished his attendance taking and passed out the vocabulary worksheets. Ed, Vince, and I were at one library table where they were simultaneously engaged in both the vocabulary exercise and the plans for Monday's hunting trip.

"Be ready to hike, man. We're going to walk about eight miles."

"Ah, that's silly. I'd rather drive the car, and you can drive right down the dirt road by the second barn."

Then Vince drew and Ed modified a map of a cornfield adjacent to a pond where the geese spend the night. "We'll have to leave by 5:30 to get there by six. Hey, Phil, you wanna come?" I declined and they went on with the map and also with the vocabulary sheet.

"Hey, what's ominous? Is that like an ominous phone call?"

He was asking me so I had to say something. "No, that's anonomous. Ominous means threatening."

"Oh," said Ed, "like a threatening phone call."

Vince was still drawing the map and the teacher came over.

"You know that one," said the teacher. " 'He *scrutinized* the signature to be sure it was really hers.' What does *scrutinized* mean?"

"I don't know, I'm dumb," said Vince.

"Well, what's a signature?"

"Like writing, when you sign something."

"Well, what do you think you would do if you scrutinized a signature?"

"I don't think, I'm dumb," said Vince.

While this was going on, Ed was writing the definition of ominous and then the teacher, who seeing that Vince had his work almost done and was just fooling, turned and left. Immediately Vince turned to Ed and said, "Yeah, but if we arrange the shooting patterns like this," and he proceeded to modify the drawing. He did not even blink when he turned from interacting with the teacher back to talking about hunting. No problem for Vince and Ed. They get their work done, they satisfy the teacher, and at the same time they plan a hunting trip.

Later in the day, they were still talking about their hunting trip and by the end of seventh period had it all decided: who would drive, how they would go, what time they would leave, how they would set up their shooting patterns, and what they expected to come home with. Of course, all the time they were going to their respective classes, doing the work the teacher asked of them, and in general fulfilling the demands of the institution.

More and more, as I continued in the school, I saw that the students' most active and alive moments, and indeed the great majority of their school time, was spent not with teachers and subject-matter affairs, but in their own small-group interactions which they carried on simultaneously with their class work. For instance, in auto mechanics class when the teacher had the students working on the car that they and the teachers were building, they would simultaneously be talking among themselves about what they would do after school that evening, this or that weekend, or something similar. While the teacher's attention was diverted to some maintenance or procedural detail, or while he was interacting with one to the exclusion of the others, there was this breaking up into dyads, tryads, or groups and this activity paralleled the subject-matter interactions.

In one particular class this was extremely evident. The situation in humanities was one in which the students were creating some filmed commercials to teach them creativity, writing, and skills in handling material. The material was quite sophisticated, a Sony TV camera, a monitoring set, some microphones, and some other audio devices. There were twenty-three people in the class, one or two of them had written the script and they were among the six involved in the skit. One more was working the camera, and another was adjusting the TV. But the other fifteen were standing around watching or rather half watching, half talking among themselves. By that time I had been in school for a month and was beginning to feel at ease talking to people, so I asked Dick, who was on the edge of the circle holding his girl's hand, "Don't you get tired waiting around like this?"

"No," said Dick, "teenagers enjoy grooving on the edge of the scene just like this. Just standing around making remarks with their friends."

"Don't you wish there wasn't so much of it?"

"No. I don't know how adults are, but we don't mind this."

"But is this all you do?"

"Well, yes. But there is nothing we can do about it. I get tired of saying we're going to do something, and talking about it. I wish we would do it."

The girl spoke up, "But we can't help it."

Then another class section came in and now there were about twelve playing with or at least interested in the machinery, and thirty standing around. Then an AV man came in and showed them how to get the proper reception on the machine, but he was talking to only three or four students, then even the actors were doing nothing but standing around.

In the academic classes the same type of phenomenon occurred. Mr. C. was presenting the material in geometry and all the students were with him, writing on the worksheets, doing the problems, and answering the questions concerning angles and lines. This lasted about fifteen minutes. Then he passed out a homework assignment and the students proceeded to work on it. Of course the rate of completion varied; while some finished quickly, the rest took longer. Those who finished then turned to one another and began talking about football. Jim, an important player, was reading the newspaper account of the previous game and making comments on the write-up. About six others in the back of the room were listening to him and laughing at his comments. In another corner two boys who had finished their work were quietly talking. Of course they, no more than Jim and his group, were preventing the teacher from helping a student at his desk. Only when Jim made too much noise, the teacher asked, "Have you got your work done?"

"Yeah," said Jim, "It was easy."

"All right, then, keep it down," and he went back to one student and Jim went back to the paper and the reading. No problem; it was not a bad class or a bad teacher. He presented his material well, students apparently paid attention for the fifteen minute presentation, but when he no longer demanded their attention, they turned and immediately went into their group interactions. When these group interactions were going on, the students were literally unsupervised; that is, they were outside of any meaningful interaction with subject matter, and since they were together and apparently enjoyed each others company, it was natural that they should begin to talk to one another. This, also, occurred in physics class and indeed in both more and less academic classes. It made sense. Students were never alone but always in the company of like individuals. They have known each other for some years. The situation demanded that the teacher be the center of the class, but the same situation demanded that he pay attention to a number of nonlearning factors and this left the students in a state of spectatorship from which they naturally gravitated into their informal interactions.

It should be admitted that the school, on the whole, seemed to be very undemanding of students. One could easily see that those who were giving only bare compliance to the academic demands were not failing, nor where they being chastized by the teachers for nonachievement.

They simply were not expected to do very much and just about anyone who gave at least a little effort could and did succeed. Bare minimal compliance seemed to be all that was necessary. Of course the degree of effort varied and some students were reputed to put out a great deal. All came to class most of the time, handed in assignments of varying worth, took and somehow passed their tests, and to some degree listened to the teachers. But even after devoting some time and energy to this, they had a great deal of time left for their private friendships.

One might wonder, as I did at the beginning of the study, how it is possible to spend only an hour or so a day with academic matters and still succeed in school. It seemed that students accomplished both goals by paying strict attention to the procedural and maintenance elements in the organization. In fact, the level of anxiety would rise only when the usual schedule and procedures were changed. At those times, one would hear, "What time is it?" "Where do we go?" "What are we supposed to be doing?" "What time do we get to eat?" These questions would be endlessly repeated by students who on normal days would go about their business without thinking or speaking of such matters. In fact, the only time the writer ever saw the entire student body upset was at the beginning of the year when instead of being allowed to leave at 2:20 as in the previous year, they were kept until 2:50 because of a change in the bus schedule. This caused an endless amount of griping and concern by both teachers and students up to the end of September when the old plan was reintroduced, and no more mention was heard of it.

Classes were the same way. For instance, in Mrs. K.'s psychology class, as in most classes, all paid strict attention when she was saying,

Now about your term papers, my first two semesters teaching this class, I used to tell them on September 3 that they should turn in a term paper on November 15. And, of course, when November 15 came around they had gotten their time fouled up and the term paper was not completed. Now, when doing term papers you have to plan your time. I might as well tell you, you can plan on at least bunches of hours spent in the library. The best thing is to use the reader's guide in this library to find out the kind of things you want to complete your papers and then you can go to the libraries either at the university or maybe downtown. I don't know, can you get in the college library? You probably can if you act like you belong there, you know you can steal the crown jewels if you act as though you belong there. Now you have to have at least five sources—books, magazines; most of your topics are so general that that won't be difficult. You can do that, then you carefully write down the sources and then when you make notes figure out some system to indicate which of the sources the note came from. The next Friday, I want to see your notes; I mean I don't want to read them all, but I want to make sure you have notes plus sources. Then the hard part comes. Whenever I write a term paper, the worst thing is to outline a rough draft from the notes. [Somebody asks about grades, not having to do with the term papers.] If you want to figure out your grades, multiply your six week test by two, and that will be close. Anyway, the reports won't be out for a while, the sheets that we're supposed to mark aren't even in the school yet and they were supposed to be here last Friday. Anyway, when they do come there will be a lot of mistakes.

Even Joe, Red, Vince, and Ed paid attention to this type of talk although it took an inordinate amount of time, but that was to be expected. All the students were concerned about meeting, in their own fashion, the teachers' and the class demands and thus gaining the future promised reward of high school graduation and, for some, college acceptance. Once the mechanics of the class were clear, the students would seem to relax and then the diverse behavior would emerge, some paying good attention, some looking at their wallets or pictures, yawning, looking around, or carrying on some subtle form of communication with their friends. If after class they made any mention of what went on or would go on in the future, the point was always about some procedural or maintenance issue, not a matter of academics. It seemed that the institution demanded not learning, but compliance with a fairly complex set of procedures. One is reminded of something John Dewey mentioned, "At its worst, the problem of the pupil is not how to meet the requirements of school life, but how to seem to meet them, or how to come near enough to meeting them to slide along without an undue amount of friction."[1]

This was never more apparent than one day when in the humanities class the teachers brought in a dean from a nearby university. The dean, an important figure in state education, was a member of the State Board of Regents. He talked for about thirty minutes about issues which he assumed were of great importance to young people: Vietnam, the draft, the hard choices faced by youth, and the challenge of the future. At the conclusion he asked for questions, and of fifteen or twenty questions, all but two had to do with the state sponsored high school exams. They apparently thought he actually wrote the Regents exam himself, and they wanted him to change or clarify some of the questions. He finally explained that he had absolutely nothing to do with state exams, and when that was clear he got no more questions. The minutiae of answering specific questions on the June exams was more important to them than any issue about which the dean assumed they were concerned.

There were some issues over which the entire student body was commonly involved and excited. One was a cafeteria boycott organized by some seniors over the allegedly poor quality of the food. Personally, I found it to be no worse than that served in the United States Army or a host of other schools, but the students, although they consumed it in great quantities, were convinced that it was poisoned. On October 2 the word went around that there would be a cafeteria boycott the next day. Signs which read "Bag it tomorrow," appeared in the busses and lavatories, and on October 3 only 118 students bought the school lunch, as opposed to the usual 565. Vincent and Rossi were in the cafeteria that noon, both leaning against the wall and looking very serious. Then the district business manager showed up and they conferred at length.

[1] John Dewey, *Democracy and Education* (New York: Macmillan, 1916), p. 184.

Meanwhile, the doors to the cafeteria were crowded with students who would hoot and holler if someone actually bought a lunch. Rossi yelled at them for this and they stopped harrassing the buyers, but continued to mill around and revel in their accomplishment.

The administrators took quick action. Rossi called a special Student Council meeting, had the cafeteria manager explain the issues of cost, cooking, preparation, serving, and so forth. Then he appointed a "special cafeteria investigating committee" composed of senior class council officers and a few football players, and the next day the committee got a guided tour of the cafeteria. Two days later the boycott ended and lunch sales once again exceeded 500. This was one time when it seemed as if a majority of students were actively interested in a school issue.

In sum, the students' active and interested involvement centered not around teacher-initiated, academic issues or even around the issues that were nationally centered. Instead, they concerned themselves with the procedures of fulfilling institutional demands, the cafeteria food, and their private in-group interactions. In general, what they did in school they did with their friends. For instance, if in class a teacher asked them to divide into groups and discuss some matter, they scurried around and found their good friends with whom they talked not about anything academic, but about their out-of-school activities. This was true not only of the nonacademically oriented students, but also of those such as Jean. In some structured interviews toward the end of the study I asked her, "Do kids seem to spend a lot of time together?"

"Yes, that's true. That's what we do, we're not very interested in school."

"You mean school, academically?"

"Yes, that's right. There isn't much to be interested in."

"Is that what you do, hang around with each other most of the time?"

"Yes, that's it. We're with our friends."

"And when you're with your friends, do you talk about school?"

"No, we talk about ourselves a lot. Self-analysis is big this year."

That interaction with one's friends was time consuming and important was substantiated time and again.

One boy who had recently entered the school told me: "When I first came, I hated it. You know, Phil, I skipped fifty-eight days last year because I couldn't stand to come to school because I didn't know anyone, and when I tried to talk to someone, we would just exchange small talk, never get down to anything. I felt like a real outsider."

"I guess you were."

"I know it. It's bad when you don't know anyone, you just walk around by yourself and feel like other kids are talking about you."

"What about the kids who don't have any friends?"

Bill was with us. "Yeah, sometimes I wonder about those kids standing around with no one to talk to. They don't say anything, but you know they see you and are thinking something. It's really sad."

"Is that the most important thing you do in school though, hang around with your friends?"

"Like I said, Phil, when I didn't have any friends, I hated the place so much I couldn't stand to come."

"I notice when you and your friends are together you don't talk about school."

"No, we have our own way of talking and we don't have much to say about teachers."

This is readily verifiable; all one had to do is walk in a room with students and listen to them. "No, last night I was with Joe on a motorcycle, all over town; he's a junior."

"Is he the one who owns a Jaguar?"

"No, that's Jeff."

And the next girl is saying, "Well, they should let me go. After all, I pay for the insurance and I'm supposed to have the car any time I want it. You know what else? Last night we, my family, bought a brand new Chevy, brand new, last night."

From a heavy girl in striped slacks, "You should'a seen what Bill did, he was choking me."

"Why?" asked another.

"Because John swatted me in the head with a paper."

"Why didn't he choke John?"

"He couldn't. He's afraid. Boy, if he'd a held up his fist, I'd a killed him."

Two rows over two girls were talking about Arlo Guthrie, "But he's awfully cute."

"I know," said the second.

By the time the teacher was ready and called for attention, all the students turned and paid attention for as long as the teacher wanted. The minute the teacher's demands ceased, all the sets of students were back into their conversations described previously.

Of course this made it extremely important for students to have friends. In fact, it may have been the single most important thing in the school. To not have friends was to have no one to be with in the corridors and classrooms, no one to walk with to class, or to carry on with before, after, and even during class, no one to eat with. The students spoke easily of this phenomenon. As Ken said, "When I didn't have any friends, I hated this place so much I couldn't stand to come." Or Dick, "In school we groove with our friends, that is, those who have friends, and most kids do." Or Pete, "You can't go to high school without friends."

After discovering this it became necessary that I begin to examine more closely the students' friendship patterns. If that is what they spent their school time doing, then that was my topic. And upon examination it became apparent that those friendship patterns were rigidly divided. One just did not hang around with anyone, or go to class with anyone, or eat with anyone. He talked to, walked with, ate with, and spent as much time as possible with his few friends and literally did not pay attention to those who were not in his group.

Therefore, the class was not simply an undifferentiated mass of students, but was a series of dyads, tryads, clique and groups. In fact, one did not even see those with whom he did not directly associate. That may sound odd to teachers who are used to thinking of students in terms of batches of not less than twenty or thirty, but it was strongly substantiated every day. If I were talking to a member of one small group and a friend of mine who was in another group approached, I might find myself in two isolated conversations since, the two students would not even recognize each others presence. In the cafeteria it was particularly noticeable. In fact, the rush to the cafeteria at noon was probably more to assure one a seat at the proper table with one's friends than it was to satisfy hunger. If one did not sit with his friends, he literally sat alone. Once when I was with Jean she mentioned that, "The worse thing that can happen is that you have to walk around the halls alone."

"What about the cafeteria?"

"Oh, that's even worse. Kids would rather not eat than eat alone."

Thereafter I frequently asked informants, "Which would you rather do, flunk a test or eat alone in the cafeteria?"

Invariably the answer was, "Flunk a test!"

I asked one of the athletes, Greg, about associating with those not in his group. The thought just did not make any sense to him. "You know like if you came here and didn't hang around with us, I wouldn't even know you."

Apparently the teacher did not see this. When asked, some admitted that the students hung around, but they thought of students in terms of the Cowpens-Winnsboro gang or the Hillsborough gang. Or sometimes they spoke of the academics and the locals, or those who were and those who were not active in extracurricular activities. Neither the teachers nor the administrators saw the class as a series of rigidly differentiated friendships. This is understandable, of course, since the teachers have their own interests.

There was an important question about those who apparently did not have any friends. One person in particular was a boy named Nick who would frequently stand around the student lounge by himself. In the first few minutes I knew him, he volunteered, "You probably noticed that I'm not too popular. I don't have many friends."

Of Nick and others like him, Bill said, "Them, they're

just standing around leaning against the wall. They're out of it." Which, as far as I could see, was a good description of what Nick did. I occasionally asked others about students who had no friends and would mention Nick as an example. Although he had been in the class for years they would say, "Who? Who do you mean?" They did not even see him, and I found that as I became closer to the members of one particular group, I, too, stopped seeing Nick.

The Group Phenomenon and Class Status

The fact that the class was broken into a series of groups had a considerable impact on the extracurricular activities section. In general it seemed to more freely allow a few students to run whatever there was to run. A number of researchers, among them Coleman, Gordon, and Hollingshead,[2] who previously studied adolescents in school, have all stressed the idea of prestige stratification among the students. They have generally found that the more athletic and personable boys, and the more good-looking, personable girls tend to rule all the extracurricular activities. This seemed to be generally true at Horatio Gates. It was not, however, just a matter of individual qualification but a matter of group affiliation. In that class of 364 members, there were about fifteen to twenty students who seemed to get elected to whatever office happened to be available and who seemed to run whatever there was to run. Since it was always the same ones, I asked about it frequently. The editor of the school paper, Marilyn, provided some good and accurate insights. She agreed that only about twenty were active. I asked "Why?"

"The rest just don't take an interest."

"Why?"

"Because they don't. You can't make them."

"Who does take an interest?"

"The power group."

---

[2] See August B. Hollingshead, *Elmtown's Youth* (New York: Wiley, 1949); C. W. Gordon, *The Social System of the High School* (New York: Free Press, 1957); and James Coleman, *The Adolescent Society* (New York: Free Press, 1962).

"What's that?"

"That's the kids who get elected to offices and run things."

"How does that happen?"

"Oh, that's it. You know what they do? There's a few of them, Joan, Sally, Betty, and them, they do this, there's a few girls who start to drive early, then they get to go around you know. Then they get a few boys; this is their sophomore year. Boys everyone likes, and they start to have parties and they drink, and the next day they come to school and tell everyone about what they did. They do fun things like, you know, tobogganing, and that, and pretty soon everyone knows about the party they had and they're envious because they seem to be the ones that are having the fun. Then, class elections come along and they put up some one of them for class elections, and then they're in and then they stay in, they won't let you in."

I asked Marilyn, who was a former cheerleader, the editor of the school newspaper, and apparently a popular girl, if she was in.

"No, I can't get in. I tried, I tried hard, but I can't do it. I can't get elected to an office. I tried last year and before that. I had a platform."

"What was it?"

"Well, I wasn't going to let Mr. Rossi run the class like he does and I was going to get some action in the cafeteria and I was going to get more kids involved."

"And they didn't vote for you?"

"No, I lost. And I was pretty bitter about it, too. Those kids won, Joan, Sally, and Betty. They always win. They vote for each other and keep nominating each other, and they've won all the elections since sophomore year."

"What about Bob?"

"Good example. He was vice-president of his freshman class, president of the sophomore class, and this year he's the vice-president."

"What does it mean to be an officer? I hang around with Bob and I never hear him mention it or do anything."

"That's just it. You're right. They don't do anything, but everyone thinks they do."

"Then what does it mean to run things?"

"It means you're in on the dances, the parties, the events, the offices. There isn't that much to do, but just a few do it all."

Talking about groups in general, Marilyn said that in addition to the "power clique" there were the jocks and the music-drama group. "And then each clique has its followers, like the jocks have the girls they go with and the power clique has their boy followers." She also said that there was an academic group who came to school to get grades, and another group of boys whose thing it was to go out and get drunk. At that she stopped and said that she had covered only about 100 students. I asked about the rest of the students. She was not sure, but assumed that everybody had someone to hang around with.

I asked Marilyn why she could not win an election by herself.

"Because the kids won't vote for me."

"But you had a platform and offered them something."

"That's right, and you know another thing? Last year at the junior class meeting when we were having elections, Rossi—I can't stand him—he says, 'Just give me one thing and I'll give you anything you want! Give me four officers I can work with!' Then he left the meeting. And you know what he meant? He meant the kids in the power clique. He loves them, he's always with them and flatters them, and then they do anything he wants, they're so flattered by his attention. He supports them and they support him and that's the way it is."

Other students supported the idea of the "power clique" who did what there was to do and excluded others. It was certainly true that the same few students kept getting elected to class and council positions, kept themselves on the committees and clubs, and were constantly with each other in school.

Marilyn's description of how things worked was as good as I could find. But it seemed that the reason a few were able to dominate was that there was very little to dominate. The range of possible behaviors and possible rewards was, in fact, so limited that involvement of more than a few was unthinkable. In fact, it was difficult to get any class member to speak of activities other than in terms of bake sales or beany sales. Regardless of the stated intent of activity, the members did little other than engage in raising petty cash with dances, sales, or car washes. For instance, I once asked Lorraine, officer of the Honor Society, "What does the Honor Society do?"

"Well, it's supposed to build character, leadership, scholarship, and service."

"How does it do that?"

"Well, last year we had a bake sale."

"What about this year?"

"Oh, this year we won't have a bake sale."

The truth is that the Honor Society did little as a society. One became a member because of reasonably high marks and a good deportment for some unspecified period of time. He attended a formal induction ceremony in which he carried a candle across the stage and received official greetings from the assistant superintendent, and then listened to a speech by that central office official, and had his picture taken with the rest of the members for the yearbook. But like the classroom, membership in the Honor Society actually demanded little, if any, active involvement. I suggested this once to a teacher, and she replied that the society did a great deal. In fact, she said they were presently starting a tutoring program in one of the elementary schools. I checked this and found that some of the members were indeed going in and acting as aides for two hours a week in an elementary school. But those who were doing it were members of the music-drama clique and were among the central figures in the fifteen or twenty who ran the class. They were doing it not as members of the Honor Society, but as members of an "in" group. Other members of the society who were not members of that group were not tutoring, and in fact, some of the tutors, while group members, were not Honor Society members. It was a case of one girl, Jean, a member of the music-drama clique being elected or appointed because of her high marks to the vice-presidency of the club. In carrying out her club duties she responded, not to the society's membership, but to her group membership. She justified her actions of including non-honor society members in an honor society function by saying that she had to get people she could depend on. "For instance, once we were having a bake sale and we appointed a junior to run it and she ruined everything. You simply have to get dependable people."

Another example was the case of student council officers. Bob, a popular boy, was a member of the council but refused to run for council office. So the other officers appointed him "sergeant at arms" and he was then treated as an elected officer of the council.

The members of the music-drama group frequently bemoaned the fact that only a few students ever became involved in activities. I suggested to one of them, Dick, who was probably the single, most active person in the class, that if more than fifteen students became involved, they would probably displace him since there was not enough activity for more than a few. He became angry at that, "That's not true. You've drawn your conclusions and now you're out to prove it."

"Then why can't you get other kids interested in your activities?"

"Because they're introverts."

"That means you have 359 introverts in the class." (There were a total of 374 students in the class.)

Dick was unconvinced, "I'm telling you, we open up our activities but still only a few kids participate."

But it was true even in the senior class president's assessment of what it took to run the senior weekend. I asked Tony, another music-drama clique member, "What do you do as president?"

"Well, for one thing, we're responsible for setting up the big senior weekend. And you have to get the place and everything."

"How many people does it take to do that?"

"I'd say five, no—I'd say two."

It amounted to calling the motel and confirming the reservation. It was the same motel that a previous class had used. Mr. Rossi took care of the band.

The president of the Student Council, also a member of the music-drama clique, one of the tutors, yet not an Honor Society member, was asked about the Student Council. "What do you do?"

"Not much. Last year we had a council dress code, but we dropped it and now the kids dress the same way."

She was right, not only about the dress, but about the council not doing much. I attended all the meetings and there was not much happening.

A few students would be charged with running something on the mimeograph, and a few would decorate the gym or the halls prior to a big ball game or dance. These were always the same few, a combination of the "power clique," most of whom were cheerleaders, the "music-drama clique" just mentioned, and some of the better football players. They were the only ones who were ever observed to be actively engaged in "student activities."

Other clubs were similar. Debbie, the editor of the yearbook, was a good girl to ask about the clubs. I was going through a yearbook with her one day and asked, "What does Future Nurses do?"

"Nothing, it's been discontinued. We didn't have an advisor."

"What does Yorkers do?"

"Nothing. We had this club designed to study the state, but that fell through, no interest."

"What does the French Club do?"

"I don't know. A lot of times you'll see those clubs and one or two names after them, but usually they get discontinued after one or two years."

"How about math or Latin Club?"

"Oh, those kids are usually the brains who take the harder math classes and the Latin classes and who get together once a week to talk about them." (I looked for meetings of these last two and could not find any record of them having met recently or planning to meet in the future.)

"How about the FBLA, what does that mean?"

"Future Business Leaders of America. They run the student store. I don't know if it's still running." (It was.)

There was considerable resentment by noninvolved students at those who ran everything. At class meetings I frequently sat in the back and overheard many resentful comments about "always the same kids," or "Why not pick someone else for a change." But these comments by non-participating students were made not to the whole class but to their own friends. No students ever challenged the right of the central fifteen or twenty students or the football players to run whatever activities there were. As was mentioned before, the total number of "active and involved" students did not exceed twenty students out of the entire class. Debbie, also mentioned previously, was the single exception. Although she was editor of the yearbook, she was not a member of the lead group. According to her, she worked hard the previous year and deserved the teacher-made appointment. But the clique members resented her severely and maintained that she just "grabbed it," and that "she was acting like a dictator."

Even Debbie, however, would liked to have been an "in group" member. "Well, yes. Most of us would like to but we can't."

"Do you have your own friends?"

"Yes, most of us just don't pay any attention to the lead group. Like me and my friends hang around together. We just don't need those kids."

In sum, there are a number of important points about the activity sector. A few ran what there was to run, but in truth there was not much to run. And while other students probably resented the "leaders," those "leaders" failed to understand the rest. All the students reacted in pretty much the same way; that is, they had their own friends and in truth did not pay very much attention to others. This raises the question of whether it is even legitimate to talk of high school classes in terms of leaders or representatives. If the few ran it for themselves, which seemed to be what happened, then looking for class leaders seems to me a silly pursuit. There was simply no one leading, nor anyone being led.

An incident occurred in a Catholic school in that same district in which I carried on a similar, although shorter study, in preparation for this one. I was sitting with a group of students who were not among the more esteemed students. Class elections had been held that morning and the priest supervising the cafeteria announced on the PA system, "Here's a list of the class officers. You can come up and check the names of your leaders." Not one boy at the table, not one member of the group, even looked up. The conversation did not even stop for a second. To them the issue of "class leaders" was not even commonly admitted. It seemed that for the majority of students at Gates that same type of situation existed.

Summary and Discussion of Chapter 3

In keeping with the format outlined in the introduction, I have attempted to provide a general and fairly objective description of the way I saw students spending their school time, and simultaneously, I have tried to avoid editorializing in the main part of the chapters. However, at this point there are again some specific questions which should be raised and directed toward those who teach or plan to do so.

It has been strongly stated that the school's organization places barriers to student-teacher interaction. What would happen if a particular teacher was not satisfied with those barriers of batch processing, maintenance details, and subject specialization, and wanted to cross them to see if he could change his students. Suppose he wanted to change Joe, sharpen up his social conscience, and get him to stop his talk about shooting people.

If it is difficult to reach such students in class; it is practically impossible outside of class. First of all, that teacher would have to get Joe alone—that means outside of class. Since keeping students for other than disciplinary reasons is not generally done, at 2:40 the teacher would have to go find Joe, convince him that coming in and talking would be in his best interests, and then proceed to set up a few sensitizing sessions on race relations. Or suppose he wanted to convince Red that the school is basically concerned with his well-being, and that the teachers really have his best interests at heart. Again, he would have to move quickly at 2:40, presuming that Red hasn't already left on early release for his job, and convince him to come in and prove that he's not just another of those "stupid people" who "talk all the time." That teacher's convictions had better be pretty strong, because Red has some good reasons for believing the way he does. Or if he wanted to convince Roger that the next time he makes a sensitive input into class, he will be commensurately rewarded, that will be a difficult task; Roger has a lot of experience that tells him otherwise. If a teacher wanted to reach any of these individuals he would have to make an "extra-organizational" effort, he would have to step out from the role of subject-matter expert, maintainer of order and discipline, and batch processer of students.

This is the same issue that was discussed in the first chapter. Horatio Gates' organization does not encourage, depend on, or even need one-to-one personal interaction between teachers and students. It does not reward teachers for attempting to reach students individually. In fact, the structure makes it difficult to do so. Also, the organization does not reward students or teachers for their individual efforts other than within very narrow boundaries. Those students who stand outside those boundaries, such as Joe, Red, and Andy, get no rewards, nor do they even receive any remedial attention. Teacher and students are allowed to play only a limited role in school. Those students who do not take a deep interest in the "student role" are, for the most part, left to their own devices. The teacher, and indeed, the whole school may just pass them over.

Perhaps one might read this and think, "If I were teaching there, I would find a way to help Joe, Red, Darlene, Andy, and Roger." But those who think and write about organizations tend to agree that people who inhabit organizational roles, as teachers do in school, behave as do others who take on those same roles. In most situations even a superior individual would tend to do what his fellows do. The lesson may be that if one is dissatisfied with the way schools are run, rather than examining individual teacher behavior, perhaps he should begin to think about the school's basic organizational structure.

For the purposes of this book, the main question then becomes, "If the many students are left to their own devices and are outside of any interaction with the teachers, are they suffering?" "Do they perceive themselves to be suffering," might be a better question. I do not think they did. Although I saw many signs of boredom, they seemed reasonably happy as long as they had their friends to talk to and be with. However, up to this point there has not been enough information presented to draw any conclusions. If hanging around in small groups was what they did in school, then my task was to begin to explore the patterns of their groups. I had to move deeper into student life by attempting to become a partial member of one or more of those groups.

CHAPTER 4

The Athletic Group

As explained in Chapter 2 the senior class was divided into groups, and because these groups were distinct from one another, it became essential for me to join one of them in order to carry out my project. If I had remained apart from group activity and attempted to maintain a large number of individual contacts among the students, I probably would have been unsuccessful. In that situation it was simply not possible to associate with everyone, or even a large number, and had I tired, my position would have become that of an isolate who "stands around leaning against the wall." The intent of the project was to explore student life, and since they grouped themselves, I followed their ways and joined a group.

During my first few days I had been introduced by the vice-principal to a few senior boys to whom I explained that I was associated with the university and wished to see what school was like "from the inside." I asked them to guide me around the school for some unspecified period of time, and although they probably had little idea of why any thirty-two year old adult would want to come to high school, they readily agreed. Since I, no more than anyone else in the school, could bear to "eat alone in the cafeteria" and because they, along with a few others constituted the type of group I was looking for, I began to associate with them on a regular basis, and subsequently they became central to the study. While my association with these few limited my time and opportunity for contacts with other students, it provided a deeper insight into the activities and purposes of at least one adolescent group in school.[1]

---

[1] The appendix will explain more fully the methodology as well as acceptance of me by the students.

This particular group was composed of seven senior boys, all of whom were important athletes. The first of the group was Jack, reported by some students and the vice-principal to be the "only one of the ball players with the brains for a college scholarship." Jack was a good student, took the harder courses such as physics and calculus, and on the basis of cumulative average, was ranked twenty-second in the class. He was an outstanding football player, was named to both first and second positions as the best defensive end in the county league, was elected captain of the football team, and in the spring played lacrosse. Jack was one of those fifteen to twenty students who was involved in class and school activities. He had been president of his freshman class, was presently vice-president of the Student Council, and frequently took the lead in school activities, such as the project to decorate the halls for Christmas and the project to collect wood for a bonfire rally prior to the first home game. He was also the one of whom a teacher, reporting in disgust about the way the student body cheered him for five minutes at a football rally, said, "And I know that kid. He can't even read!" But Jack could read and very well. What seemed to irritate the teacher was the fact that the students showed more enthusiasm for Jack and football than they did for her and American literature. The cheering was an indication of Jack's status among the students. Jack demonstrated that status on a number of occasions. Once at a senior class meeting, the members were going through the process of selecting someone to lead the annual variety show. Tony, the class president, was presiding and had received two or three names when Jack, who was sitting in front, stood up, turned around, and said, "All in favor of Dick say 'aye.'" Then he started to clap, a few of the boys around him and approximately thirty of the 200 others started to clap. "Well, OK," said Tony, as he moved on to the next matter, "Dick is the head of the senior variety show." Dick was the logical choice since he was president of the Drama Club and took his acting seriously, but no one else could have done what Jack did to assure his election. Another incident occurred at a Student Council meeting when the agenda called for election of officers.

The president of the junior class turned to him and asked if he wanted to be the president. "No," said Jack, "that's too much work; I want to be vice-president." When the nominations got around to vice-president, the junior nominated him, and he was easily elected.

The second member of the gang and one of my initial contacts was Jim, regarded by some as the "biggest screwoff in the school." Jim did not take the harder academic courses, but neither was he strictly enrolled in the business or vocational sequence. He took ceramics, humanities, and was repeating sophomore geometry for the third time. Although his academic record, grades, and class standing were poor, Jim was accepted in college and planned to become a policeman. He was an excellent football player at offensive tackle and won all-county honorable mention, which, according to a number of his teammates, was an underestimation of his ability and performance. While he, like Jack, was an important ball player, Jim was not one of those involved in other school activities, never served as an elected officer, and when proposed as a candidate for the student council, received only a few votes. He was noted for gross and dirty jokes, for constantly fooling around, and for a general lack of seriousness about school. Although as he and I became friends, I found him to be an intelligent and sensitive person with a strong sense of propriety.

The third member of the group was Bob, another football player and another one of those who seemed to be automatically elected to class offices. Bob was vice-president of his freshman class, president of his sophomore class, currently vice-president of his senior class, and appointed sergeant at arms of the Student Council. However, Bob gave no evidence of being involved in any of this. In fact, while I associated with him almost every day, only once or twice did he do anything that indicated he had any specific duties to perform. Once he said he had to make a phone call, another time he had to go to a meeting.

Bob was a halfback but he was overshadowed by the performance of another group member who also played halfback. As a wrestler, however, he had taken his weight class in county competition for the two previous years. He had chosen not to compete for the present year, and this irritated Rossi. "We have three football players who won't go out for wrestling because they think they're going to get a football scholarship. Can you imagine that? Those guys getting scholarships?! What's Rick's average? About 70? And Bob, he reads on the third- or fourth-grade level. I don't know who puts that garbage in their heads."

Bob was enrolled in the academic sequence, took physics, Math 12, and humanities, but was generally a poor student and maintained an academic standing of only 212. According to some of his teachers, Bob's reading level was extremely poor, but he was accepted into a community college where he hoped to start on the football team. He had a reputation for being "a real wildman in a fight," and on occasion lost his temper in school.

The next member of the group, and another excellent football player, was Rick, who had been a close friend of Jim, Jack, and Bob since grade school. Rick, too, was named to honorable mention in the all-county football team and was reported by other players to be "strong as hell." Rick was a vocational student taking auto mechanics, drafting, and humanities, and maintained a class standing of 321. Although a member of the group, Rick spent a lot of his school time with his girl, Mary. He ate with her in the cafeteria and was with her at lunch and before and after school. While not one of those who was extensively involved in activities, Rick was elected to the Student Council twice and was frequently involved in the school projects and committees.

The final member of the central group of five was Greg, the only non-football player, the only black, the only basketball player, and the only one who did not live in or go to school in Hillsborough. Greg was a member primarily through his close association with Jim. He was listed as an academic student, took French III, sophomore geometry, and humanities. Greg maintained moderate marks, had a class standing of 70, and was accepted into one of the better universities in the state on a special program for black students. While a strong, group member in school, Greg's outside time was taken up at a local TV station where he worked thirty hours a week as a cameraman.

There were three other boys, also football players, who while not as close as the first five, were usually present and were always included if they wished to be. The first of these was Max, an outstanding halfback, named to all-county team, the leading ground gainer in the county, and the player who overshadowed Bob. Max, named best looking boy in the class, was one of those who was often elected to class office. He had been class treasurer in his sophomore year, president of his junior class, and was the one that those outside the group named as the leader of the football players. An academic student, Max took Math 12, physics, and humanities, and maintained a class standing of 162.

The final members of the group were Pete and Ralph. Both were football players, although Pete received a serious knee injury in the first few weeks of practice and was lost not only for the fall football season, but also for the winter basketball season and the spring track team. It was said that his loss may have been the reason why the football team gained second rather than first place in county competition. He was reputed to be a real fighter. According to Bob, "Me and him are the toughest kids in the school. We get in more fights than anybody." Ralph, too, played football and had previously played basketball. Both boys were academic students taking physics, Math 12, and humanities. They were also very close friends and went with girls who were also best friends. Pete's class standing was 159 while Ralph's was 174. Pete planned to attend a nearby community college while Ralph wanted to join the Marine Corps.

Jim, Rick, Ralph, Pete, and Max all came from middle-class homes and their fathers were employed in factories, crafts, or in Rick's case, the family farm. From all indications their families were fairly stable. Greg's home, however, was different. His father was dead and in addition to her three children at home, his mother took in foster children from the county. Greg, therefore, was the oldest remaining son in a home which included seven or eight children. Jack and Bob came from broken homes; Jack lived with his mother and Bob with his father, who had married a succession of women since Bob's mother left. In the group, however, such matters as parents, home situations, or brothers and sisters were rarely mentioned and never pursued. In fact, only after associating with these boys on a daily basis for two months did I learn that the president of the school's sophomore class was Greg's step brother, that Bob had a sister who was a sophomore, or that Jim's parents had both been in the hospital that term. These personal matters were simply not topics for group discussion.

Therefore, beyond these few remarks about home background, this chapter will not deal with the boys' family life, nor will reference he made to their individual scores on achievement tests, personality inventories, IQ ratings, or other such personal information. Although that data was available and Mr. Vincent said I could have access to it if I wished, it was never even systematically collected. This should be explained. First of all, these things were never matters of group discussion and therefore were not pursued because the intent of the project was to find out what the group members seemed to care about, not what I presumed or guessed that they cared about. But more importantly, the premise of this chapter is that consideration of the group as a whole will capture something usually missed in observation of individuals. The group was, after all, a real unit. It had its own meeting places, roles, patterns of communication, topics of discussion, and was definitely purposive. That is, as the boys associated with one another in school they worked out a pattern of collective behavior which enabled them to fulfill some of their personal needs. The intent was to examine the group as it operated and carried on its processes in relation to the school environment, not to deal with the individual characteristics of each boy.

The first thing that immediately became evident was that the group had a long history; that is, the boys had been associating with each other literally for years. Jim,

Bob, and Max grew up in the same neighborhood in Hillsborough and had been in the same class and on the same athletic teams since third or fourth grade. At the age of 11, Jack moved to that neighborhood from the central city where, according to his account, he was one of the toughest kids on the block and the leader of a group of older boys. As an athletically talented individual, he joined with Jim, Bob, and Max when they were just beginning to play football for the junior high school. If there was any question of his acceptance, no one ever mentioned it and when they moved into the ninth grade he was elected class president.

Rick also joined at that time. He lived on his father's farm outside of town but was bussed into the school from the seventh grade and there joined the others in the same class and on the same teams. The last to join the group was Greg, whose family had also moved out of the central metropolitan area to Winnsboro. According to his account, "We moved to Winnsboro and I didn't have a car and there weren't any busses, so sometimes I'd hitchhike into Hillsborough. But I was pretty much alone except for a couple of guys I knew out there. But when I came to this school, I was playing freshman football and freshman basketball and that's when I met those guys."

The final members, Ralph and Pete, both came from Cowpens. They had been the best of friends since the first grade and their association with the others started in the ninth grade where they too played football, basketball, and wrestled. In sum, the group of seven boys had been together for between four and eleven years by the time they were seniors, and therefore had had a long time to build up a network of interactions and understandings.

The Internal Dynamics of the Group

This particular group of athletes, like most groups, was not a collection of evenly organized individuals, but a complex network of best friendships. At the time the study was being carried out, the closest of these seemed to be between Jim and Greg. According to Greg:

You know, me and Jim, we hang around together all day. We have second period in study hall together, then during third period we're in math, then fourth and lunch and fifth and sixth is all in humanities classes, then we have another study hall together. So we're together all day, and we got to be real good friends, real close. Before this year we knew each other but not that close. Like last year Jim was hanging around with Jack a lot. But Jack's different, he travels, he hangs around with lots of kids, but we don't. We hang around together. Lake this weekend, we're talking about going to the mountains for skiing. Now last year, maybe he and Jack would have thought of it, and then I would be invited. But this year, me and Jim started it and now we'll invite the other guys."

Greg's account of spending his day with Jim was true. From the beginning of the morning when they would accompany each other to their lockers, to the end of the day when Jim would have to attend football practice and Greg, basketball practice, they were together. Occasionally Greg would skip his first period French class and Jim his first period ceramics class and they would walk around or go to the student lounge. That, of course, meant they were together the entire day. During this time together, they carried on their own particular brand of fooling around. They frequently skipped classes, almost as frequently got caught, but because of their personal popularity with teachers and administrators, were rarely punished. Once when Mr. Rossi caught them skipping class, they told him that they had been only ten minutes late, but that the teacher had already sent in the attendance sheets. Mr. Rossi told them to get a note verifying that from the teacher. "So, you know what we did?" said Greg.

We knew that Mr. C., the math teacher, was in the teachers' lounge so we went in every single room in the school looking for him. We must have come in the student lounge three times and we'd look around and say, "Gee, he's not here. I wonder where he is?" And all the time he's right next door and we know it but we don't go in there. Then we go back to Rossi and tell him, "We looked everywhere, we don't know where he is." And all the time we're laughing our ass off. So he told us to go back to class, took the note, and we left.

Another time when a substitute was teaching geometry class, they walked in late and instead of sitting down as they were supposed to, they pretended they were sent around to pick up the names of missing students. So they took the absentee cards, which, of course, included their own names, and left. They then threw away the cards and went to the lounge for the period. Greg and Jim maintained good personal relations with most of the teachers and this made it easier for them to do as they wished with impunity. They consistently skipped seventh period study hall, and once, the teacher, Mr. Williams, asked them, "Do you think you could possibly make study hall tomorrow?"

"No, we can't. That's too much, you're simply asking too much," and they walked away.

Of course, he continued to place them on the absentee list and Mr. Rossi continued to call them in for "talks," but their behavior changed little. Actually it was difficult for Mr. Rossi to punish them because they never did anything so terrible that they could have been suspended. Once Jim took an inkstamp with the word ILLEGAL imprinted on it from the office. For the next two days everywhere one looked, on walls, windows, lockers, and lavatories, could be seen the word ILLEGAL. Jim and Greg made no secret that they had done it, so Mr. Rossi called them in, made them give the stamp back, and decided to punish them by making them clean up their markings. So they took some Windex and cloth, and during sixth and seventh period, instead of going to class, they entered various classrooms and cleaned all the windows. Of course, they had a good time, they laughed, the students in the class laughed, the teachers laughed, and the punishment was turned into a farce.

Jim and Bob were also close. Of the entire group they, along with Max, had been together for the longest time, since third grade in the same neighborhood. Now they played ball together, double-dated with girls who were best friends, and following school worked as janitors in a steel warehouse. Bob's courses were different from Jim's, but before school in the morning, during homeroom, the two or three humanities periods, lunch, and football practice or weightlifting, they were in each other's company. Greg and Bob were not close at the beginning of the year, but as they more closely associated with Jim, they became better friends, and by the beginning of the second semester, they were associating with each other both in and out of school on a regular basis. It was with these three that I most closely associated during the field work phase of the study.

Another close friendship was between Rick and Jack, despite the fact that except for humanities they took different courses; Rick was in drafting and auto mechanics, Jack in math and physics. They really were not together that much in school, since Jack had his activities with other students and Rick was often with his girl, Mary. Also, it may have been that for Jack and Rick, both of whom were 18 years old and serious about girls who were serious about marriage, the time of best friendships was ending. Still, they managed to remain close, participated in out-of-school activities together, and at the time of realignment of groups in the humanities class, they went to some lengths to be sure they stayed together.

The group was not only a series of dyads, but Jim, Jack, and Rick also constituted a triad. While their school activities were separated by Jim's friendship with Greg, Rick's girl, and Jack's other activities, they spent large amounts of time outside school in one another's company. In the school, however, the series of dyads were more common.

These issues of dyads and triads and the general internal dynamics of the group often seemed to hinge on the question of the group's leadership, and therefore that issue should be more fully explained. It was obvious that Jack was the group's past leader, but as Greg explained, he had been moving in other directions. As vice-president of the Student Council he was one of the few students who interested himself in the school's internal politics. Also, he steadily dated a girl who had previously graduated, and since she apparently did not want him to be part of a high school gang, he spent his Friday evenings with her instead of in the bar with Jim, Greg, and Bob. During the first semester, Jack was the only one of the group who did not elect to go into Mr. Summer's humanities section.

Jack was also differentiated by his athletic talent and the possibility of gaining a scholarship at a "name" school. He was receiving invitations to look at such schools as Pittsburg and the University of Pennsylvania, while the others were not getting any attention, not even from the community colleges. Of course, he was aware of his prestige. "All the kids think I'm sort of God around here ever since I made all-county. Eddie made it, too, but none of the kids know him. They don't realize I'm just another kid."

While these alternatives gave Jack a number of extra-group interests, some of the distance between him and the rest of the boys may have been due to the fact that he was the one member who expressed open disgust with the whole process of schooling. He once remarked, "I hate this sitting around all the time. This is the biggest waste of time I ever saw. This whole place is a waste of time."

Greg replied, "Aw, next year you'll miss this place. You'll be in some big school. No one will know who you are. You'll be going out for football practice, and no one will greet you or slap you. You'll be just another freshman player. You'll hate it and wish you were back here where your friends are."

"No," said Jack emphatically, "I can't wait to get out!"

On another occasion he mentioned his thoughts about being locked in school:

Well, most kids don't think about it. But at the same time they see things. Like they tell us we can't go out because of insurance laws, but we went out last year. Kids don't say anything but they see these things. I asked Rossi if kids could have a say in what teachers were hired, but he said, "Absolutely not. That is the duty and right of the Board of Education." But I think it would be good. After all, it's to the kids' advantage to have the best teachers.

School never bothered the others, or at least they never mentioned it. Jack's apparent indifference to the group may have been just another reflection of his personal impatience with the school processes. The result was that the group was actually leaderless and instead of a cohesive unit was broken into a series of loosely connected dyads. Associations consisted of Rick and Jack, Rick and Jim, Jim and Jack, Jim and Greg, Jim and Bob, and Greg and Bob. There was a noticeable lack of friendship between Greg and Rick who, once when we were watching a basketball game, mentioned, "I didn't think niggers were supposed to be smart, but Greg's not dumb at all." He sounded genuinely surprised. This same lack existed between Jack and Greg, who were only rarely observed alone in one another's company in or out of school. Bob and Rick also seemed, other than the football team, to have little in common, perhaps a mutual respect but no close friendship.

As it turned out, Jim, while he was the more dependent member of the dyad between him and Jack, had the most contact with the others as individuals, had the least amount of other interests, and was closest to being a leader. Jack's presence, however, still placed a strain on the group, at least upon that part of the group that revolved around Jim. For instance, when Jim, Greg, and Jack were putting up the Christmas tree in the hall, Jack told Greg to go get a saw from his car. "Go get it yourself," said Greg. Jim seemed uneasy. If it were just he and Greg, they would have gone to get the saw together, but in Jack's presence he sided with Jack. "Com'on Greg, go get it." Greg balked, but finally went and took his time getting the saw.

On another occasion we were on our way downtown one evening when we saw Jack and his girl. "Hey Jim. There's Jack. Aren't you going to run after him?" chided Bob. "Fuck you," said Jim.

When we were going on a field trip to the university there was a lot of indecision among all of us as we waited to see what bus Jim would ride, and Jim was waiting to see what bus Jack would ride. It appeared that Jack, who would have been equally popular on either bus, was torn between his different sets of friends.

The other three members, Max, Ralph, and Pete, need some explaining. Pete and Ralph, having grown up together, formed an independent dyad. Their strongest link to the previous five seemed to be with Bob. All three would recount with delight the stories of their fights against twenty other boys who were making trouble for a friend, or the time Pete hit another boy who dated his girl and to make sure no one interfered, Ralph hit anyone who tried to break it up. On numerous occasions they would tell about the time that Ralph actually hit the former principal. "We were playing J.V. basketball and Pete hit some kid and all of a sudden everyone's fighting. So Murphy [the former principal], he's out there, too, so I went right over the top of two guys and belted him. He never even saw who did it."

Bob was the only one of the central five who associated with Ralph and Pete outside of school. In fact, at a wrestling match, Jim, Bob, Rick, and Greg would attend together and Ralph and Pete would attend together, but unless there was some specific event, like a party, the two sections of the same student group would not get together. In fact, they barely spoke to each other.

The last member was Max who is important because of his popularity and his football and general athletic ability. He was also present in humanities and at lunch. There was some hard feelings directed toward Max, especially by Bob who resented his newspaper headlines and the big yardage gains made when he was sidelined. Also, Jim frequently referred to Max as a "pansy" who was too easily knocked down and failed to make the gain that he should, considering the size of the hole in the line that Jim had made. Max was also the butt of jokes about this having to go to church and confess his dirty thoughts, and about his girl, who previously had gone with both Jim and Bob. Jack liked him, however, and he was respected by many students outside the group. After humanities class had realigned in January, even Bob told me that, "The teacher tried to separate me, Greg, and Max, but he couldn't. We didn't let him."

Graphically, the group as described looked like this:

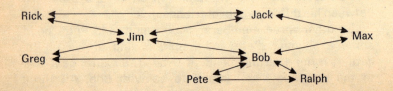

The position of the athletes in the school's prestige structure was secure. They were at the top. However, the whole concept of prestige stratification may be misleading. There was very little activity on which to base prestige and most students did not even bother to compete. Instead they got their school rewards from other sources, mostly from the friends in their groups. The athletes' prestige was not based on any kind of power or authority, since as students they too were at the bottom of the organizational hierarchy. Instead it rested on the fact that they were among the few students who involved themselves in an activity that demanded participation and therefore had something to differentiate them from the majority. For instance, when the ninth-grade teams played football, the coach would ask two varsity players, usually Jim and Jack, to referee the game. They, therefore, would get to take an active official role in an important activity unlike the remainder of the students, who, as usual, only sat and watched. At the annual winter sports rally, Jack, awarded the Most Valuable Lineman Award and Max, the Most Valuable Back Award, walked the entire length of the basketball court carrying their huge tropies while the students who filled the bleachers on either side cheered. It was the one perfect example of what it means to be a sports hero. Of course they were aware of their status. As Greg said, "When you're walking down the hall and a teacher stops you and says, 'You did a good job Saturday or Friday,' that does a lot for you. And they do it, too."

Jack said, "Oh, yeah, see, we're the biggest kids in the school and other kids sort of look up to us. So when we get into trouble Rossi is always telling us we're setting a bad example."

They received respect as individuals also. Once, when a large group of seniors was getting ready to choose up teams for a basketball game, Bob simply announced, "Ok, me, Greg, and Phil will stand these three guys. The rest of you go down to the other end." And everyone (including myself) did just as he said.

Of course, they received preferential treatment from the administrators and teachers. As Greg told it, "We don't pay any attention to Rossi. Like last year, you could do anything you wanted in the office. There were kids in there all the time, they just walked in. But this year they said that was all going to change. At the beginning, you know that big window where the secretary sits? Well, kids were supposed to get what they wanted there and not go in. But shit, that didn't last at all. Now we walk in the office whenever we want and they never stop us. Like Jack and I, the other day went right in Rossi's office and talked to him and he invited us right in. He's really a pretty good guy."

I asked him if he didn't think that athletes received special favor. "Yeah, that's probably true," he replied.

The Group in School

Having established the fact that there was such a thing as a group—that is, that there were a number of individuals who met frequently, maintained certain communication patterns, had places of meeting, and shared a sense of common participation—the question becomes what did it mean to be a member of the group in school. Of what importance was the group in the lives of these boys, and how did that groupness assist them in that institution? How did belonging to a group help them to fulfill some of their needs as human beings?

To begin to answer these questions, we need to consider what it was that they did in school as a group. First of all, it was obvious that they did not walk around en masse all day. There were only a few times when they could all be together, but one could usually manage to be with at least one or two of his friends all the time. Jim and Greg have already been mentioned. Rick and Jack shared a humanities project; Jack, Bob, and Max a physics class; Pete and Ralph another physics class; Max, Bob, and Greg a later humanities class; and Jim, Jack, and Rick a play that the class was putting on. So, while the entire group met only once or twice a day, in the beginning of humanities and at lunch and possibly at football practice, any single boy, unless he was with his girl, could be found in the company of another member.

The main meeting place of the group was the cafeteria, where the last table in the corner was unofficially reserved for the senior athletes. Only two juniors ever sat there, one was the quarterback of the football team who sat there only after the third game when he took over starting position. The other was the president of the junior class and a team halfback.

The conversation and activity at the back table was probably the key to understanding the group, and it was always the same. It revolved around what the boys did as a group. They talked about the games they played together, the parties they went to together, the time they gathered wood for a bonfire rally or went downtown after skipping school, past and future football games or wrestling matches, of the draft lottery, or they spoke of fooling around in school. They never mentioned books, teachers, papers, assignments, homework, or anything academic.

After a particular humanities class, Jack came to the table and wanted to continue a discussion they had just had concerning the Vietnam war. "Hey, did you see that stuff Milner was passing out? It told how much it cost to kill a Vietcong! $20,000! And how much the war is costing a year—$30 billion a year." He was shaking his head about it and obviously wanted someone to respond, but no one did. It simply was not picked up, even when initiated by Jack, the leader. The conversation passed to Jim, who was making some remarks about a girl across the way.

When Max came to the table one day he wanted to talk about physics. "That Fresino, he's a good guy. He doesn't want anyone to flunk. He even marks on a curve."

Pete said, "A curve means that someone has to flunk." And despite the presence of Jack, Bob, and Ralph, who all took physics and all had Mr. Fresino for a teacher, the conversation was dropped.

Even on report card days no mention was made of marks. I asked Greg once when report cards were due. "Last week, you were here." I was there, but since I had seen only the group members and they had not mentioned it, I didn't know.

Not only were the conversations group-centered and

noninvolved with academic matters, but the group went to lengths to avoid any kind of interaction that would disturb the stability of the group. When Rick, at the next table with his girl, got mad, stood up, slammed his tray, and walked out, not one person commented on the fact that he and his girl were having a fight. It was not an accepted topic for group conversation. Instead we went on with the usual banter. "Hey, you got new pants. Did your father finally get a job?"

"His father gave me a job last night."

"Man, are you growing a moustache or did you braid the hairs in your nose?"

"What is this shit they're giving us?"

"Better that you get at home."

"At least I don't live in a barn."

The topics would go back and forth like that with Jim and Jack talking the most, Ralph, Pete, Bob, Greg, and Max less, but still actively involved. Anything personal or serious was avoided. As previously stated, the group never spoke of their families and as much as possible avoided cases of anger. For instance, Ed was a junior who on occasion sat at the table. Once he was talking about an incident in which a class member had been struck by a car and killed. "Who did it?"

"I don't know," said Ed. "Some colored guy. Oh, excuse me, Greg."

Greg flared immediately. "What do you mean, 'Excuse me?' What'd you do, insult me or something? Just because some guy does something and he's black, this is a bad mark on me?" Although Greg was getting redder, he then shut up and looked down at his plate. No one said a word for a few seconds. Then Jim grabbed the kid with one hand and jerked him back from the table. "Go 'wan. Get outta here. Don't come back, we don't want you eating back here with us."

"Com'on Jim, cut it out. I didn't mean anything."

Jim was getting madder as he continued to hold the boy back.

"No, man, I didn't mean anything," pleaded the kid as he pulled himself back to the table and shut up. Then

Jim stopped and went back to his meal. The rest of the boys looked very uncomfortable. A few seconds later Jim motioned to Greg, they got up and, leaving their unfinished meals on the table, walked out. The rest of us were very quiet for a minute and actually, it seemed as if everyone were embarrassed. Even Bob, Pete, and Ralph, to whom fights were a common occurrence, did not say anything. We then went on with a conversation about wrestling and never mentioned the incident there or anywhere else. The boys simply did not even recognize such an emotional issue in the group. When Greg's feelings were involved, he and his best friend Jim simply left.

A similar incident occurred when Doug, who used to sit with us and who had a habit of showing his distaste for the food by spitting it out, did so while sitting across from Bob. Bob, who did not like Doug anyway, jumped up. "Goddamn you, you ever spit on my plate, I'll fuckin' kill you." Bob threw his chair aside and started coming across the table to get Doug, who by that time was standing behind me. But he did not. He controlled himself, threw his milk carton on Doug's plate, and sat down. Pete, Jim, and I simply wiped the spattered milk off our shirts and everyone, including Doug, sat down. About six months later Bob and I were talking and he referred to Doug as about the only kid in the school he disliked, but that remark was not made in the group, but in a personal conversation between Bob and me.

It seemed that anything, such as feelings, fights, or other emotional issues, that could possibly upset the usual pattern of group interaction was ignored or met with an embarrassed silence. It was not that the boys disapproved of fighting—they were all football players and would speak lightly of getting into fights with players from other teams and other schools. Also, they were all involved in a couple of basketball game brawls, so it was not a case of fearing violence. It simply was a matter of taking great care to maintain the group structure which in school meant avoiding emotional issues.

The group also took care to avoid trouble with teachers. When a member came into conflict with a teacher over any issue, he was not supported by the other group members. Once when Jim became particularly gross with Miss P., a student teacher, even Greg would not support him. "Jim shouldn't have done that, not to a teacher, it's not right. She'll tell Rossi and he could be thrown out." Had the teacher involved not been young and pretty, it would never have happened, because as much as Jim fooled around, he knew enough not to cause unnecessary trouble for teachers.

After a food throwing incident in the cafeteria, a frustrated and angry teacher erroneously blamed Jim for starting it and told him to stay and pick up the food. Jim did not say a word, he barely showed his annoyance at the teacher's error, and when he finished eating, he picked up the thrown food and left. Of course, nothing was said of the incident.

Bob, however, was not as cool as Jim. It was prohibited to push the cafeteria tables next to one another, but Bob was late once and did so in order to have a seat with the rest of the group. The teacher on duty came by and told him, in a hurried manner, to put the table back.

"All right, all right, I'll move it."

"What'd you say?" the teacher snapped.

"I said, you don't have to talk like that, I'll move it, but I respect people who respect me." Bob was getting redder and redder.

The teacher, who obviously didn't want it to go any further, said, "Listen you, just move the table." Then he left, not waiting to see if Bob did as he asked. Rick then derided Bob sarcastically, "I think you had him scared, Bob." Jack shook his head, the rest of the boys just went back to eating. All seemed genuinely relieved that nothing serious had happened. Later, both Jim and Greg said, "Bob shouldn't have done that. He shouldn't talk that way to teachers." Their point was that the teacher was a good guy just doing his job, but, of course, they had not said that at the table, they were the ones who, after the teacher left, started the conversation about a boxing match that Max and another boy had held the previous night.

Avoiding conflict with teachers was a safe way to avoid trouble with parents and administrators, but it was clear that the boys had no common opinions of most teachers, and therefore, had no common perceptions to discuss. There was one teacher whom I thought did very little instructing. In fact, he did none. He would begin with some topic and almost immediately relate it to his war experiences, his hometown, his school days, or his brother-in-law and would just ramble on meaninglessly all period. But after class the boys would say nothing about his performance, no more than they would about any other teacher, even those who did good jobs. Or, if one did say something, as Max did one day, "that Tomaso, sometimes he's an asshole and sometimes he's OK." "He's always an asshole," said Jack, and that was the end of it. That same teacher insulted Ralph one day by making a sarcastic remark about Ralph and his girl who was reputedly wealthy. "Watch out for Ralph, you can always find him next to the smartest person in the class, that or the richest." Ralph was infuriated, "I'll kill that sonofabitch someday, he better never meet me alone." He said this to his best friend Pete, and me, and Pete said nothing. In fact, Pete actually liked Mr. Tomaso and elected to stay in his humanities class.

It was the same case with the librarian who was particularly crabby most of the time. I asked one day, "How do you stand her?" "Her? She's all right," Bob replied. And no one volunteered anything more. In the beginning of my study I thought that perhaps my presence was keeping the boys from revealing their true feelings about the teachers, but their behavior was consistent over the entire semester. While occasionally a teacher would be mentioned by one member, the topic never became general. Nor were related topics of marks, grades, academic work, or assignments ever made topics of general conversation. The boys simply had no common definition or understanding of those things and therefore, in the group settings, they avoided them.

There was only one teacher who was heartily disliked by all. Pete told me:

Like that Johnson. You know what he did the other day in study hall? He says, "I don't want to hear a sound in here. I just put one kid on detention and I would just as soon do it to another. I can't play favorites. Not that there's anyone in here I'd ever favor." Just like that. Can you imagine? I don't think most kids caught it, but me and Rick heard it. If I ever meet that sonofabitch alone, I swear I'll kill him.

This issue of Mr. Johnson was interesting because he was one teacher who on three different occasions was mentioned by individuals as being a poor teacher. Jim, Greg, and Pete all considered him bad. Once Jim and Greg together talked about him. Jim said, "I'm not going to class, that asshole Johnson is talking."

"What's he teach?" I asked.

"Nothing, he doesn't teach a thing. Just a bunch of bullshit," said Greg. And yet, even though he was one teacher of whom they held some common opinion, he was mentioned in a group setting only that once.

Bob hated one particular teacher, Mr. Smith, who, when he heard about Bob dating Marlene, called Marlene's mother, suggested that she have her daughter checked for VD, and that she stop the relationship. That earned Bob's undying hatred. "I'll kill that sonofabitch. Someday he'll say something and I'll do it, I'll kill him." But when Smith passed us in the halls, Bob would only look away, and although everyone knew his feelings, no one ever said anything. In fact, the others did not feel that way. That same teacher liked and was liked by Jim, and at Christmas he helped Jim get a part-time job.

There were other topics which the boys avoided. One was an individual member's relations with his girl. When Jim was with Betty, or Rick with Mary, or Bob with Marlene, the others would not even talk to him. He and his girl would be left strictly alone, and no mention was ever made of their relationship.

On the other hand, the best friendships were able to take care of many of these issues. As I became closer to individuals, such as Jim, Greg, and Bob, we would have small conversations in which teachers, girls, families, grades, or the future would be discussed. With Bob alone one night, he told me the story of his father, his mother, his stepmothers, and spoke at length of his relations with his girl. Alone with Greg, I heard him talk about his family, the way he and his mother handled the house, and the problems they had with his stepbrothers. But when one of those stepbrothers came and sat with Greg at the back table, Greg absolutely ignored him and thus discouraged him from returning. Jim, too, would talk about his concerns about the health of his parents and his desire to go to college. But these things were reserved for the close friendships, not for the group. As Greg said, "All these kids think me and Jim just fool around, but they never see us talk serious."

The way the group dealt with other students was interesting. While they recognized their own position of status, and received some resentment from other students for "not speaking," it seemed to me as if they behaved just as other students behaved. That is, from all appearances they did not even notice other students.

I asked Greg about it and he agreed. "Like, if you come here and didn't hang around with us guys who are on the top, I'd just think you were another new kid, I wouldn't even know you."

If I asked a particular member about some other student the reply would frequently be, "Who? Who do you mean?" I could only conclude that they somehow did not even see those with whom they did not associate. And I found that as I became more a member of their group, I too stopped seeing many of the students I had met in the first month.

The boys never made an attempt to include any but their own few friends in activities. Their acceptance of me was due to my status as someone from the university who was approved by administrators and teachers. However, I had to go slowly beginning with Jim and Greg before I was generally accepted.

The group's reaction to other outsiders who stumbled into the group was predictably harsh. As mentioned, Greg simply ignored one of his stepbrothers who made the mistake of sitting with us. And on the occasion of our going to the university, Jack and I struck up a conversation with a boy who was not generally recognized by the group and who was trying to sell one of us a used motorcycle. When the class arrived at the place, it split into its various groups and this same boy was somehow left with us. It turned out badly. First, we went to the local McDonald's hamburger place, Jim, Rick, Jack, Greg, Bob, myself, and George, the outsider. All the way down the street there was a decided uneasiness—we hurried, no one was relaxed. Jack seemed tense, Jim made no jokes about the college girls. Then when we were all eating there arose a dispute over where we would go. I mentioned a few possibilities; the art museum, the natural history museum, or the media center. Jack grabbed Rick and said, "Com'on, you, me, and Phil will go to the museum." I agreed, since there was little alternative, and off we went, leaving Jim, Greg, and George, the outsider.

As Jack and I were going out the door, Greg and Jim got up abruptly and started to leave another way. George was simply left sitting alone. He could not have followed. It was too obvious that he did not belong. Later Rick, Jack, Jim, Greg, Bob, and I joined up at the natural history museum and spent the rest of the day together. Of course, no one asked "Where's George?" They had not even overtly recognized his presence.

Even when a member would initiate some talk of an outsider, it would not be discussed. One night when John, Rick, Bob, and I were out, Rick expressed some resentment against Dick, who was running the senior play. "That guy, I didn't even use to know that kid and now he's running everything."

"Com'on Rick, cut it out," said Jim, who was not about to let us go into a conversation of personalities. Dick was mentioned on one other occasion by Bob, who regarded him with easy tolerance. "That guy's an asshole—but to direct a play, you gotta be an asshole."

In sum, by meeting frequently within school, taking care to avoid personal or emotional issues, and sticking to common and familiar friendship and conversational pat-

terns, the boys were able to maintain their group structure in the school. In fact, that was what they did in
school most of the time. It was not always easy. There
were conflicts between the school's demand for compliance and the group's need to carry on familiar activity.

An incident occurred one afternoon, just prior to
Christmas. As vice-president of the student council, Jack
was responsible for decorating the building and asked
Mr. Rossi if he could go get a tree with Jim and Greg. Mr.
Rossi said, "No."

"We're going anyway," said Jack.

"You do and you'll get suspended."

They went and returned an hour later carrying a large
freshly cut tree on top of Greg's car. Mr. Vincent called
them into his office and Jim's version of the confrontation
went like this.

"Vincent says, 'This time you guys have gone too far,
go see Mr. Rossi.' Then we go in Rossi's office and close
the door. He says, 'You boys are going to get a little vacation, about five days worth.' "

" 'Bullshit,' I told him."

" 'Don't use that kind of talk in here and, furthermore,
I don't like your attitude,' " said the vice-principal.

"I said, 'Fuck that, what do ya mean my attitude? If I
didn't give a shit about this school, I wouldn't have bothered to give you that fight and song I gave you. If I didn't
give a shit about this school, I wouldn't have gone to get
that tree. Bullshit, we're not getting suspended.' "

"Then Jack started in on him and Jack can put out the
words when he wants to. He couldn't say nothing. He
couldn't throw us out of school. Shit, if he throws Greg
out, he'll have a race riot on his hands. I told him, 'I
know I fuck around a lot in class, but that don't mean I
got a bad attitude.' "

That was Jim's version, which was generally supported
by Greg. "And when we got into trouble for that Christmas tree thing, Vincent told Jim that he should cut it out
because his parents hadn't been well and Jim started
swearing and I thought Jim and Rossi were going to start
swinging and Jim said, 'That's none of your business.' "

"And Rossi yells, 'Don't you talk like that.' "

"And Jim says, 'I'll talk anyway I want to.' And then Rossi looks at Jack and starts laughing and then Jim starts laughing and then it's all over."

"Jim says, 'Don't laugh, I've got something to say and I can't say it unless I'm mad.' But then we all laughed. Then he told us we had to come after school for three weeks and we came for one week and each day we'd eat cookies and drink milk in his office and he would talk to us and after a week he told us we didn't have to come anymore."

"Would he have thrown you out?"

"I was scared because he told us not to go and then he stood there and watched us go out the door and yelled at us that we were gonna get thrown out if we went. But Jack kept going and Jim kept going and so did I. Then when we came back, we were going in Rossi's office and we passed Lorraine [a popular cheerleader] and she asked us what we were doing and we said we were gonna get thrown out and she said, 'Okay, I'll get a petition and we'll put it all over school.' She would have, too; they didn't dare do it."

Mr. Rossi did call Jim's mother and told her his behavior was going from bad to worse, but there was no improvement. Greg was most hurt by the incident because the vice-principal told the basketball coach, who benched Greg that evening and for the next few games on the basis of his "poor attitude." Shortly after Christmas he quit playing. Since football season was over, Jack and Jim were free from similar sanction.

Immediately following the confrontation, the three went out and put the tree up in the hall by the office. Jack would ask the advice of every teacher who came by, "Do you think this is all right? Is it straight?" Then, to me he remarked, "Shit. They throw us out of school and this school would fall apart. We do everything around here."

About a week later another incident occurred. Jim and Greg were sneaking out the rear library door clearly marked STUDENTS DO NOT USE THIS DOOR and ran directly into the principal. "Have you guys got a pass?"

"Sure," says Jim. "Which one do you want, the one signed by Mr. R., Mr. M., Mrs. P., or Mr. T.?" All the time Jim was pulling these passes out of his wallet and laughing at the joke.

"This time you guys have gone too far," said Mr. Vincent. But nothing happened; they were merely told to go back to class.

Jim and Greg were the members most determined that the school routine would not interfere with their own activities which were built around associating with one another. They used to meet during seventh period study hall and go to the lounge, gym, or through the halls greeting their friends. Greg told me what happened when a teacher tried to stop them. "That Johnson, I hate that sonofabitch, you know what we, me, Jim, Jack, and Rick did yesterday? Well, Johnson gave us the pass to go to the guidance office see, and we went to the gym and got caught. So Johnson in the study hall today had to tell everybody about it. Then he calls me up to the front and says, 'I guess you're going to have to stay in this study hall for two weeks. You made a mistake.' I says to him, 'Well, you made a mistake, too, you're not supposed to let me go to the guidance office without a presigned pass from them.'"

"And he says, 'Yeah, you're right. I made a mistake, too, you're going to pay for it. You're not leaving this study hall for two weeks.'"

"And I told him, 'Uh huh, I ain't staying in this study hall.' And I won't either, I can't take that shit. I'm telling Rossi I won't and if he don't like it, he can throw me off the team. They're always threatening to; let 'em, I don't give a shit. I won't stay in that study hall."

Mr. Rossi was coming down the hall, and Greg talked to him. "I told him," he said later.

Another time in the same study hall, the teacher, seeing Jim leave, chased after him. Passing Jack and Rick at the door he told them to catch Jim for him. Of course they agreed and for the next fifteen minutes, to the great hilarity of all present, they chased Jim around the auditorium. They finally captured him, "We got him! We got him!" and carried him bodily back to the study hall. The teacher, of course, could do nothing without eroding his authority further.

Jack, Jim, and Greg were difficult to punish. Jack was the most popular boy. Greg was a confidant of the vice-principal when it came to the problem caused by a boy who was placed in the care of Greg's mother. Jim's mother was president of the PTA and his father of the Booster Club. All three were well known and well liked by students and teachers and as such were perhaps outside the normal sanctions of the school. And, too, Mr. Rossi would have had a hard time defending the expulsion of students who "went to get a Christmas tree" or "who didn't have a pass," or who "skipped class." So he dealt with them as best he could.

Flagrant abuse of the rules and regulations, however, was usually restricted to Jim and Greg and occasionally Jack. The rest of the group went along with the rules and regulations with no questioning or resentment. Only twice did this change. The entire group, on one occasion, was part of a group of one hundred seniors who skipped out to breakfast and came in late. Another time the whole group went to the basketball game after a few hours of drinking and turned a slight scuffle into a full-scale floor brawl. When it was over, they left for the evening and the following school day nothing was said from the office about the incident.

Other than this instance the group as a whole rarely exceeded the bounds. In fact, when the other members thought Jim and Greg were going too far, they took steps to stop them. One morning the entire humanities class was having a concert and after we had all filed in, Jim and Greg decided they could not take it, so they got up and left. Jack, Rick, Bob and, I were still sitting. "Those guys are getting away with too much," said Jack.

Bob called Mr. Tomaso over and said, "Hey, Mr. Tomaso, see anybody missing?"

Jack said, "His name begins with J." Tomaso looked around. "He's our other buddy," added Rick.

"He and the tall kid that hang around with him aren't here."

"Where's Pete?" asked Mr. Tomaso.

"No, not Pete. He's in the hospital."

"Jim and Greg, where are they?"

"They skipped out, but we didn't tell you, right?"

"You didn't find out from us, did you?"

"We didn't tell you that they're in the lounge, did we?"

Tomaso left to get them and both Rick and Jack agreed that, "Those guys skip too many classes."

The teacher found Jim and Greg and gave them a lecture on responsibility. Rick, for some reason, went and informed Jim that Jack and Bob had told on him, but did not mention that he had done it also. Later when Jack and Bob informed him that Rick, too, had participated, he said, "That fuckin' Rick, he's getting too wise," and a week later Jim led about five other boys, got Rick in the bathroom, and took his pants off. Rick was angry, but he and Jim had been good friends for a long time, and they later laughed about the incident.

The Athletes in Class

The only class where most of the members got together was in humanities class. At the beginning of fourth period every day they, along with the other 107 humanities students, would enter the large group instruction room and take their seats wherever they pleased. Of course, the group sat together which was natural. Anyone who knew the class members immediately saw that the entire class of students arranged themselves so that each, together with his few friends, would be sitting in the same place every day. It would not even make sense to speculate on what would happen if an outsider sat in a spot usually reserved for a group member. It just never happened. After the first few weeks of school the places were settled upon and they never changed.

During those first ten or fifteen minutes when the three teachers would be taking attendance, answering questions, and giving general instructions, the students would be sitting with their friends and doing what they wanted to do. What they chose to do, as always, was talk to each other in their usual pattern. They talked about the previous football game or the coming football game, about Bob who was sidelined, that is "on the Red Cross squad," about how someone else who had Bob's number was making the headlines, or about Pete's injury or Jack's webbed feet, which he proudly displayed. Or, if someone said something they would make fun of him. Once Bob, for instance, said, "Some sonofabitch stole my log book and if I catch him, I'll kill him."

"Oh oh, watch out for Bob. He's got the rag on today," said Rick and everyone started hitting Bob, which made him all the madder, but then he too would laugh.

"Same old shirt, when's your father going to get a job?"

"You guys laugh, but my father's a quadruple amputee."

This would go on until the teachers were through taking attendance and told the students to go into the small groups. The humanities students had two assignments. The first was that each individual was to maintain a log of his daily class activities. That is, he was to write down the activity and his subjective impression of it. The second was for the students to break into small groups and work on independent study projects. This was an attempt on the part of some teachers to try to utilize the students' self-motivation, although as previously noted, the project did not have much support from the administrators. The teachers had decided that one way to begin would be to choose a broad concept and let the students go to work developing a project around the concept. The teacher had not made any attempt to separate the informal student groups. It would have been difficult and would have involved knowing more about the students than the teachers knew. So, after general instructions were over, Jim, Greg, Pete, Bob, and Rick would cross the hall along with twelve other students and would enter Mr. Summers's room. The first thing they did in the room, of course, was sit together. The other twelve students would sit and work with their friends also.

Somehow in the first week the athletic group had decided to study the idea of success as understood by the inmates of the county penitentiary. They proposed the idea to Mr. Summers, who agreed that it was basically sound and told them to go ahead. Exactly how they intended to study the issue or what connection they made between prisoners and success was never clear. The idea was simply there and they went at it, or rather they played at going at it, for the first twelve weeks of school. The boys really did not know how to start. It was terribly slow and painful, but toward the beginning of October, Bob, Rick, and Greg were making some attempt. During class they were to think up questions to ask and ways to approach the inmates. There would be some shuffling around as they looked at one another, waiting to start. Bob, who was willing to work, said, "Let's start. Let's write down some questions."

So Rick took out a piece of paper and a pencil. Greg, Pete, and Bob watched him. "How do you get in here?" was a question Bob suggested. Rick wrote that down and the rest of us watched. Jim was looking competely bored, and while Rick was writing, Greg said to me, "We're trying to keep Jim out of this thing. He'll fuck it all up."

"Why are they in jail?" said Bob and Rick wrote that. There was a painful silence. Jim was getting more bored. "What else will we ask?" said Bob. Then he said something to the student teacher. She came over and everyone stopped to look at her. That was all Jim needed. "Are you working on your log?" she asked.

"I wish you'd work on my log," Jim responded. She turned red and left, but the laugh he got raised spirits. Then he made a couple of cracks about prisoners and started being funny. He made some gross remarks about the student teacher, and said he would try to get her before she left. Then, when he had everyone's attention, he continued. Rick put down his pen and turned to Jim and listened. Then Pete told about the time some girls hid his and Ralph's clothes when they were swimming and so they laid across the hood of the girls' car naked and all screamed. That was the basis of the conversation for the rest of the period. Mr. Summers and the student teacher, trying to follow through on their policy of non-interference, left the boys alone. This proved futile. The next day we started with the questions again. Bob or Pete asked, "What'll we ask the inmates?"

"Ask 'em if they bend over in the shower," said Jim.

Patty, the student teacher, spoke up, "Com'on boys, do your work."

"Ask 'em what kind of soap they use," said Jim. And everyone laughed as Jim did an imitation of someone bending over to pick up the soap. After all, he was the leader and was apparently doing what the group wanted to do.

Until Thanksgiving, when the boys were supposedly spending an endless amount of time "working on their project," what they actually did, with Jim as leader, was what they had been doing together for a long time: talk about cars, sports, girls, and group interests. It was not just Jim's "bad influence." One day when he was in the guidance office talking to a college recruiter, the group did not suddenly become work oriented. With Jim gone, it was a little awkward at first, but only for a minute. Bob was telling Pete something and then turned and included Greg and me in the story. It dealt with his summer job and the way he cut off the end of his thumb, applied for compensation, and was promised $600 for a loss of four weeks work. He never received any, so he was telling us how he went to the compensation office.

There's this old lady sitting in the corner eating candy and smoking and I says, "I'd like to ask about compensation." She looks through her file and says, "Don't worry, we do our job." I got pissed off so I [Bob was pretty animated now] flung this chair across the room right in her direction, then I tipped over a table and yells, "God-dammit, I want my money and I been waiting long enough." You should have seen her, she about shit. She goes through the book, told me she'd take care of it, and Wednesday I got a check for $125.00. Then I asked her about my hearing, I want some money for my thumb, that guy was covered. She told me January, and I told her that if she tries to put me off I'd be back. I'm going back on Monday, I'll probably wind up in jail if i do anything else, but . . .

Then Pete warmed to the topic and told how he punched out a salesman at a local department store on Saturday for fouling up his tires for three and a half hours. Briefly, the man sold him tires, never delivered the order to the garage, finally ordered the wrong tires, then accused Pete of not paying cash. Pete punched the salesman, got his money, and left.

The humanities project dragged out long enough and the boys got Mr. Rossi to take them over to the penitentiary on the bus. There they met the superintendent and got the official grade school tour. There was no opportunity to talk to prisoners. In order to write it up, Jim and Greg took notes and Rick's mother typed the two and one-half page report. That was the small group humanities project for twelve weeks of school.

One might conclude that the teacher should have worked more closely with the group, but when a teacher tried he was simply unable to influence them. Mr. Summers once suggested he call in the district psychologist to talk to them about the "criminal mind." So Rick, Greg, Jim, Bob, Pete, and I went to meet him one period at noon. Jim and Greg at first waited outside the door and Mr. Summers laughed, "They're waiting for Bob. They'll get him to do the talking." Bob came and did as they wished. He started the session and the psychologist answered his questions, speaking generally of psychology: clinical, experimental, Freudian, and so forth, for about twenty minutes. The boys listened, then Jim asked a question about thieves, then another about rapists, then Bob was talking to Jim about someone they knew and what this person had done. Then Greg was talking about some kid he knew who did a certain thing and by the end of the period we were back to our usual conversation. Even I was ignoring the psychologist, who was literally reduced to the position of spectator to the group interaction. If he had known more of what the boys wanted, or if they had even known what they wanted, it probably would have taken the group longer to co-opt him. I have no doubt that it would have happened in time. The group's strength and solidarity was just too much for an outsider, even a teacher, to try to bend.

In a later humanities class the group often went to the library to study some material on communication. They would go to the reading room with some magazines and start looking at the articles and pictures, but it never lasted more than a few minutes. Soon someone would start fooling around in general patterns that they understood and study would be forgotten. They would lapse into their familiar patterns of talking about a particular girl who was after Pete, about Max's car, about what they would do next year, their prospects for athletic scholarships, or about a particularly funny past incident which they shared. When asked by a teacher to do some academic activity, the group was unable to break the interaction pattern that had been set up for so long.

To some degree the fact that they could not work together bothered individuals in the group. Greg once mentioned that he was disgusted with Jim's unwillingness to take class seriously. Jack remarked after a particularly fruitless session, "They ain't ready for it. These guys don't know how to study by themselves." He expressed particular disgust once in reference to the group's performance on the project. "When they tell these kids to go to the library and study, they just go to the lounge and dick off . . . They aren't prepared for this . . . They aren't doing their projects at all."

And Bob at times would be genuinely disgusted with Jim's performance. He came in the lounge one day and began berating Jim for skipping class. "You're going to flunk the first marking period, Jim, don't you know that?"

"Screw that—I'm not even here today—I got here at 10:30 and they didn't mark." "Yeah, but Summers knows you're here." It discouraged Rick, too. He said once, "We never do anything around here."

Yet when the group was together in school, whether in class or elsewhere, they could not make a learning experience the center of their conversation. Sensing that the group was doing nothing in class in November, Mr. Summers asked the whole class to come up with some suggestions for improvement of the humanities class. "Now for the next twenty minutes of this period, I'm going to leave you alone and I want you to talk about the class, what the good points are, what the bad points are, how the class can be improved. Bob, come up here and be the chairman."

With that he left the room. Those that were left included the group, two other boys, Sam and Charles, and three girls in the back who were doing some of their own work. Bob wrote on the board, "*Pros* and *Cons*." Taking his chairmanship rather seriously said, "All right, what are some of the good points of the class?"

Greg was reading *Playboy* up to that time and passed the magazine to Jim. Charles said, "Freedom," and Bob wrote "Freedom" under pros.

"More interesting," a girl said.

Bob wrote that under "Freedom" and asked, "What else?"

Greg turned to me, "Com'on Phil, help us out." But, as usual, I refused to say anything.

Jim was looking bored and said, "We're not used to this type of setting," but he was really not participating, he was looking sort of sullen and irritated. He was then becoming interested in *Playboy*, but added, "We should change groups. Like next time we're going to be in something different."

So Bob wrote on the board "better groups" under con.

Same spoke up, "Yeah, but we should realign the groups, like we should break up differently."

"That's what I said," said Jim sharply. "Next time we'll be in the education group, but who gives a shit about that. We have to change the ideas."

"Yeah, you're right," said Sam.

So Bob wrote "better groups." It was awfully slow but he was still trying. He added "Should have more push from teacher" under cons and then looked at Jim. By this time Sam, who had started out sort of enthusiastically, had given up. Greg said, "Com'on Phil, you know this stuff."

I just said, "Jim's right, the groups should be changed."

Jim ignored it. He and Rick were deep in the magazine.

Bob was still trying. "What else?"

"It's the first year," added one of the girls in the rear and Bob wrote "First year" under cons.

That was the end of the discussion. Bob was looking as though he wanted to do something with the idea, the other two boys were watching but saying nothing. The center of the class was Jim. They were all looking at him, but he was looking at the magazine. They were really immobilized without his leadership. Through his position as the other member of the dyads, he and Greg, he and Bob, and he and Rick, Jim controlled the interaction in the group. And neither the two boys outside the group nor the other class members could challenge him. He controlled the group and they controlled the rest. When Greg wanted me to help, my refusal was a result of my role as a researcher. I did not want to make a difference. But I doubt if I could have turned the group. Jim was the leader, not I. Finally Bob got irritated, "Jim, you know last time you got an 89 because of Patty [the student teacher], but you ain't going to get it again."

"Bullshit," said Jim. By this time he and Rick were at the centerfold and were looking intently at the nude. For the next few minutes, Bob read Jim's log book in a deriding manner.

He was really aggravated and yelled at Jim, "You don't do anything, Jim, you're going to fail."

"Bullshit, I did as good as you." But he was still looking at the magazine, not at Bob. That was the end of it. For the last five minutes we did nothing but sit. Jim and Rick read the magazine. Bob looked at Jim's log and continued to deride him, but to no avail. Greg, myself, and the rest did nothing.

After class I saw the teacher down the hall. Having passed twice to look in the window, he looked disgusted. "They couldn't even take fifteen minutes, could they? They couldn't even keep it going."

"No," I said, "They couldn't."

"Sometime before you go I have to get your impressions of the whole thing. I just don't understand why they can't work by themselves."

If Mr. Summers had appointed Jim as the chairman, I do not think he would have made that much difference. It was not just he who discouraged group participation in academic affairs, it was simply that the group had no way to handle those matters. Even Jack could not motivate the group academically. And had Jim even tried to lead the discussion, he would have been so far out of his usual role, that I doubt he could have succeeded. It should be noted that Mr. Summers introduced me to Jim, Rick, and Greg as my starting place and thus he recognized their "groupness," but it was plain that he did not understand the group's nature. Of course, that was not his job; he was paid to teach English, not to run sociological studies.

However, as individuals the boys did their academic work and at times even expressed interest and enthusiasm for it. Greg was proud of the number of books he read in his January–February humanities project. Max or Bob would occasionally mention an interesting problem they were pursuing in physics and even Jim spoke of his humanities musical experience as one of the best in high school. And although they seldom referred to homework, most of them did at least a minimal amount. Jack and Greg each reported working an hour a day. Rick was conscientious about his mechanical drawing activities. Those who took physics and math always did their work, and all the boys did their logs for humanities. During second period Jim and Greg would go into the study hall for about fifteen to twenty minutes to do their geometry. In the first few minutes of the humanities class, some would be doing their logs; that is, writing down what they did, their impressions of what they did, or adding news articles to fill them out. All of this took little time or effort, and most of the boys had assistance. Rick, Ralph, Bob, and Pete all had girls who did part of their work. Ralph's girl did his entire humanities log and made sure he got credit for the project on which she and some other girls worked. Max did the same for Rick. When the humanities projects or logs were due, there would be some scurrying around to get unfinished work completed, but the efforts were equal to the demands; that is, they were minimal and they did little to interrupt the general group activity of talking, joking, making plans, reminiscing, or simply being together.

As individuals they recognized the necessity of making grades. In the humanities class when they were having a test on *Babbitt*, Pete, Rick, Jim, and Greg had study guide versions so all could answer the questions by reading the outlined version rather than the book.

In humanities Ralph was concerned about his girl doing his daily log and about the difficulty of getting his Math 12 grade up to passing. Greg would occasionally talk to me about his grades, his problems of getting his French III grades up to the eighties, and his trouble with his teacher. Max was worried about his low physics grade. But that was an individual, not a group interest. This changed on one occasion. Bob, Greg, and Max worked hard on their second project which was to create a motion picture of Christmas decorations. Greg had the technical skill and the equipment, and for a number of evenings they went around and shot the film. They talked about it at length and finally showed the film in class, but Mr. Tomaso's reaction was that it was "sloppy," and that "anyone could have done that." Greg was totally disheartened, but he crossed it off simply by saying, "That asshole, he doesn't know anything." However, there was no more talk of "group" projects.

As stated earlier, Jim was a central figure in the group, and the fact that the group did little work together was not merely a result of his influence. In a later humanities class with Bob, Greg, Pete, and Max, when Jim had elected to go into the play production section, there was still no talk of books, grades, learning, or carrying out the common assignment. Pete, Ralph, and Bob, who formed an independent triad, also avoided all talk of academics. So this phenomenon of noninvolvement with the aims of the formal organization was limited not only to Jim and his influence, but ran through the entire group. It was plain that the boys knew well enough how to comply with or get around the basic requests of the institution without letting it interfere with their group activities.

One of the most interesting incidents occurred when the group was actually faced with its inability to work together on academic matters, as well as the fact that they received different grades. On the field trip to the penitentiary Jim and Bob took notes, but Rick, who also went along, did not take notes because he thought the others would. When the time came to write it up and Rick wanted to be included, Jim, Greg, and Bob refused to put his name on it because he had not taken notes. They had a big discussion on the issue with Jack agreeing that Rick's name should be included, and Jim, supported by Bob and Greg, saying, "Why should we? He didn't do anything. We took notes, he could have, but didn't."

In the end they worked it out. Jim and Bob gave their notes to Greg, who wrote it and then turned it over to Rick who had his mother type it. Then they turned it in and all got the same mark, C.

A few weeks later Mr. Summers asked, "Do you want your report card grades?"

"Yeah," said Bob.

"You got 87."

"Good," said Bob, smiling.

"What did I get?" asked Greg.

"90. You got a higher mark because your log was better." Greg smiled.

"And Jim, you got 76."

"I didn't ask," said Jim.

"Well, I told you anyway," said Mr. Summers. "Here's your project."

"Did we get a B?" asked Greg.

"You were lucky to get a C," said Mr. Summers, and he threw the paper on the table. "It was only three pages."

Jim was mad about the fact that Bob and Greg got higher grades. He picked the paper up and looked at it. "Shit. We could have made the margins wider, we could have triple-spaced it, we could have put in that stuff we got from the school psychologist. Look at this. Rick's old lady didn't even spell Freud right—F-R-O-I-D."

"I'm happy," said Bob.

"So am I," said Greg, and both of them laughed at Jim.

Jim went on: "Rick's old lady didn't even spell peniten-tiary right, p-e-n-i-t-e-n-y-u-a-r-y."

He wanted to do the project over, and wanted the others to help him, but Bob and Greg just laughed at Jim's low grade. They even got up and went to the other side of the room and made loud plans for their second twelve-weeks project and Bob kept saying, "We don't want you, Jim, you're not one of the smart kids, so you can't work with us this time." Mr. Summers laughed, some of the other students laughed, but Jim just fumed. It seemed that they were getting some revenge on him because he had dominated the humanities class for so long and had prevented them from doing better. Apparently they thought that he deserved a low mark. For Jim it was a bad twenty minutes.

The next day Greg told me, "Hey, Phil, Jim quit the group because me and Bob were giving him such a bad time."

Bob laughed, "Yeah, he went where his talents would be more appreciated."

It was true. Jim was hurt by his low grade and by the fact that his friends had actually made fun of him over it, and the next day he left that section of the humanities class and joined another section with Rick and Jack. Also the next day in the cafeteria Jim, for the first time that year, was not taking the lead at the back table. He did not even sit there. He, his girl Betty, along with Rick, Mary, and Jack were at another table. Bob derided him, "Hey, Jim. Aren't you gonna sit back here with us guys? Are we too smart for you?" Jim did not even look up.

After lunch, when we all gathered in the halls that day and for many days thereafter, Jim was with Betty, not with Bob, Pete, Greg, or me. Of course, this was difficult for me also, because in the absence of a leader, the group center started to shift, and I found that at times I would be asked to decide on some activity. I stayed quiet, and Greg and Bob took over the center of the group.

It was also difficult because Jim and I were good friends, yet when he was with his girl, I could not be with him, and, besides, Greg and Bob expected me to be with them. I

elected to stay with Bob, Greg, Pete, and Ralph because
that was where the most action was, but Jim was hurt.
Whereas before he would simply say, "Com'on you guys,"
and all of us would go, now he would ask me, "Hey, Phil,
come down to the music section of humanities class, if
you have the time." I was hurt too because I genuinely
liked and respected Jim, but the lesson was there. The
teacher in his official capacity had penetrated the group,
made them face the fact that they received different grades,
and openly stated that the group's purpose was antithetical
to academic achievement. This had done possibly perma-
nent damage to the group. Greg read all my notes the following June and told me then that he and Jim were never
again as close as they were preceding the incident.

The group was not destroyed, the boys were still friends,
but the friendships realigned. Greg was with Bob and Pete
more, while Jim was with Betty, Rick, and Jack more. Jim
had to be with Betty in order to hang around with Rick
and Mary. It was like a double date. Jim, Jack, and Rick, as
a result of the humanities class, began spending more time
together.

With Jack and Rick, Jim was no longer the undisputed
leader and as such had to make an adjustment. Two weeks
later, however, he was back at the table, participating in
the conversation which, as always, was about sports, girls,
sex, cars, and group activities. Thus, while there were
subtle changes in its internal dynamics, the group continued in its usual pattern until the following June.

Summary and Discussion of Chapter 4

The athletes were unique in Horatio Gates, but they are
not unique to American high schools. Every secondary
school probably has a group of senior boys who are athletically talented, popular, attractive to girls, and who receive
a large share of the available rewards. Because this phenomenon is so widespread, I appreciated a chance to see
how it operated within this one school.

That they were fairly respected among the students is

understandable. What surprised me was that they were equally popular with, and possibly even influenced, teachers and administrators. This raises the first of a series of questions that I consider important for teachers: "Do these popular students seriously influence the actions of teachers and administrators?" And, if so, how do they do it? I might simply ask: "Would Mr. Rossi have dared to suspend Jack, Jim, and Greg knowing that Lorraine was circulating a petition to the class members asking for their immediate reinstatement?" Personally, I don't think he would have; it was simply not in his own or the school's best interests. He was supposed to maintain a smooth-running organization, not be vindictive about punishing errant students. Given that other students might have taken action, it simply would have been more trouble than it was worth to try to punish them. Even with teachers this was true. When Jim and Greg went into rooms and were cleaning the windows, no teacher reported them or even chastized them for fooling around. Instead, they laughed with them. Of course there were teachers whose rooms they would not have entered—they knew their own boundaries and avoided exceeding them. The athletes defied nonsupportive teachers, also. When Greg skipped study hall and Mr. Johnson tried to punish him, Greg won. He did not spend two more weeks in the class, and, as far as I know, the teacher just dropped it. Continually trying to punish Greg again would have been more trouble than it was worth. The teacher might succeed only in embarrassing himself.

This is not to imply that these boys were completely free from the organizational sanctions. For instance, when Jim carried on in the geometry class described in the second chapter, the teacher did not challenge him; but Jim did not challenge the teacher when the teacher wanted to teach either. The two reached an unspoken, but clear agreement. These boys knew their boundaries, but it seemed that their boundaries were a little wider than those respected by the average students. Had Joe, or Red, or Andy, or Darlene gone out and stolen a Christmas tree, or refused to come to a study hall, or interrupted classes, they very likely might have found themselves suspended from school.

Part of the issue was revealed in Jack's comment, "Shit, they throw us out and the school would fall apart—we do everything around here." The athletes thought that they made a significant contribution to the school, and as such deserved special consideration. Are they wrong? Considering the importance of football and wrestling in that school, and the attendance at the games, I would say they were not wrong. They were important in the school, and the fact is that the administrators and teachers, in an extraofficial manner, treated them that way.

When one of these prestigious students walks into a classroom, the teacher should remember something. There are now two people in that room who deserve respect, the teacher and that particular student. Since an additional authority figure is now present, the teacher must not let his own authority slip in any way, or that student is capable of taking over. Or should the student decide to challenge the teacher, it would behoove the teacher to have his authority already strongly established. In many cases, teachers have to strike a compromise with the more prestigious students.[2]

Then there is the second matter concerning this particular group as a group, rather than as a collection of prestigious individuals. That the group never discussed anything academic surprised me. That was apparently their way of maintaining the cohesion of the group in the school, but it raises one important question for teachers. "Does the fact that the students have a group structure limit the teacher's ability to influence them?" I would say "Yes." That the group under consideration had a long history is important. Having been together for years, they had their group routine all worked out, and they just did not need the additional input from teachers. In fact, those teachers that did try to make inputs earned themselves nothing but trouble. It did no good for the teacher to call the girl's mother about Bob; it did not stop their dating, but only served to earn Bob's hatred. Nor did Mr. Tomaso increase his instructional ability by making remarks about Ralph

[2] See C. W. Gordon, *The Social System of the High School* (New York: Free Press, 1957) for further discussion of this point.

and his girl. It seemed to me that if a teacher, however inadvertantly, crossed over and interferred with the students' social and group lives, he did himself and the students no good.

At this point I should return to the comment in the second chapter about teachers walking down the hall and ignoring the students. The teachers who did so respected organizational constraints, but they were also respecting the informal, student structure which did not need, and indeed had little use for, their input. In fact, their input was not a positive contribution; rather, it was regarded as interference, and as such, was politely ignored. For instance, if a teacher on cafeteria duty said something in a friendly manner to Jack or Jim or Greg at the back table, the conversation would stop, the teacher would be politely listened to, and when he was gone, the conversation would resume with no comment about the teacher. Therefore, we might say that the student group structure may serve as a barrier to student-teacher interaction, just as does the organization.

A third issue, and a very important one for a prospective public school teacher, is "Can you actually use the group structure for instructional purposes?" That is, if the teacher encourages the students to "break into groups and develop a project, or discuss the material," can he expect them to do as he wishes, or will they merely form into their already set-up informal groups and carry on group business? It may be that they will succeed only in cases where the informal leader wishes to pursue the academic material. This success depends upon the informal leader being a motivated student. What if he isn't? What if his leadership, like Jim's, depends on a number of other things? That was what happened in the humanities class. Mr. Summers said, "I don't understand," and what he didn't understand is that the purpose of the student group is to give the individual members some personal and human rewards in the school, not to gain academic achievement. The students, therefore, in order to maintain their groups, have to keep a delicate balance between the demands of the organization and the maintenance of their group. I would tentatively say that unless a teacher is willing to experiment and learn about the group structure, he should forget trying to utilize it. He simply cannot rely on it to help him in any way.

This is not to imply that the athletes and their group were completely apart from the school's official structure. Indeed, had it not been for that official structure and the importance of athletics, those students may not have been among the most prestigious. There were many other points of interaction. Jack, Rick, and Bob used Mr. Tomaso to put Jim and Greg in line. The group took action to assure that its members respected the organization, and the most revealing incident occurred when Mr. Summers' action as a teacher ruptured the group. Although there were points at which both the school's organization and the students' social structure were integrally related, both teacher and student seemed happier when each stayed clearly on his own side of the line.

CHAPTER 5

Some Other
Student Groups

When this project began I was aware, as are most teachers, of the importance of peer-group relationships among adolescents, and, therefore, I was not surprised to find strong, group structures in the school. I was not prepared, however, to find that what the students in Horatio Gates did, for a major part of their school day, was interact with one another in small, isolated, social units. Yet, evidence supporting that fact emerged consistently, whether I was dealing with the athletes of whom such behavior might be expected, or nonathletes, among them even the high achieving students. To further explain this phenomenon, some other students and their group structures will have to be explained.

Bill's Friends

Among the other groups with which I came into contact, the most interesting were Bill and his friends. I had an open invitation to become an associate of these boys almost from the beginning when I met Roger and Ken, but I stayed away, partly because it would have interferred with my association with the athletes, and partly because Bill and his friends spent a great deal of their time stealing. Cars parked in the large lots around shopping centers were their favorite targets, and from them they stole tires, wheels and all; credit cards, money, tape decks, and anything else they could haul away safely. Of course this made them too risky to associate with, but it also made them an interesting group because it provided a chance to compare them with the more typical athletes. Many times when they were in the same vicinity in the classes or cafeteria or halls, I took the opportunity to talk to them. This did not impinge on my membership or participation with the athletes, because as individuals they too had interests and activities outside the group.

Bill was an extremely personable boy who seemed to be one of the most popular students in the class. That he did not get elected to office and committees was the result of his unwillingness to try, not a result of invisibility or unpopularity or even his illegal activities. He affected modish, hippy clothing, a moustache, often carried a guitar, and obviously cared little for study. Although he was listed as an academic student, as far as I could see, and even by his own admission, he did no work. Nevertheless, he was reputed to be one of the most intelligent members of the class. Others in his group recalled the time when they were sophomores and were taking biology. "Bill never even opened a book all year; he took the state exam and got a 96." That accomplishment was cited as irrefutable proof of his academic potential. In reference to his actions in school, Bill said:

> Not all the kids fool around like this. Some of the guys going to college are really serious about their grades and their future and, let's face it, if you want to go to college, you have to have the high grades. But me? Couldn't care less about going to college. You've probably noticed, Phil, our group is very interested in music. I know if I could spend my days taking guitar lessons, I wouldn't be here, I'd be there.

The second member of the group was Ken who transferred into Gates the previous year after being expelled from a nearby parochial school. Ken was personable, smart, and quick. His principle activity in school was bookmaking. He passed out the parleys on Tuesday, picked up the money on Friday, and made his payments on the following Monday. He was reputed to be under investigation for gambling, cashing bad checks, stealing, and using stolen credit cards, and was frequently absent from school because he had to go to court. Some of this may have been exaggerated, but no one ever found any flaws in his stories. He carried a wad of money which he flourished around the halls, drove a flashy car, and constantly talked of his gambling. Ken took humanities, business math, and typing. He carried an average of about 67 and a class standing of 340.

It was Ken who most clearly articulated what it meant to be a group member:

> I came here last year—you know, from St .Charles. I was in a low class, and they really bust your ass over there. They work you hard, but then I came here after being thrown out of there. When I first came, I hated it. I didn't know anyone. You know, Phil, I skipped fifty-eight days last year because I couldn't stand to come to school, because I didn't know anyone, and when I would try to talk to someone, we would just exchange small talk, we never got down to anything. I felt like a real outsider. And it's bad when you don't know anyone. You just walk around by yourself and feel that the other kids are talking about you. But it's okay now, I got my friends, and I'm all right."

And, indeed, Ken was "all right." I do not think anyone enjoyed school more than he. Everyone knew him, if not first hand, then by reputation. And while he did not have the kind of status that Jack, Bob, or Max had, he was extremely popular for one who had been in the school for only one year. While other students, such as the athletes, regarded the stealing that Ken and Bill carried on as dangerous, they regularly placed bets with Ken and would make a point of dropping in at his father's restaurant and bar for a talk when Ken was working.

The third member of the group was Roger, who was particularly helpful to me. He was the son of the area's chief real-estate developer and his car, clothes, and pocket money reflected his father's wealth. Like Bill and Ken, he did little in school, and while he was always promising himself that he would get going and work up his marks for college acceptance, it never happened. He was listed as a vocational student and carried only a 75 average with a class rank of 285.

Next came Fred, whose average was 73 and class ranking

was 300. Like Bill, his main interest was music, and he spent three hours a day practicing on the electric bass. Fred's attitude seemed to be one of complete detachment, and he frequently expressed utter contempt for school:

> I have to go to the guidance office. I go once a week and tell her how much I hate school and hate the teachers and hate the whole place. She listens and nods her head. She thinks she's helping me. Actually, she must be disappointed because my marks have been real shitty for three years. But now I have a B average. She'll be disappointed to learn that.

Fred seemed to take pleasure in the fact that he did so little. "Hey, Phil, is 120 a high IQ?"

I told him it was.

"That's what mine is, and the teachers know it and are always telling me I have the ability and could do something if I wanted. But I don't give a shit. I won't even graduate because I lack two credits."

The other two members were Steve and Tom, both of whom spent more time engaged in illegal activities than anything else. They stole from cars, houses, and even from each other's families. Steve was usually on the verge of being thrown out by the vice-principal for either not coming or not caring when he did come. Perhaps the only thing that kept him in school was his mother's position as an employee of the system. His class average was 79 and his standing 125. Tom stayed with the group while in school and participated in some of the same activities, but he was quieter than the others and had other friends with whom he was frequently seen.

Like the athletic group, Bill and his friends, with the exception of Ken, had grown up in the same neighborhood in Cowpens and had been associating with one another since they were in grammar school. Roger gave a brief account on the history. "Well, it started with me and Fred. We grew up on the same street so we've been friends for a long time. Then Fred started hanging around with Bill and I sort of was out of it, you know. But then I started again with Steve and Bill and we've hung around ever since. Last year when Ken came everyone thought he was a real ass-hole, but I don't know. Somehow we got to know him and we really like him. He's one of us."

The Dynamics of the Group

Bill was at the center, and the group depended on his presence for its existence. If some of the boys wanted to go out to eat, whether they went or not depended on him. If he agreed, they went; if not, they stayed. If he chose to hang around the lavatory and smoke rather than eat or go to class, the rest stayed, smoked, and talked with him. When he chose to study, they tried to do the same. When the humanities class was leaving for its tour of the university, Bill was missing. In his absence Fred, Steve, and Roger could not decide if they wanted to go or not. "Is Bill going?" "I don't know. Where is he?" "What are we going up there for anyway?" Then they left to see if they could find Bill and since they had not returned when the busses left, I assumed that either they could not find him or when they found him he chose not to go. If Bill was not there to decide on the group activity, the others were prac-tically immobilized. Individually he was the one the others would name first when they talked about the group. Mem-bership in the group depended on him. As Fred said, "If he didn't like Steve, no one would."

Fred, Ken, and Steve personally regarded Bill as their best friend, and Roger would always check with Bill before making a decision on some action. Also, Bill seemed to associate more easily with members of other groups. He was close to the members of the music-drama group, who will be described later, and also many of the more popular students.

Apart from Bill the boys had some hard feelings for one another. Fred was close to Ken and Bill, but did not like Roger. Of Roger he said, "You know who's a typical senior? Roger. He's always worried about something; his clothes, grades—everything. He's probably the most disliked guy in the group. Like he always says, 'Let's do this or that,' but he doesn't mean it, he doesn't do anything."

Fred also had trouble with Steve. They had had a fist-fight in January, and Fred told me he was looking for another chance to hit him. Fred had other interests, however. He was becoming involved with a girl and in early February Roger reported that, "Fred dropped out of the group. He never goes anywhere with us. He's always with his girl."

Ken was close to Bill, Fred, and Roger; Steve was close only to Bill; Fred was friends with Bill, Ken, and Steve. If diagrammed so as to show the interaction patterns of Bill's friends, the group might look like this:

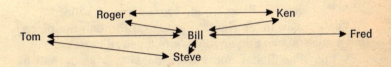

Bill's Friends in School

Regarding schoolwork, none of the members made any real effort. Fred was the only one taking an academic course, Algebra II, which he was repeating. The others took courses such as typing, business arithmetic, humanities, music, and drama. Instead of working they, like the athletes, busied themselves with their group activities and spent their school time together. Roger explained it, "Well, yeah, in our free time—in my free time—I'm with one or two of those guys, but not all the time. I pick up Fred in the morning since we live on the same street, and then before class we're together and during lunch hour we're together and then sometimes in the halls."

"Yeah, but you all take humanities and you're together all through that."

Roger laughed, "Yeah, you're right, we do spend most of our time together."

"I noticed when you're together you don't talk about teachers."

"Well, some teachers are pretty good, like Mr. Phillips. He always fools around with us, but he gets the kids to do all their work, because they like him."

While admitting that most of the teachers were pretty good and that the kids liked them, he still agreed that the group didn't talk about them.

Then, referring to some of the rules and regulations, I asked "Well, there are things in school that you guys don't like. What about them? Do you ever talk about them?"

"There's a saying around here. It's like this—Vincent's law, that's it. 'What can you do, they got you and you can't do anything about it.' If I don't like what Summers is doing, then I can't do anything. If I don't like what Tomaso's doing, I can't do anything. No kid can, you just have to take it."

"Is that why you hang around together all the time?"

"Yeah. Yeah, that's right. You just go through the place, that's all. You can't do anything while you're here."

By this time Roger and I were passing a study hall in the large cafeteria. "Look in here. I'll give you a good example. Look at how many kids are in there studying. How many do you think?"

There were about fifty students, and I guessed twenty-five.

"Yeah, but half of those you say are studying are just dicking around on the paper." (Roger was the boy who was mentioned in the second chapter as saying, "That's why I sit and jack off all day.") I asked him if he put much effort into class, and he simply said, "What's the use? You do say something and no one listens."

Bill agreed, "We have our own way of talking and we don't have much to say about school or teachers." And later Ken added, "School is not part of our group thing. We might do schoolwork by ourselves, but as a group we do our own thing—not school."

As did the athletes, they rigidly segregated themselves from other groups. Bill explained, "I feel that I can talk to those other guys, but still, we don't talk very seriously, not like we do with our own friends."

Also like the athletes, they had their own topics of conversation. For example, one day Steve received a threatening letter from a former employer telling him to pay back the $50 he took from the cash register or else face criminal charges. For the next three days, in and out of class, the boys talked it over. What to do? Put five dollars with Ken, who would attempt to increase it through the parley; rob a gas station; reciprocate with a threatening letter telling the store owner to lay off or have his store burned down; or forget it? That was what they talked about in school for three days. It should be noted that they did none of these things. Their burglaries were minor and they avoided hold-ups and arson.

When Bill was out one night, he hit seven cars, just going around town bumping into them. The next day he explained, "It was that asshole Fred's fault. No wonder. I was talking to him, didn't see this guy in front of me turn, and I hit him at about fifteen miles an hour. Then that was that so I hit a few more." For the next three or four days the group discussed the event, how it happened, how someone got Bill's license number, how he was charged with failure to stop, how only three of the seven complained, what could happen to him if he pleaded guilty, what would happen if he used up his youthful offender status, what judge would be expected to hear the case, and on and on.

Fred's personal interest was in figuring out ways to steal things. He had a job at a restaurant and would say proudly, "I've managed to cheat some people on the change; they order two and I charge them for three or I return a one instead of a five or a ten dollar bill. But that's small. I've got to find something else."

When Mr. Thompson was asking for volunteers to go down and act as stage hands for the opera company, I suggested they might enjoy it. "Hey, Phil, can you steal things, too?" asked Fred quietly.

Doug once came up to Bill in the bathroom, "Hey, do you have those tapes?"

"Yes," said Bill. "They're in the trunk of my car."

"How many?"

"About sixty."

"Do you want to go to the car and see them?"

As Doug, Bill, and I were moving down the crowded hall toward the door, Bill was saying, "My insurance agent was pretty shook up. My guitar that was worth 400 dollars

—or it was insured for that much—was stolen. I reported that Friday night, and then Saturday I had to call him and tell him that I had an accident and that it was my fault."

"Did you get a summons?"

"No. I don't know why. He wrote it up but left no ticket with me. Maybe it was because the car in front of the one I hit stopped suddenly and it was actually his fault. If I get another ticket I'm through. I already got to go to the JP's house and talk about the one I got a week ago." Then Doug and Bill moved out to the parking lot to examine the tapes. Referring to the guitar theft, Bill had previously planned to insure his instrument, claim it was stolen, and then collect the money.

Or they would make plans, such as the plan to bring some bread, cheese, pepperoni, pop in a wine bottle, candles, a tablecloth, and have a real Italian lunch. "What will you bring?" "I'll bring the table cloth and the silverware. Fred, what will you bring? You guys won't forget, will you? Wait'll Rossi sees this. He'll raise hell with us."

Or when Ken bumped into me. "Shake my hand, Phil. You might not see me for a long time."

"Why?"

"Tomorrow's my hearing."

"What for? The forgery thing?"

"Right." Ken had been using a gasoline credit card that unfortunately belonged to someone else.

This is not to say that these boys disrupted the organization. While occasionally they would pull small pranks like falling down in the hall and laying on the floor until a teacher would tell them to get up, or coming to school in old clothes and waiting until Rossi told them to go home and change, their behavior was never disruptive enough to attract serious attention or risk suspension by the administrators. In fact, while they did have trouble with the office, it was not because they stole or did poorly in class, rather it was because they frequently skipped school. In school they were much more compliant with the general routine than Jim or Greg. They realized that it would be much easier for Rossi to suspend or even expel them than it would have been for him to suspend or expel a popular athlete.

For instance, there was a rule that food should never be taken out of the cafeteria. The boys always took care that they finished their milk or ice cream in the inside and were never seen eating in the halls. Or in class, if any teacher asked them to be quiet or even for their attention, they would make a momentary attempt to comply. While most of the time they would quickly drift away mentally, they did not do anything to interrupt the teacher when he was speaking or when another student was answering. I was quite surprised one day when the librarian reprimanded them for going out the wrong door. Fred, who thought nothing of jacking up a car and stealing the wheels, appeared nervous about it and said he might go apologize. "Do you think it will do any good?" he asked Bill.

"No," said Bill and Fred did not do it, but the fact that he seriously considered it was an indication of his general compliance with the wishes of the teachers and his respect for organizational rules. Bill's friends did not share Jim or Jack's attitude that their presence was a favor to the organization.

In many ways, however, their school behavior was similar to that of the athletes. Like the athletes, this group never made mention of personal issues. Fred's father had a heart attack one morning and was in serious condition, but Fred was in the cafeteria with his friends at lunch, and when I asked if he was going to the hospital, he replied, "No, what good would that do? Hey, Ken, lend me some lunch money." And he went on with the group conversation.

Or when Roger's young uncle was killed while snowmobiling, even that did not interest the group. That day they were more concerned because Ken had received another summons.

On those occasions when they were unable to interact with one another in class, Bill usually paid attention. In fact, when another student read Spencer's poem, *The Cit-*

izen, only Bill of 112 students volunteered to answer to the teacher's question, "Why didn't the man have a name?"

Roger, too, would pay attention and would occasionally volunteer a thoughtful answer. Fred did his homework in all his courses, and admitted that for him intermediate algebra was not difficult. But Ken, Steve, and Tom, as far as I could see, did absolutely nothing. If left by themselves they would look at their wallets, at the parley sheets, at the last issue of *Parade Magazine*, or simply drift off.

For all the individuals the high point of any day seemed to revolve around some planned group activity. For instance, although it was forbidden to leave school during the lunch period, in September Bill and his friends were regularly going out. The plans for this venture alone would consume at least two previous periods. "Hey, you going out?" "Yeah." "Is Bill going?" "Phil, you going with us?" "Where'll we go?" "When do we have to be back?" "Hey, they're having a movie sixth period so we can skip and stay out two periods." And so on until Bill made up his mind and if he wished, they would go. Then when they came back, if they were together, they talked about what they did when they were out. I went with them a few times, and while it was fun, I have to admit that it tired me out.

One particular time in humanities class Fred said to Ken, "Hey, we goin' out?" "Yeah. Phil, you goin' with us?" "Yeah, we have two periods because no class fourth period in here. Okay, we'll go."

Then Ken asked me if I had seen the accident. I asked what accident, having been out of town, and he said, "Oh, man, five kids on Boulevard were killed. You know, where the pizza place is above Bill's Cycle Shop. This Dodge Charger, 383 cube, came dragging another car up there Friday about 10:00."

"No, it was 7:30, I remember," said Bill.

"No sir, buddy. I was coming down to the Holiday Inn from the dance and had the radio on and it said 10:00 or just before. Anyway [looking at me] they were dragging about 110 and hit a little bump, you know the one I mean. Then they flew in the air, hit a tree broadside, and the car split and the front end traveled for 100 yards—blood and bodies all over the place—five colored guys and two white girls. One guy bailed out when the car hit the tree and lived. I'll show you the spot when we go out." He said this in front of Mr. Summers, who paid no attention, but who was still asking the athletes about their project.

At 11:50 the bell rang. We went—Steve, Roger, and I in Roger's car. Fred, Bill, and Ken went in Ken's car. Out of the lot, around and down Cowpens Road. Ken first, Roger behind, 70 miles per hour. I got nervous. Roger was not that good a driver, he was just following Ken. Around a few corners, speeding up, stopping—more speeding, and then we were at a local hamburger drive-in.

We lined up and ordered. This was quick. There was some talk of the accident. Bill was explaining. Then Ken and I went and sat in Ken's car, and Fred, Bill, and Steve came. We were all listening to "Alice's Restaurant" on a stereo tape. Roger and Tom got in Roger's car. We all ate, no noise, just laughter at Arlo Guthrie and his jokes.

"I want to go to the Head Shop," said Bill. "We don't have time," said Fred. "I have to be back sixth period." "Shit, that doesn't start until 12:45. We have plenty of time." The record was ending and Ken said, "Let's go. I have to be back, too. We'll make it." Roger was told of the plan. "No, I don't think so." Then Fred got out and said he would go back with Roger, the rest of us were going to the Head Shop. Fred got back in, "I'm going, too." Off we went. Roger followed.

Then we went speeding over Thompson Road, over the bridge by the plain. A Camaro went by. "Get him, Ken." The driver was sitting by the light, he turned right. "Too bad, can't get him," said Ken. Roger pulled up and rolled out. A race! Ken hit fifty-five and Roger quit. "Ahhhhh, I love to cut him," said Ken. Then it was over. There was no talking. It seemed as if we were all thinking of Ken's driving —fast, too fast—but not bad, not like Roger who was less experienced. I could trust Ken a little more than I could trust Roger.

Next, a right turn toward the downtown metropolitan area. "Phil, I'll show you where this accident was. Let's see, there's five of us, we need one more to beat it." Roger pulled up and signaled for Ken to slow down. "Screw him. He's always telling us to slow down when there's nothing to slow down for." "Yeah, lose him, go 'wan," said Fred. "He's a pain in the ass," said Bill, speaking of Roger. "Always scared he's going to get caught." So down Boulevard we went, hitting sixty. Roger was still there. Passing the scene of the accident, we got a running commentary from Ken. "Wow! Look at that tree—yeah, a hickory tree. I'd rather hit a brick wall than a tree, they don't move. A brick wall will at least give. Yeah, five colored guys, two girls. WOW!"

Next we took a left turn on Elm. "Lose him, Ken," said Fred, referring to Roger. "Make the light and make him miss it." So we rolled up to the light and made sure Roger did not have time to make it. Down Central Avenue we laughed about losing Roger. "Ha, haaaa, we lost him, that bastard. He won't run lights. He'll never find us." Left on University, then up and around. "Hey, where's the Head Shop. Ask those two kids." Fred stuck his head out and asked. The kid said it was on Central and Court, next to Sid's.

"Go up and around Timberlane," I told Ken. He did. Roger was nowhere in sight. "Lookit the chicks. Hey, Phil, how is it here?"

"Fine," I told him. Up Grand River, right on Timberlane, down Harrison—Ken was still losing Roger, who, by that time, had managed to catch up. There was much excitement in the car. Roger and Ken were doing about zero to fifty in one block, then stopping for a sign and hitting zero to fifty again. Ken lost Roger by Central High School. "What do you think of his driving, Phil?" "Smooth," I agreed.

Then we went around down Central and parked across from the Head Shop. We got out and looked. It was closed. Bambu paper, clothes, incense, paintings, handcrafts in the window. "Wow," said Fred, looking in the window, "Look at the clothes." "Yeah," we solemnly agreed. Roger and Tom finally came up, Roger looking hurt and angry. "Nice guys." (I was embarrassed, but I was the only one.) "Let's go," said Ken.

So we ran to the car and started again. Crossed the

street—off and down, around, up Linden and across Grove
—all the time losing Roger again and looking for the Music
Box (a discount record shop). I misled them a little, but
nobody cared, the enjoyment was in racing around in Ken's
car with Ken driving—very cool.

"I wonder what they think of us townies," said Fred,
looking at the college students. Around and down Court
and over Park. We drove in a No Parking zone across from
the drugstore. We got out and someone mentioned the No
Parking sign. "I don't give a shit, I just tear tickets up,"
said Ken. "Oh, wait," he got in the car and brought out an
old ticket, placed it on his windshield and we all laughed.
"Ain't that cool. I always carry one," said Ken.

In the discount record shop I looked at magazines because I really did not care about records. But the others
were very quiet, very respectful, and very serious. There
was no talking, just looking at records and reading the record sheet pamphlet. Like, "Look at this. I heard this about
two months ago." "Have you heard this?" "Ohhh—man—
look." This was a serious business, much more so than
school—no jostling, no joking, not even any talk of stealing. Fred bought a Carole King record. He was very proud
of it. He also read the record paper he bought. I never saw
Fred so serious or concerned about anything. The rest were
the same way—no grouping. Individually they went to
check out what they wanted to read and see, and the
counter where Fred was paying became the meeting place
again. Roger and Tom came in. Roger was a little quiet,
just like the rest of them (I was still embarrassed). We left
the shop and went down the street to the new clothing
store—all seven of us.

We walked in and looked at the clothes. The clerk was
watching us closely. Again, the boys were quiet and respectful. "Wow! Look at this. Phil, ask him how much it is,"
said Ken. I did—$85.00 "Phil, that record playing, ask him
if it's the Byrds," said Fred. I did; it was. (Neither Ken nor
Fred would ask the manager a civil question.) So we
looked, quietly; Ken with belts, Roger and I with ties; Bill
and Steve with shirts.

Again out we went to the car, all the time laughing about

Ken's fake ticket. Back in the car and off down Hoffman, over Central, down Water Street to Winchell to the Boulevard and on to Cowpens. Ken talked all the way: "Fuck you, lady. Get your ass out of the way. What the fuck are you doin' lady?" "Goddamn you buddy." This from Ken who was hitting sixty in a block and then braking; hitting sixty again, then braking. Fred was seriously interested in his record and told me about its history. "It's five years old and was extremely advanced for its time. Have you ever heard it?" He was reading his sheet. Tom and Steve in front also were reading their sheets. I was surprised at the profanity from Ken, only because I seldom heard it from anybody in the group, including him, and also at the seriousness with which the other read their copies of *Crawdaddy*, and their record covers. I never saw them so solemn over anything.

Going up Boulevard again there were more comments. Then there was a running description of the accident and some jokes about us hitting the same tree. Then we were almost to school and had to decide whether to sneak in or skip the whole day. "We'll never make it. Let's forget it." "Are you kidding, we got fifteen minutes." "What if we get caught?" "Rossi is already after me," said Fred. "I got caught skipping gym this morning. He says he's going to see me at noon to see if he's going to throw me out of school." Fred did not appear too worried.

"What if coach is there? He already caught me skipping this morning and sent me to Rossi," said Fred. Back in the lot, no coach. We got out out of the car and split. Fred and I headed up straight; Ken, Bill, and Steve went to the gym door. The length of the walk between the lot and the school was about forty yards. It was always problematic whether Rossi or Vincent were there waiting. "Phil, you be my excuse. Say we were looking at your cycle," said Fred. "No, we don't need an excuse, there's nobody there." "What will they do to you?" I asked. "I don't know," he said. "Well, what have they done to others they caught?" "I don't know, they never caught anybody that I know of."

I was surprised at the way these boys were afraid of getting caught, although they disdained the idea of punishment. As Roger said another day when we were hurrying back to school. "Aw, what can they do? Put you on detention? Big deal. I've been here for three years and I've never had detention yet."

The next day Fred asked if I would like to be included again. "We're going out again this noon. We're going over to this girl's house to eat. She's got booze and everything. Want to come?"

I refused because it would be risky to continue with that group. A participant observer's status in any social system is dubious and always open to challenge. He has to be very careful of his actions and should, if possible, avoid activities that bring attention to himself. It was just as well that I refused that day because Tom and Steve came back drunk, and the rest made a lot of noise about what they had done. It was shortly after that Mr. Rossi told Bill, who was allowed to come in at 9:00 in the morning because of his airport job which lasted until midnight, to stay in during lunch or lose the privilege of coming in late. So the group stayed in for the rest of the year.

In school their behavior continued as before. Walking down the hall I ran into Charlie, who asked me if I were going to the football game between the two eighth-grade teams from Cowpens and Hillsborough. I did, and Bill and his group were in the stands making a lot of noise. Ken wore a service station hat. They got up and acted like cheerleaders and got a few laughs. Then they saw the eighth graders coming and went over to raid them. "Hey, let's go raid them. Com'on, Phil." But I did not go, it was too much. They danced, played "grabass," leapfrog, and went from one activity to another. They grabbed Steve's shirt and tore it apart—he just laughed and went shirtless. Then there were more cheers. They never did raid the freshmen; if they caused any trouble, the teachers would have said something. Then they played jump rope, always moving and laughing; it looked a little forced to me, but they did it that way all the time. Watching them made me glad that I had resisted being one of them.

During January their past activities were catching up with the group. Bill had to cut his hair and shave to appear before the judge for the third time. Ken had to appear in court because of a gambling raid in which he was arrested. Steve was finally expelled for a combination of things, one of them being that he took large doses of some kind of pills. Mr. Rossi called Tom's father about his son's absences and Fred was going with his girl and sort of dropped out of the group. This caused some realignment. Two boys I had not known previously began hanging around with Bill and his friends, but the in-school activities did not change. Bill was still the center of a group and the boys' school activities were centered around their friendships.

Bill's Friends and Academic Requirements

Bill and his friends did their school work as individuals, not as a group. They took it less seriously than the other students, but still did enough to avoid failure. Bill explained in December, "You know that project we were supposed to be working on for two months? I stayed home yesterday morning and did it. I handed it in the same day and still got a C." He put Steve's name on it, too, but that was too much even for Mr. Summers. He failed Steve and then laughed. "Steve's mad because I wouldn't give him credit for Bill's project. Those guys are a bunch of winners."

Roger's reaction to the humanities project was to plan the history of rock music with Fred. And so he would sometimes go to the library and try to work. But it did not happen. Bill, Fred, and Steve would come in the conference room and the group would begin to carry on as previously described. Roger seemed to mind a little. Once in that room he said, "Phil, you gotta help me. How does this sound?" He handed me his essay. It was awful, even for a high school student. It was two pages long and two-thirds of it had been copied directly from an article in *Parade Magazine*. The rest said nothing. So I passed it off. It would not have done any good to help him. I would have had to move far beyond my role, and it would not have been accepted. Roger was discouraged and did not know what to do. He just put his head down saying, "I don't know why I even try. I never do a fuckin' thing around here."

However, he never stopped talking about trying. After

the first report card period Roger decided to study. Mr. Tomaso was complaining about students skipping class, and I asked Roger if he and his friends were the ones to whom he was referring.

"No, we got there on time, for once. But we're going to cut the bullshit for a while anyway. You know—start getting to class and stop fooling around—all that. These next six weeks are important to me."

"Because of college?" I asked.

"Yeah. These are the last marks that will go on my transcript before I start applying, so I've got to get going. If I get B's I'll be happy."

I thought he meant it, but he did no more the second twelve weeks than he had the first. The interesting thing was that they even stopped being so close as friends, because Bill quit school and ran away to New York for three weeks. Even in his absence, which was their main topic of conversation, the members did no additional work and their marks did not improve.

Only once did Bill's friends become excited about grades. That happened when Mr. Tomaso theatened to flunk Steve on the semester humanities grade. Since humanities counted for three classes, a failing grade would have prevented him from graduating. Bill and the rest became quite angry about this and made some loud threats around the halls. They were "going to get Tomaso"—meaning they would slash his tires, burn his house, make obscene phone calls, and so forth. These threats were apparently heard by Tomaso, who called Steve in the next day and asked, "What do you want for a grade?"

"75."

"Okay, you got it."

Whether Mr. Tomaso was actually intimidated I cannot say. But Steve got his 75, and the boys were absolutely convinced that they had saved Steve from failing.

The only serious case of trouble between a group member and teacher occurred between Bill and Mr. Tomaso. One day in January he took a pack of cards away from Bill. Bill then grabbed them back out of his hand. "I wish I could get you outside," said Mr. Tomaso.

"Let's go," said Bill and toward the door they went. Half way there Mr. Tomaso stopped and said he did not know what got into Bill or why he was so much trouble. That was the end of the confrontation. The group members related this as an instance of a teacher backing down. They were proud of Bill. Other than this one instance, they continued their usual pattern of avoiding confrontation with teachers.

Bill's Friends and Other Groups

Like the athletes, Bill's friends did little interrelating with other groups. When I told this to Roger, he disagreed. "Not anymore. I mean in the sophomore and junior years, it was really like that. Everyone was in his own little group and a lot of people did not even know each other's names, but now it's not like that. Something happened. Like around the time of the variety show last year, kids started to know other kids like they didn't use to, then they got to find out that most kids around here are pretty good. And they started to accept them more, at least that's what I think."

"Was the variety show the turning point?"

"No. There weren't that many kids, there were just about fifty in the whole thing, so that wasn't it." Roger thought and then added, "It used to be that there were three classes of kids: the high class, the middle class and the low class [he meant both academic and socio-economic class] and if you were in one class then you got to know and hang around with those people. Like my brother, he played sports and was in the harder classes, so he got to hang around with the jocks, and those were his friends. He just didn't know a lot of others."

"Does the social class thing exist now?" I asked.

"No. Like I said, it used to be that way, like those girls, Betty [Jim's girl], and Marlene [Bob's girl]—it used to be that I wouldn't dare speak to them; they'd think I was being wise. But then, I don't know, I got to know them and they're all right. We talk and get along."

"And Mary and those real classy girls—Pam and Sally and them—it used to be that they only went out with athletes, but that stopped. It started to break up when I introduced Janet to my best friend and she started going out with him; then other girls in that crowd started breaking off, and now it's sort of like one big group."

For the next few weeks I watched to see if Roger was right, but there were no indications. It was still a series of groups, centered primarily around neighborhood associations. Even Roger admitted that kids hung around with other kids from their own places or neighborhoods.

Also, I asked him about prestige stratification, since that would be related to some clear separation between groups.

"Is there a lead group among the boys?"

"Well, the athletes, they stick to themselves pretty much —those guys, Jim, Rick, Charlie—but I get along with them. I can go sit with them in the cafeteria, and I don't feel funny."

"What about kids that aren't like you. Kids who don't have others to hang around with?"

"Well, that's the way they want it. If they wanted to get along they could do it. Like this Horace, he's a new kid. At first people were feeling him out, like they did to you, but now he seems to be getting along. A lot of guys think he's okay, if the guys don't want to hang around with anybody that's their fault."

"But," said I, "Some of these kids must be really lonely."

"Yeah, I suppose. I try to talk to some of them sometimes but like Fred will say to me, 'What are you talking to that guy for?' But Fred doesn't understand some of the things I do and I suppose he understands a lot of things I don't." Roger kept stressing the idea that the students were not as rigidly segregated as I thought they were.

Some of the teachers agreed that the class had once been broken into a series of isolated groups, but that around the time of the class variety show, which was put on when they were juniors, things had changed. Of course I could not say what the class was like previously, but during the time of the study there was very little intergroup relations. Roger might say he could go eat with the athletes, but neither he, nor anyone in his group ever tried it. He and his friends elected to go into the same humanities class with the athletes, but the seating arrangement always looked like this:

Teacher's Desk

		Dick and Some of the
Athletes		*Music-Drama Kids*
Jim	Greg	
Bob	Pete	Janet Dick
Rick		Mary Sylvia
Me		

Ed's Friends

Bill	Roger
Fred	Steve
Ken	Tom

Two Best Friends

Sue   Margaret

Never was there any indication of open communication across the groups. In fact, once in a conversation with Bob I mentioned Steve and he said, "Oh, is that that kid's name?" He did not even know Steve although they had been in the same class for six years and neither Bob nor any other athlete ever mentioned that the other group existed. Each elected to go with his friends.

In class they developed projects independently; when the test on Sinclair Lewis's *Babbitt* was coming up, even the cheating was a group activity. The athletes used their copy of the outline guide to answer the questions; Bill and his friends used theirs. The only times I actually saw conversational contact between the athletes and Bill's friends was when Ken was passing out the parleys and collecting the money, or once in the large, group room when the athletes were in one row, Bill's friends were in the row in front, and Jack and Bill were having a brief discussion over a musical event. The rest of the members of each group sat and watched the two leaders talk.

Although the athletes got most of the rewards that were available to students, as Roger indicated they were not resented by Bill's friends. I asked Bill and Ken if the class were prestige stratified, and they did not seem to find it that way.

"Well, you know Mary, she's one girl—about the only girl—that I would say is stuck up. She has her group, but then I get along with most of them except her," said Bill.

"What about the boys?"

"No, I don't think so," said Bill. Ken agreed.

"What about the jocks?" I asked.

"Well, those guys stick together pretty much, but that's because they all play sports. I wanted to for a long time, but my parents wouldn't let me," said Bill.

"Yeah," said Ken. "I played football at St. Charles and would have gone out for it when I came here but for the eligibility rules."

"And," added Ken, "The girls that go out with the sport joes wouldn't go out with anyone else."

"Who?" I asked.

"Oh, Mary, Marlene—those girls. They wouldn't go with a guy who didn't play sports. A guy could be the dumbest guy that ever came along and if he plays sports, if he's a sport's joe, they'd go out with him and think he was the greatest. On the other hand, you take a real sharp guy who doesn't play sports, he's sharp, good looking, smooth, and still they wouldn't look at him."

Bill added that that was breaking down a little. And Fred, too, admitted that only a few ran things, but crossed it off by simply saying, "Most kids don't care to run things—the plays and all that."

Fred asked me one day which group I would rather hang around with, him and his friends or with Max and Bob and them. I told him I liked both. "Yeah, but those guys are tight. They're the typical high school seniors, not like us guys. We're losers."

I asked Fred what he meant but he did not give an answer, just went on talking about his friendship with Bill and with his girl. (Sometimes looking for well-articulated answers just did not work.) But he said the term "losers" without resentment; rather, he said it with pride.

One thing did surprise me, however. Bill's friends, when speaking of the athletes, would first mention Max as being in the center of the athletic clique. They really did not understand that Jim or Jack was the center. I was really surprised that one group would have so little understanding or knowledge or even concern for another group.

On the other hand, the athletes were somewhat aware of Bill's illegal activities and would shake their heads in amazement at them. Occasionally we would all work in the library and Bill, Fred, Roger, and Steve would describe their latest break-in, or credit card theft, or their chances for swiping a pair of skiis off the slope that night. While they carried on, Bob, Pete, Jim, and I would just sit and watch them. Later at lunch someone might remark, "Those guys are crazy." But no one ever condemned them for it and like all remarks which were about other students, it was readily forgotten.

Like the athletes, Bill and his friends maintained a strong group structure within the school which took up and served to satisfy their individual needs for participation, interaction, and activity. Also like the athletes this group structure was the central activity in school. While as individuals they gave the school's productive-academic structure a sort of minimal compliance, so they were not prevented from graduating, they saved their time and energy for their group activity.

The Music-Drama Group

An additional group that would be useful to describe was the music-drama clique. Some of its members, unlike the athletes and Bill's friends, were among the high achievers in the class. Its name stemmed from the fact that it was composed of a core of five individuals who made the music and drama activities their prime interests in school. Partly as a result of those interests, and partly as a result of their talent, they controlled most of the activities in the class.

Dick was the leader. Although he was a nonacademic student, with grades in the low 70's and a class standing of 122, he was reputed by his teachers to be one of the smartest boys in the school. When the scores of the annual achievement tests came out, he scored very high, and when the state exams results were announced, he had a score of 92–96 percentile and received a state scholarship. Dick was president of the Drama Club, director of the musical play which the humanities class was sponsoring, and director of the Senior Variety Show. Those activities made him the single most active senior in the school, and for all practical purposes, he had more individual responsibility than any other student.

He read and talked knowledgeably about a great many subjects, and if an opportunity for class discussion occurred Dick always seized it. When I first arrived, he introduced himself, immediately began talking about the issue of student power, saying that they had little but hoped to get more, and offered to be of assistance if I needed it. His interest in school issues led him to form the political committee of the Student Council. Despite his brains and talent, however, Dick did not study. "My grades are shitty. I haven't kept a notebook for four years; I just don't care."

The second member of the group was Jean. She was vice-president of the Honor Society, and through her association with Dick, had an active role in the Student Council political committee, the Drama Club, and the Senior Variety Show. Jean was ranked number one in the class and maintained an average of 97. In her junior year she had caused quite a stir in the school by gaining acceptance at Vassar.

The third member of the group, Tony, was president of the senior class and winner of a state scholarship. Tony planned to go to a nearby college, had a class standing of 26, took humanities, music theory, drama, and speech. He was an outstanding singer; his music teacher said he was the best tenor in the county. Tony was fresh from Winnsboro, and his election as president of the class represented a break in tradition, for the previous class presidents, Jack, Bob, and Max, were all varsity athletes from Hillsborough. Tony was well-liked by most of the class. He was extremely active in clubs and played J.V. football for three years.

The next member of the group was Carol, the president of the Student Council. She was from Hillsborough, had a class average of 83, and was ranked 64th in the class. She was an extremely attractive girl, although some of the students seemed to think of her as "stuck-up" or "power hungry." However, these expressions may have been just resentment because she stopped going with her former friends and sorority sisters who were in the "power clique." As she admitted, "I don't go with the party crowd anymore." She took humanities, physics, and typing and wanted to go to one of the better state universities.

The last member of the group was Larry. Larry was new to the district in his junior year and explained his entrance into the group as a result of his involvement in the junior musical production. He, too, had a good singing voice and with Bill, Dick, Tony, and Roger formed a rock singing group. He also took humanities, drama, and music. He referred to himself as a drama major and planned to go to a community college.

In addition there were one or two others who took an active interest in music and drama, but they were not in the inner core and were not in recognized positions of student power. I could not really tell much about the internal dynamics of this group with which I never associated that closely, but I did maintain good relations with individual members such as Dick and Tony and Jean. They seemed to appreciate my interest in their activities, and when an event of some importance was about to occur, such as a Council meeting, or the Honor Society induction, they would invite me to come. On a number of occasions, such as when they were planning to confront Mr. Rossi over some issue, they would tell me, "We'll have something to tell you later." And later they would relate the event.

In some ways this group was similar to both the athletes and Bill's friends. That is, all but Carol were from Cowpens and had been associating with each other since early grammar school. As opposed to the other groups, they did not seem to constitute a group outside school. Rather, their groupness evolved directly from their common interests in school-sponsored affairs. In fact, outside school, Dick, Tony, and Larry joined with Bill, Roger, and Fred to form a larger group. Carol had friends who had graduated previously and Jean had some friends who went to other high schools and who were interested in publishing a county-wide "student" newspaper.

In school, however, like the other groups, the music-drama crowd spent their time interacting with one another. Jean, of whom Dick said, "She's a real radical, she hates the place," expressed this probably more articulately than any other class member. When I asked her if she and her friends spent their school time hanging around together, she said:

"Yes, that's true, that's what we do. We're not very interested in school."

"You mean school, academically?"

"Yes, that's right. Well, there isn't much to be interested in."

"What do you mean?"

"Well, you've been in classes, we don't really learn anything. Like you were in our French class with Mrs. M. What we did in there could have been done better with tapes or something. We really don't have a class. And in humanities, we don't do any real work in there either. It isn't school really, it's a farce—something that Beckett would write about. Here we are all running around with no one really learning anything."

"Do you hang around with each other most of the time?"

"Yes, that's it. We're with our friends."

"And when you're with your friends, do you talk about school?"

"No, we talk about ourselves a lot. Self-analysis is big this year."

"What about last year? Was it the same way?"

"Well . . ., not for me. Last year I really worked. I got good grades, got accepted in college, and then this year, I've relaxed."

"Did you learn a lot last year?"

"Well, we had this one teacher in English. [Mrs. J.] She's no longer with us, but we had this group that were in her class. We put out a literary magazine. Maybe you heard of it. But we only did it once. That was a terrific class. You know what happened to Mrs. J.? She got asked to resign. Partly because of the literary magazine."

"What was it? Somebody call it subversive or something?"

"But it wasn't subversive, it was good. But you know Rossi is no literary critic. They're so conservative out here. Like, when I told the guidance counselor I wanted to go to Vassar, she just about fainted. She didn't even want to give me the catalog. She kept giving me recommendations to those state schools. It seems that everybody is so stuck out here that they resent you if you're going somewhere."

"How about other classes?"

"Well, we had a history teacher who spent the year telling us how dumb we were and how we didn't know anything and how we'd never go anywhere. Do you know Mr. Phillips?"

"No, what does he teach?"

"Well, he teaches English once in a while, when he feels like it—which isn't often."

Then Jean continued explaining how poor she thought the teachers were, and although she had received consistently good grades, she had not learned any more than anyone else. "But, I'll be able to go someplace because I play the game. It isn't really fair at all."

Jean was the only student who ever expressed any personal animosity toward the administrators. "What was Vincent—a football coach? And Rossi—a music teacher? I mean, what can you expect?"

Regardless of these often expressed sentiments, Jean dealt with the productive structure in an apparently ideal fashion, was studious and attentive in all her classes, and was highly respected by the teachers.

Dick, who referred to himself as "pretty conservative, more so than Jean," seldom expressed resentment at the organization. Since he received very low grades, I asked if he found the work difficult.

"No. One thing you have to know, that is how to fake your way through. You have to know the little gimmicks, the little tricks. And if you know them, you can get through. Look at me. I might get shitty grades, but I haven't kept a notebook for four years."

"Is it true that you spend about four-fifths of the time in the school hanging around with your group?"

"For seniors, that's true. It might even be a little conservative."

"What does school mean to you?"

"School is where I can go and do things I want with my friends."

"Yes. But is that all you do? Isn't it just too much of a good thing?"

"Well, yes. But there's nothing we can do about it. I get tired of saying we're going to do something and talking about it. I wish we could do it."

But he added, "School is all right because you're with your friends—it's a big picnic all day long—we just hang around together."

Dick really was quite happy in school. As was mentioned before, he took advantage of every opportunity for classroom discussions. During the Vietnam moratorium, the humanities class had a discussion. Dick was the first among them to decry the lack of justification for American involvement. In the speech class he was the most eager to do the improvisations, the poetry readings, and the skits that the teacher set up. He took his speech classes and music class seriously, although the business of doing an assignment or a log book was simply beyond him.

"Guess what, Phil? I flunked humanities and drama."

"Nobody can flunk humanities, Dick."

"Well, I just didn't write anything. I never hand anything in and when you're a senior, you really have to do the writing. I read all the time; you know that. But I never do the log or progress reports on the project. I just can't stand to sit down and write. I read; I remember. I must read four books a week. At night I just go home and read and play the guitar, but I never write."

"But you don't have to write that much."

"Oh, you do. Have you ever seen those log books?"

"Yes, and five minutes a day would finish them."

"Well, you have to write down everything that happens and then what you think of it."

"Yes, but it's not that much."

"Well, maybe you're right; I just can't."

While he admitted he knew the system well enough to get through it, he found it difficult to comply with the most minimal academic demands. However, even while not complying, he got by and was accepted at a local community college.

The Group in School

While some of the group members took different classes, they were together before school, in the cafeteria, during humanities, during lunch, and at their meetings after school. As did the other groups, they spent their time engaged in their own interests and systematically excluded any discussion of academic activities. Jean complied and got the highest grades. Dick failed. Yet, they were the best of friends. They simply did not consider the school's academic demands and grades an integral part of their group. As Dick saw the school, it was a setting "where I can go to meet with my friends."

Jack articulated this same thing. I asked him how he kept his class standing of 22. "I don't do any homework, but it's not that hard. Classes just aren't demanding." I then asked him how most kids felt about classes. "Most kids don't think about it. They just accept it. You go to school—it's a job."

"Do you get bored?"

"Sure. Like the kids can't stand lectures. You ever been to any of the biology lectures? They're terrible. When they started everyone thought they were going to be great, but they aren't. No kids like lectures, they just can't keep your interest."

Even Tony, a very able student, agreed that four-fifths of the time in school was spent interacting with his friends over matters of group importance. He had a larger view of the phenomenon, however. He compared Gates unfavorably with a nearby school in a suburb where the students cared more, and he said that the parental push was lacking in Gates and, therefore, kids just did not care.

As with the other groups, the music-drama people adhered to or failed to adhere to the rules and regulations as individuals, not as group members. Dick was frequently late for class because of his smoking in the lavatory. Tony believed in following the rules rigidly and was often asked by the administrators to help in enforcing something like keeping the lounge clean. Jean, as demonstrated, thought little of the whole process, but her high grades and excellent behavior in class made her immune to the sanctions invoked against those who flaunted the rules and regulations.

Except for Jack, Jean was the only student I ever found who expressed real resentment against teachers. Even Dick who reported, "I got a lousy music theory teacher, but I can't do anything about it, so why try?" did not express any overt resentment against the teachers or the organization of the school. Carol, who admitted that school "was just a social thing," did not seem to think it should be anything else. The members of the music-drama group were like the members of other groups. They took as many of their classes as possible—drama, humanities, and chorus—together. Tony and Jean also took physics; Carol, calculus; Jean, French III, so they were not together the entire day, but they managed to be in each other's company for at least four of the seven hours.

In addition to the play and shows they made school politics a part of their interest. In fact, they were the only students to do so. Once when a new boy, Horace, was told to shave his upper lip or leave school, Dick, Jean, Tony, Carol, and Jack went into Mr. Rossi's office and told him he could not make Horace do it, and if he did they would have a sit down strike. Horace and his moustache stayed. When the superintendent came and talked to the humanities class, the athletes wanted the football field fixed, others wanted a choice of desserts at lunch, but Dick, Jean, and Carol forced a discussion of student rights and got him to admit, "There may be some contribution that students could make to the running of the school." Despite their conviction that they did nothing in school, they went to the Board of Education and suggested that parents be invited to school so that they would be encouraged to vote affirmatively for the next budget. It was they who, through Jean's presidency of the Honor Society, worked on a project to provide high school tutors for elementary pupils.

Dick was all for exercising more power. After a large number of students skipped for the October moratorium, Dick remarked, "What can they do? Throw us out of school?" Yet he was never able to work up any enthusiasm; all descried the lack of involvement on the part of other students. Although when I attended the script writing meeting for the variety show, or the Drama Club meeting, or the Council meetings, it was evident that there was simply very little to do. I remained convinced that the "student activities" sector of the school was not worth the involvement of more than a few.

Despite their protestations to the contrary, the music-drama clique was just as isolated from other students as anyone else. Dick actually denied that the groups were split. I asked him once if the cliques were divided. "For the first three years there were different cliques; now there is just one clique with a few outsiders—those guys you hang around with [the athletes] are a clique only on the football field. The rest of the time they are part of the main senior clique. All it takes to join the clique is that you be a decent person—not mind a few gross jokes, have a certain amount of patience, and get along. It's really not broken up into little groups anymore, not like it used to be."

I disagreed and mentioned the cafeteria seating arrangements, saying that the class was rigidly divided, and Dick admitted, "You never see the cliques you're in, so maybe I'm wrong."

Tony agreed that their clique was tight, that it had been for a long time, and that if you were not in, you were not likely to get in.

The music-drama clique behaved in a fashion similar to both the athletes and Bill's friends. The focus of their group activities differed, but they too dealt with the institution by giving some individual degree of compliance while saving most of their time, energy, and enthusiasm for their group relationships. Despite their statements about desiring more involvement with others and their leadership positions, their behavior was as an isolated social unit.

The Power Clique

As in many schools Horatio Gates had a group of senior girls who, for the entire three years in high school, managed to keep control of most activities. By others they were called, sometimes with bitterness, the "power clique," a term which apparently referred to the way they manipulated the class elections, the committees, and the staff members. I did not take them too seriously, because although they did get elected to class office, their members had little to do with the activities that seemed important during the time of the study, such as the senior play, yearbook, and newspaper. Apparently this was the first year they had missed anything, and they still controlled class elections and the out-of-school social life. The yearbook editor, Debbie, was a good person to ask about the politics of the class. She had, with a combination of hard work and cleverness, secured her editorship which was, as far as I could see, the only position in the whole extracurricular structure that demanded any time or talent, and her perceptions of the power clique seemed fairly accurate. I asked her once if there was a "lead group."

"I'm probably a good one to ask that question. Yes. There is a lead group and it's run by one girl. And yes, other kids would like to get in it but it just can't be done. It's a group of girls, Sally, Kathy, the Martin twins, Gloria, and Ellen, and they keep everything pretty tight. Like Tony is the president of the senior class, but it's Sally who actually runs things. She tries to keep Tony right under her thumb but he doesn't like it. In fact, Tony is sort of the link between the rest of the school and the lead crowd. But it's Sally who's the big wheel in school."

"How does one get into the lead crowd?"

"Well, like Alice got in because she's a friend of

Dotty's, and Barbara is a friend of the twins and they are in with Sally and Kathy, the two leaders."

"Could you get in?"

"No. I'm not in the lead crowd and never could be. It's funny because my friend and I were talking about this with my mother and sister. The lead crowd is really different. Like they drink, fool around, don't study and they're clique, and most of them smoke, too."

"Do other kids want to get in the lead clique?"

"Well, yes. Most of them would like to, but like me they can't. So most of them don't pay any attention to the lead group. They have their own friends. Like me and my friends hang around together, we don't need those kids."

"What does it mean to be in the lead crowd; what does a lead crowd lead?"

"Well, they just take everything for themselves."

"What do you mean, *everything*?"

"Well, the class offices. They get those, they run the class that way."

"You mean they get *all* the positions? What about Bob and Max?"

"No, not just that. They might not get elected to *everything.* But they influence everything. Like they're the ones who keep nominating Bob and Max and keep getting them elected. If they don't get elected they still influence those who do."

"What things?"

"Like the proms, the dances. Tony actually has done a good job this year. He isn't influenced by them. He's resisted them and that's good, but he's the first."

"They also have big parties to which they invite only their friends, you just don't get invited unless you're in with them and the parties are a little wild. They drink and smoke and carry on."

"Like me, I'm proud of my family and my religion and my work. I do my schoolwork. I'm what you would call a square."

"Do they run the yearbook?"

"No. And they're not going to."

"Do the boys have a lead group like that?"

"Oh, yes. The football players. They're in a class by themselves. But they don't run things the way the girls do. They're actually nicer; like Jack, he always speaks to me."

I would like to have known more about this group, but a male adult, even if he is running a school-approved study, should not associate too closely with a group of teen-age girls. Also, some of these girls dated athletes and I did not want to get between any of the boys and their girl friends. As far as I could determine, there were six girls who formed the clique: Sally, Kathy, Lorraine, Mary, and the twins. In addition there were three or four who were frequently, though not always, present. They ate together everyday at a table close to the one the athletes used, associated with one another in the humanities class, chose to work in the humanities sections that others in their group chose, and dated boys who were best friends. Their leader, Sally, went with Ralph and her best friend, Kathy, dated Pete. All belonged to the same sorority. Three of them were cheerleaders, and most were high on the lists of senior superlatives: best dressed, Sally; most popular, Janice; best dancer and most personality, Lorraine, and so forth. From all appearances, like the athletes, they constituted a tight group with a strong idea of what they wanted in the school. Also like the athletes, they did their best to turn the situation to their advantage so that they could continue to maintain their togetherness. They walked around and talked together in the halls, lounge, and cafeteria just as the athletes did. They seemed to share their own set of interactions and, as far as I could see, seldom dealt with other students.

One should not get the impression that these girls were busy with activities, because it just was not true. I watched them a number of times, and toward the end I even got to know a couple of them quite well. Their actual involvement was like Ray's; that is, one rarely saw them doing anything that indicated serious responsibility.

I asked Pete once how Kathy kept getting elected to things. "Well, she's pretty well liked, but you know she doesn't do anything. It's that she's in the clique; she doesn't do anything but type things."

I asked two of them once why they ran everything. They first denied it, saying that the kids in the music-drama clique ran things (like the senior play and the talent show), which was true. But after considering the matter, they admitted their existence as a clique and further admitted that they were in a lot of school activities. They quickly explained that they ran things because the rest of the kids did not want to and there was no sense in trying to make them. "If we don't do it, who will? We're the only ones with any school spirit."

This point was even agreed to by outsiders. At a class meeting at which the clique members were taking the lead, a girl behind me remarked, "Jesus Christ, it's always the same kids." Sam was next to me at the time and I asked if there were resentment of the "clique." "Yeah, there's a lot but one thing, if you nominate these kids that are complaining, they would refuse. The clique members at least do things."

Being in that group did mean something. One day we were in the lounge and someone brought in a plastic belt. The idea was to put the belt around two people and then watch them struggle out without unbuckling it. The members of the power clique started playing with it and everyone else watched. When those two dropped the belt on the floor they backed off but no one moved. There were, twenty of us, lined up in three rows to watch the two girls. When they finished we still stood there and simply watched the empty belt, waiting for someone else to do it. Sure enough, the only ones who would come forward and perform were two more girls from that clique.

In addition to the athletes, Bill's friends, the music-drama group, and the power clique, there were large numbers of other groups. There were a number of boys from Cowpens who spent a great deal of time hunting. There was a group whose members spent their time and energy on their cars. Others hung around a pool hall downtown; a number were interested in music; one group had a rock band; and there was a fairly large number who could have been classed as deviants. One group, which I would have liked to explore further, was the "Executioners," a motorcycle gang of approximately twelve boys, one of whom owned a Honda 90, the remainder of whom wore embossed denims and dreamed of future Harleys. My appeal was solid. I rode a real motorcycle and was promptly invited to join. One Executioner, Rainy (apparently the second in command) sought me out, asked if I were "the new kid with the Bultaco," and thereafter we spent some time talking about cycles.

Later he invited me to go with him to meet someone. He walked into the on-going shop lab and motioned to another boy (apparently the leader) who promptly put down his tools, came out, and we talked cycles and cycle gangs for a while. He impressed me by citing his personal interactions with the members of two, older, opposing cycle gangs who were having a series of minor shootouts on the streets of the downtown area, and then he asked me if I wanted to join. I politely refused. About a week later Rainy asked me what I was going to do that Saturday. I mumbled something, waiting to see what would happen, so he asked if I would be interested in driving to a town thirty miles to the north to meet another motorcycle-less gang, one of whom had impugned the integrity of an Executioner. I declined, since being wheel man for a gang fight was not part of the study.

I would like to have learned more about the Executioners and their school perspective. After all, what does the school mean to students who join a cycle gang? But there was no time and to become attached to such a group could have become troublesome. It would have made the staff members suspicious and one complaint to the principal or superintendent, and I would have been out.

There were interactions between the athletes, Bill's friends, the music-drama group, and the power clique. That is, the athletes dated girls from the power clique and Bill and his friends associated with Dick, Tony, and Larry out of school. When the big senior events came up (the prom, for instance), Tony and Dick and Jean would work with the girls from the power clique. Also, in the plays (the humanities' *West Side Story,* and the Senior Variety Show) Dick and Jean wrote and directed, Tony and Larry and Sally took the leading roles, and Bill, Ken, and Roger helped make up the supporting cast. However, this did not mean that groups were breaking down. Except for these interactions, they still ignored each other in the halls, cafeteria, and classrooms. It should be added that in none of the aforementioned activities was an "Executioner" invited to take part.

Summary and Discussion of Chapter 5

In addition to the athletes there were a large number of groups in the school, from the music-drama clique to the Executioners. In fact, almost everyone, as Marilyn said in Chapter 2, "Seemed to have someone to hang around with." Although these groups were made up of different individuals and centered around different interests, all seemed to have a common way of dealing with the organization. Their individual members would comply, as did Jean or Jack, or fail to comply, as did Dick, Jim, or Bill, but the group would not allow an individual's degree of compliance or non-compliance with the academic sector of the school to interfere with its activities.

Furthermore, the groups in school were separate and distinct social units. There was very little cross-group communication except where boyfriend-girlfriend relations were involved. That is, individual athletes interacted with individual power clique members in that Max dated Mary, Bob dated Marlene, and Jim dated Betty.

Many individuals probably had other friends outside school. Jim was close to and sometimes associated with a group of boys from downtown Hillsborough, but like other students, he rarely spoke to his nongroup friends in school. In fact, I was particularly surprised to find out in November that Dick and Bill and Tony and Roger were friends. In school I rarely saw them together. I know they never ate together. If their groups interacted at all, it was centered around some senior class project, and even there the group lines were clearly drawn.

There are two sets of issues and questions I would like to raise in reference to the descriptions in this chapter. The first issue has to do with teacher-student relationships, the second with student-student relationships.

In reference to the first, I should reiterate the point that it is terribly difficult for a teacher to penetrate any of the groups, either in or out of the school. First of all, it takes a great deal of time: it is simply not possible to be a sometimes group member and expect to maintain any influence. When I was associating with Bill's friends, at no time did my opinion make any difference. Of course I did not try, but had I tried, I could not have done it. They enjoyed my interest in their activities, had no hesitancy about telling me what they did, but had I tried to influence them, I would have become an outsider. And, of course, I was not acting as a teacher. Had a teacher attempted to do what I did, and simultaneously tried to be "directive" or "teacher-like," they would have excluded him. Thus, as long as individuals stayed within their groups they were actually "protected from teachers." The groups actually insulated individuals from contact with teachers and administrators.

Let me try to make sense of the whole process. It was already stated that the organization and the role taken by administrators and teachers leaves students to their own devices. It seems they reciprocate by building social units or maintaining those that have been previously built outside school, and these social units give the students the activity, interests, involvement, and participation for which the schools make no provision. But then the process continues. The units then prevent teachers from being involved because the teachers' presence and influence might upset the group's delicate balance. However, a teacher might "get close to" an entire group if he would to some degree do what they do. But how many teachers would enjoy a noon hour with Bill's friends, a Saturday gang fight with the Executioners, or an evening in the bar with the athletes? Few at most, and I certainly would not try to make "participation in student groups" a job requirement. So any interaction of students and teachers would have to be teacher-, or at least, institution-centered, and that too closely resembles a classroom situation. The answer to the question, "Can teachers get close to students," may not be "absolutely no." Certainly some teachers do it, and many others think they do it, but it is clear that the student group structure works to discourage teacher-student interaction.

There is another question: "Are the students suffering from the absence of teacher contact?" If we define "suffering" as meaning lost, directionless, and alone, the answer is surely "no." The groups satisfy the students' human needs. As a participant, I found that Dick was right. It's fun being with your friends.

We might consider the more positive function that the group performed for the school. It served not only as a barrier between student-teacher interaction, but as a way of dealing with certain organizational characteristics, such as the maintenance and routine procedures. Bill's friends took care of Steve when he was in trouble. The group members, Jack, Rick, and Bob, reported Jim's and Greg's absence and this kept them in line with the rules. All the groups exchanged information within their ranks about meeting the organization's basic demands. The groups provided orderly activities for their members so they relieve the teachers from having to worry about students all the time. Thus the groups were "functional"; that is, they served definite purposes for both the individual members and even for the organization.

There is one additional question about students and school. "For what reasons do students get into trouble?" I thought it was significant that when Bill's friends got into trouble, it was not for gambling or stealing, but for skipping class or irritating a teacher through some breach of organizational routine. Staff members knew Ken gambled, the administrators knew he was picked up in a raid, and a number of teachers knew that all the boys stole, but they did nothing to prevent it. They just ignored it. This point strengthens my belief that the school has a difficult time touching students in any personal way. It demands only that they respect the organization's standard operating procedures.

What about the relationships between students and students? Personally, I thought that having worked in public schools for eight years, I knew something about the "adolescent society." What I saw in Gates, however, surprised me. I had previously seen adolescents in any particular school as socially homogenous. While I knew there were more or less prestigious students, achievers, and deviants, I had thought that they had more in common with one another, and had some common interests about which they communicated. That wasn't true of students in Gates. The groups there really were discrete social units, narrowly bounded not only by age, sex, and neighborhood, but chiefly by interests. The athletes made no attempt to communicate with any other group, nor did Bill's friends, and the music-drama clique, although they asked "Why don't other kids get involved," did not attempt to involve them. Even those who were termed "class leaders," such as Max, Bob, Rick, and Jean, and the power clique girls, never, to my knowledge, communicated with those outside their group.

Concerning the matter of class leaders, if no one was leading nor anyone being lead and the individuals communicated only with their small groups of friends and kept themselves isolated from the rest, where is this "adolescent society" of which we speak? The data suggest that rather than a society or even a subculture, there is a fragmented series of interest groups revolving around specific items and past patterns of interaction. These groups may be the important social referent, not some mythical subculture or "adolescent society."

Once an acquaintance of mine asked how my study was coming and added that he heard that, "All the kids over there are popping pills." I assured him that this was not the case, but when I reflected on it, I realized that considering the fragmented nature of the student experience, I would not have known about a drug culture unless I associated directly with students who took part in it.

There were students who took drugs, but they and their activities were not even discussed or considered by those with whom I associated. Only Steve took some kind of pills and if he talked to anyone about what they were, then that person was probably Bill, his friend. I would suggest that when we hear it said that "all students are taking pills," "getting religion," "smoking grass," or "turning on to this or that current fad," we should reflect on the nature of the adolescent experience, remember that cross-communication among adolescents may be very limited, common activities and interests very rare, and perhaps conclude that there may be no such thing as "all students."

CHAPTER **6**

Some Isolates

I have stated repeatedly that it was extremely important for any single student in the school to have someone with whom he could associate, but unfortunately there were a few students who seemed to have no close friends and who were not even allowed follower status in any group. I would like to have known a number of these individuals, but at the time I could not study them. As emphasized earlier, one engaged in participant observation must choose his associates carefully for he will be initially judged and accepted or rejected according to their status. If I had started by associating with friendless students, I would not have had any chance to enter the groups. To attempt association with everyone would gain me the trust and friendship of no one. However, I did run across a small number of these students and I feel that one brief chapter should be devoted to describing what I learned about them. There are two reasons for this. First, I think in order to understand how important it is to have friends, we should consider what happened to those who had none, and secondly, their school experience may be typical of a significant number of adolescents.

During those first few weeks, in addition to going to class, I had few acquaintances and a lot of free time to walk around. During that period there were students who, having heard that I was in the school doing some sort of study, sought me out to ask why I was there. These were not the more popular students. They were the ones who seemed to have few if any friends, and they were probably anxious to talk to someone who would respond to them. The attempts at conversation were awkward. One day in art class I sat next to a tall, slim girl who dressed poorly and had an acne problem. She looked at me sideways for a while and finally said, "Our phone doesn't work." "That's too bad," I replied. She said nothing for a few minutes and looked away, staring alternately at her nails and the teacher. A few minutes later, "Next month we're moving to Detroit where my father has a new job." "That sounds good." She looked away again, this time putting her head down and later in the period said, "We use my grandfather's phone." By then I didn't know what to say to her. I didn't want to start a conversation in the middle of class for fear of irritating the teacher, and when the bell rang she left quickly.

I watched her later and she behaved as did other isolates. In the halls she would not stand and talk to anyone, but kept moving and was seldom seen "standing around leaning against the walls." That was understandable. If you keep moving and act as if you have somewhere to go, no one will notice your aloneness. In class, or those rare occasions when I saw her in the lounge, she would sort of half eavesdrop on the conversations of others. I soon stopped seeing her and presumed she moved to Detroit.

Perhaps she had just moved in and out of the district and therefore didn't have time to make friends. But, it wasn't only the transit students who were alone. There was Nick, who had been in the district all his life, and who, at 5 ft. 5 in. and about 105 pounds, was one of the smallest boys in the class. Later when I wanted to ask other students about those who had no friends, I would suggest Nick, but I found that most of the others did not see him, nor were they even aware of his presence.

I first noticed Nick in the student lounge where he would sit against the wall and watch the others talking or playing cards with one another. Nick was always alone, and a few times I made a point of sitting next to him. He would ask how my study was coming, and I would tell him it was fine. Once, when he asked what I was finding, I told him the kids seemed to spend a lot of time together.

He replied, "You probably noticed that I don't have many friends around here." But he dropped that and went on, "See that girl? She's a new girl. I feel sorry for her coming to this school."

"Why?"

"Because she'll have to put up with some of the girls around here. Like those girls. They're really rough. The language they use and the way they talk in the girls' lav. I'd like to meet her though." Then he added, "Not the girls in our class though. Some of them are really wonderful."

He was silent for a few seconds and I asked him what he did in school. He replied that he worked hard, took five classes—English, social studies, retail business, a vocational technical course, and shop—and that he had only two free periods in which to come to the lounge. "That takes most of my day." He also talked about his job, "I got a job now at the liquor store, starting tonight. I don't look old enough, but I am. I'm eighteen but I'm real little."

At that time Jack and two other football players were getting rough. They would pick up one of their friends, carry him around, take off his shirt and shoes, and deposit him on top of the coke machine. Nick did not like it. "Those guys are too rough. They pick on everybody else. This lounge is going to get closed because of them. Like I'm not too popular. I don't hang around with those big kids. I hang around with the less popular kids, like, see that kid in the yellow shirt playing cards? I hang around with him some."

Jack and the boys were getting rougher and they were right next to me. "They're always picking on everyone. I wish Rossi would come in when they're doing that. Like me, I'm not concerned about my size. I don't care. I walk by this school proud. . . . Look at that. The way those guys tear up the furniture. That was new last year, but last year's class never did that stuff. They kept the lounge good. But those guys don't take care of anything."

He was referring to Jack and the three others who were now wrestling on the couch. Rossi did come in then, looked disgustedly at the horseplay and just said, "Why don't you save that for the Georgetown game?" Then he walked out.

Nick was silent for a few seconds then went on to say, "It's hard to stay in school and hard to stay out of school."

I asked what he meant and he replied, "It's dull hanging around all day, but you need a high school diploma to get a job."

"Is that what you do—hang around all day?"

"Well, I work. The classes are pretty hard and you have to do your work to pass."

At this point, another boy, Ed, whom I knew came up and started talking to me. There was absolutely no recognition on Ed's part of Nick, and I was involved in two conversations. By the time I turned back toward where Nick had been, he was gone.

While watching Nick a few times in class, I noticed that he paid attention fairly well. He did his assignments, maintained a class standing of 110 and an average of 82. In all these ways he was complying with the organization in a very acceptable fashion. Yet when he came into class or left class or stayed in the lounge, he was always alone. He was very open about it, admitting that he would have preferred more friends, and seemed very conscious of other students, as his remarks about the "rough girls" and "those guys" showed. His accusation that, "Those guys pick on everyone," however, was not true. The football players carried on horseplay only with their friends.

Later I asked Nick what he thought of school. While other, more popular students would speak of school in terms of their friends and activities, Nick always discussed his school days in terms of his official role. That is, in terms of his classes, his work, his grades, his desire for a diploma and the hope it offered of a good job. He apparently had some hopes of working at the liquor store permanently, but he had no luck there either. When I saw him a week later, I asked how he was doing . . . "Ah, I quit." "Why?" "The guy told me he'd pay me minimum wage and then after I worked all week he only gave me $10. So I quit." I suppose I could have probed, "What is it like having no friends in a place like this?" However, it was obvious that Nick's school days were lonely.

Another fairly isolated student was Andy, a boy referred to earlier as replying, "I don't know. I never know what you're talking about," when a teacher asked him a question. Andy was another student who tried to get to know me when I first went to the school. He was eighteen years old and worked fifty hours a week in a discount gas station, but in school he seemed totally lost. At the beginning of the year he was wandering around taking only English and social studies. The rest of his day was spent in study halls. He was supposed to be having a double class in vocational education, but during the first week of school he went once, the teacher was not there, and by mid-October, Andy had not bothered to return. I wondered then if there were many students like Andy wandering around taking only one or two courses and spending the rest of the time in study halls. Andy said that sixty-five percent of the students were doing the same thing, but he was the only one I ever found. Why Andy did not go and straighten his schedule out I do not know. I asked and he said he would get around to it sooner or later, and in November he finally went to the guidance counselor and was placed in the right class. Even then the majority of Andy's time was spent hanging around. Like Nick, to whom he occasionally spoke, he would lean or sit against the wall. If he saw me with Jim or Greg, he would come over to talk a little, even when it meant being a target for Jim's wit. I asked Andy what he thought of school. "Well, you gotta have the diploma. I'll need a high school diploma to get a good factory job."

"But what do you think of all this hanging around?"

"I don't mind. It's dull, but I get a chance to sleep a lot, and I need that." Then Andy would tell me how much he was making and what he was buying with his money: clothes, radio, and possibly a car. In that respect Andy apparently had his own interests.

Sam was another example. He was in humanities class and chose to enter the small section with the athletes. Sam, however, had no specific friend there and as a result, he and one other boy became involved in their own project on which they did a fairly respectable job. The other boy was not an isolate. He was a semi-professional musician and attended school only a few periods a day, saving his afternoons for practice and his evenings for work. Thus he kept his relationship with Sam class-centered. Sam, like Nick and Andy, would have preferred some friends. He, too, would initiate conversations with me by asking how the study was coming. When I told him I was finding that kids hung around together, like Nick he spoke of his inability to do that. "Not me. You haven't seen me do that. I don't have any friends around here."

After we had talked two or three times, Sam attempted to make me his friend. That is, he tried to hang around with me in the cafeteria, class and lounge. I was there to do a study not to be a friend to those who had no friends, and if I had started hanging around with Nick, Andy, or Sam, I would have made one student the basis of the study. That, of course, is a real problem in the methodology of participant observation. Had I gone in only as an occasional visitor to collect some information, I would have had very limited contact with both Sam and Jim, Andy and Jack, and there would have been no issue of involvement. By making a conscious decision to become personally involved, I had to choose carefully those with whom I associated, and to choose an isolate like Sam would have severely limited, even destroyed, the study's purpose.

Sam tried to be in on things but it did not work. When, as illustrated in the second chapter, the small humanities class under Bob's appointed leadership was trying to deal with the issue of improving the class, Sam made one comment and was silenced by Jim. Then he gave up. Another time he was part of the class preparing for a production of *West Side Story* and was one of a group singing the "Officer Krumke" song, Sam took the trouble to try to imitate the movie version and was signing some lines in a falsetto voice. He did it twice in practice when the whole chorus was standing around the piano, and while he was singing others would look at one another, shake their heads, and grimace. After he did it the second time, Jack turned to Chris, another football player, and said, "You take that part, Chris." Chris did, Sam drifted into the back of the chorus, and no more was said about it. Personally, I did not think his singing was so bad. Certainly it was no worse than Chris's. But for Sam to move to the front of any activity was apparently, unacceptable to other students.

Another time Sam tried to initiate a going-away party for Patty, the student teacher who had been assisting Mr. Summers in humanities. He talked about it with Mr. Summers, picked the last day of her assignment for the party, and decided to bring in pop and doughnuts to the small class section. Sam told me about it that morning, collected a dollar from me and two other people, and went out to get the refreshments. During fourth period he brought them into the class where Jim and his group, Bill and his friends, and Dick and some of his girls were. It was an embarrassing flop. No one but Sam and I even ate the doughnuts. Jim and Greg left to talk to a college recruiter. Bob entertained Rick and Pete with a story, Bill and his friends left for the library, Dick went to a meeting and Patty, the supposed center of the party, put her head in a book all period. Mr. Summers was absent.

Sam really tried. He passed the doughnuts saying loudly, "Have one, Phil, you might as well, you paid for them." I suppose he hoped that if he could engage me, then others would follow, but that did not work and he gave up. I was very embarrassed for him, but that is what happened when a non-popular, groupless student tried to initiate some activity. It is sad, it really is, but that is what happens to those without friends.

There were probably many more lonely students. I know Charlene was one of them. She was new to the class and was not getting anywhere with friends. I was nice to her a few times. That is, I acknowledged her and talked to her, but that just encouraged her to start hanging around me, so I had to do my best to avoid her. When we did talk she would frequently refer to her former school and her friends there. When I asked her how she liked Gates, she would speak disparagingly of the clique-ness of the kids. According to her, students at her previous school didn't do that. Later she fell in love with a university student and seemed to spend most of her time either writing him love letters or reading the ones he wrote to her.

At the Senior Variety Show practice session I saw a good example of what happens when an isolated student tried to move into an in-group activity. At the practice there were forty-seven students present, thirty-three of them girls, mostly power clique or music-drama group members. The boys were either football players or Bill's friends. One girl I had not seen previously was waiting to practice her song. She looked small, shy, and was sitting alone until she came up and asked Dick if she could try out for the show. He apparently said it would be all right because she got up and started singing "There's a Place for Us" from *West Side Story.* Personally, I thought she was better than any solo singer I had heard in that school, far better, in fact, than the two popular girls who took lead parts in the humanities' production of *West Side Story.* I was even beginning to enjoy her song. But the other students started giggling and tittering. Joan and Dick were grimacing at each other, Jim and Doug started burping, and the twins started giggling. The further she went, the worse it got. Then she stopped and asked Dick if she could start over and go all the way through. He turned to us, rolled his eyes, grimaced and said, "Sure, Marian," and on she went. Then he came back to where Max and Mary were sitting, and they told him, "We haven't got time to listen to her. Tell her to do it some other time."

He replied, "What can I do? If I tell her she can't sing, she'll, like, have a traumatic experience right on the stage."

Then Mary just told him, "Get her to sit down, Dick." So he said, "All right." And called to her, "Marian, can you come tomorrow night? We have a lot to do tonight and really can't spare the time."

"Oh, sure, Dick," she said, and sat down. I do not think she returned because I did not see her in the final production. I asked later and was told that she was a real "weirdo," overly talkative, given to some sort of seizures, and at times difficult to deal with. Apparently that justified her exclusion from the show. It is only fair to add that not everyone was excluded. Janet, an attractive black girl, got up and did a blues number and was genuinely cheered by all. Janet was not an isolate, she was close to a number of other girls and seemed to have a strong personality in her own right. Dick or Mary would not have dared to tell her to sit down.

It may be said of Nick, Andy, Sam, Charlene, and Marian that every day they were faced with the brutal fact that they were friendless in a friendship-based society, and during the time when others were engaged in group or friendship activities, they just seemed to be "standing around leaning against the wall." Ken's comments on why he skipped school for fifty-eight days actually made a great deal of sense. Kim, another boy, expressed the same thing when I asked, "Do many kids walk around alone?"

"That's what half of the kids are absent for. They don't have anyone to talk to in school."

It is important that one avoid equating "unpopular students" with isolates. There were a few students whom I think were genuinely unpopular. Two of these, Liz and Betty, dressed in long tight slacks, undersized sweaters, high heels, and maintained exaggerated hairdos. John and his group referred to them as "goddamn whores," and the more popular girls referred to them as "studs who got caught somewhere in the 50s." "Stud Queens" was the term used by Marilyn to refer to them. But Liz and Betty had each other, were always in the company of one another, and after school would be picked up in the parking lot by some men in their twenties. That they were unpopular didn't seem to bother them at all. They were always engaged in animated conversation over something, and as far as I could see, they paid absolutely no attention to the other students. Unlike Sam and Marian they made no attempt to join other students in school events.

Summary and Discussion of Chapter 6

Again, there are a number of issues concerning the isolates that I would like to bring up and direct to the attention of those that either teach or plan to teach. I said before that an individual's group seemed to protect him or at least stand between him and the organization. He could use that group to intercede for him, to bend the organization to him, to give him some human rewards. Not so for the isolates. They were alone with virtually no protection. I think that is why Nick wanted Mr. Rossi to catch the ballplayers fooling around. He wanted the organization to come and protect him, to be closer to him.

Others in the room where Jack and his friends were being rough paid little attention. They knew that the ballplayers picked on only the other ballplayers, not on students in general. They didn't need Mr. Rossi to protect them, they were with their friends. When Nick spoke of school, he did so not as Jim and Dick and Bill who talked about their friends, but in terms of his classes and homework. They were all he had to be involved with. Nick actually wanted more from the school. He wanted and needed personal relationships. But he did not get it. In fact, it was those students who were most prestigious and popular in the student sector who most often received that personal relationship with the official structure. When Rossi came in and reprimanded Jack and his friends, he did so in such a way as to recognize their positions as athletes. "Why not save that for the Georgetown game?" Nick, who needed Rossi's recognition, was not even noticed. Rossi probably didn't know his name. It is perhaps paradoxical that it was Nick who behaved as the organization said a student should, but it was Jack and his friends who got the rewards.

I found it painful to watch isolates get hurt, especially

in Sam's case. I think that if Sam had been a group member and had his friends around him, he would have had clearer ideas about the norms for acceptable behavior. Group members who went too far had friends to help them back into line; that was a functional purpose of the group. They acted as guides to members' behavior. But Sam had no friends, so he had nothing to protect him, nothing to guide him gently, or to act as a restraint on his behavior.

The point is that the organization is, with its rules, roles, and regulations, far removed from an individual student. If students were kept active and involved in academic processes, being an isolate would not be so terrible. But they aren't; they are left to create their own world, and it is a social world of groups, cliques, and friendships. In that setting, to be an isolate is extremely difficult. The organization doesn't provide personal interest in students. Even teachers, as pointed out, have no way of getting to individuals like Joe, Red, Nick, and Andy. Their instructional role passes right over the students' heads. Therefore, the group is necessary. It helps the student *adjust to* the organization, and even, on occasion, can *adjust* the organization to the student. Andy's case is proof. If Andy had a group, as did Steve and Jim, he would have had someone to tell him about going to class and getting his schedule straight. But he didn't have a group, so he drifted for two months. It seems to me that teachers rely on informal student groups for more than they recognize. They don't even seem to be aware of the fact that if those groups weren't present, those students would be demanding more interest, personal involvement, and even information from them. Therefore, we might say that the student group is an important and purposeful social unit in the school.

Again, let us ask: "What could a specific teacher do for an isolate?" Andy told the teacher, "I don't know what you're talking about, I never know what you're talking about!" What did the teacher do? He explained, of course. Teachers always explain, just like that—in words, in sentences with subjects and predicates and stated from a subject matter point of view, in a very reasonable way. But that isn't what Andy needed. He needed some personal interest, some behavioral direction and involvement. But was it there? No. Could the teacher give it? Maybe, but he didn't, and that's what matters. He chose to maintain his teacher role and kept a stream of words between himself and his student.

"What about those teachers who want to change things?" We must remember something. Teachers are not really different from their adolescent students. Jim, Jack, and Greg were talented and personable individuals. Small wonder that both teachers and students liked them. I liked them. I frankly enjoyed their company, and so did the teachers, and so did Mr. Rossi. When they and I were together with Mr. Rossi, we had a personally satisfying time. We enjoyed each other. But Andy, Sam, and Nick were not as personable, as interesting or as enjoyable to be with. Not for me, not for the teachers, and not for Mr. Rossi. So now the question: "Can a teacher take as much personal pleasure from interacting with students like Andy and Nick as he does from Jim and Jack?" Remember, he is more than a teacher. He is a human being subject to his personal likes and dislikes just as are the students. Asking him to put aside these personal likes and dislikes and become involved with those that have no friends will be hard, maybe impossible.

Marian is another matter. How could a teacher protect her from the embarrassment of exclusion by the other students? Is that even possible given that the teacher made a genuine effort to let the production be "student run"? Perhaps, perhaps not, but it won't be easy. If teachers are to help any of the Marians and students like her, it will demand conscious effort and a great deal of thoughtful planning, possibly some radical changes in the school's basic organizational structure.

CHAPTER 7

Integrating
the Student Groups
with the Organization

What has been presented is a picture of Horatio Gates as an organization composed of two separate entities. First, there was the official, school system with its administrators, teachers, classes, grades, and routine where the student was relegated to the roles of learner, watcher, listener, and subordinate. Secondly, there is the evidence in Chapters 2, 3, and 4 indicating that within that environment, the students created an extra-official, group-centered social system which consumed a significant amount of their time and energy, and which offered most students a set of rewards different from that offered by the official structure. Even the existence of a few isolates does not change this. Though alone, their remarks and behavior affirmed the fact that the students' world was group- and friendship-centered. In addition it was demonstrated that the students themselves seemed to go to some lengths to maintain distance between the official system and their friendship patterns, and thus by their actions, encouraged the existence of two separate structures operating in the building.

That there was a dual system is not surprising. Anyone familiar with organizations is aware that within any institution—a hospital, office, school, or large bureaucracy —there is an officially designated, organizational structure, sometimes called the "formal organization," with recommended roles, channels of communication, patterns of authority and expected outcomes. Simultaneously there is a *de facto* structure characterized by the way people in that organization interact and deal with one another on a daily basis. The latter is commonly called the "informal organization."

However, this dichotomy is oversimplified, and should not be used in an attempt to explain the behavior of the Gates seniors. First of all, by equating the students' group structure with "informal" organization, we might imply that their groupness is a natural and unavoidable phenomenon and ignore any attempt to explain it by simply saying, "Everyone knows kids hang around together." Secondly, we might be lulled into overlooking an important point; that is, for those with friends the group seemed to consume more time, energy, and enthusiasm than the academic side of school. When the participants in any organization admit, with apparent honesty, that their private, non-task–oriented activities take up two-thirds to four-fifths of the energy and enthusiasm they expend in that organization, one should no longer accept that behavior as "natural and unavoidable." Rather, he should begin to look seriously at the entire organization.

In reality the "formal" and the "informal" organizations are not at all dichotomous, but because they occur in the same place, during the same time, and their activities are performed by the same people, they may be regarded as parts of a larger system. It follows that we must attempt to look at this total phenomenon of groupness among these students and attempt to explain it and its effects, not only on individuals, but on the total school organization.

Since a system may be defined simply as a set of component parts in interaction with one another, our central concern is the interaction of not just one or more groups and the school, but with the phenomenon of "groupness" as it relates to other elements in that environment. In doing so, of course, we will have to deal with the basic characteristics of the institution that were explained in Chapter 1. Hopefully, that will allow us to say something about the total organization of Horatio Gates and eventually, about its effectiveness as an educational institution.

The Student Social Structure in Class

In the first place, it seemed that Sam, Andy, Nick and other isolates were often excluded not only from clique activities but also from class involvement. Those, like Jack, who were popular and who belonged to groups could and did exercise some control over formal classroom situations. It frequently seemed that those who were members of a prestigious group would, if the teacher were not taking strict charge of the class, just take over with their group. In doing so they would exclude isolates and less popular students from participation. The example in Chapter 2 in which there were twenty-three pupils and one Sony TV camera, and the eight who were doing anything with it were all in-group members serves to illustrate this point. Or the time in the gym when the physical education teacher was absent, and Bob proceeded to organize us and tell us who would play was another example.

This also occurred in a class where Mr. Lilley, the drama teacher, set up a role playing situation in order to develop a discussion on communication. The situation was a mock school board meeting. He assigned one group of students to be parents, one to be students, one to serve as board members and a few individuals to be school administrators. He contrived a situation in which the parents had voted down the budget and the board was trying to revise it. Mr. Lilley did some explaining to each group about their role and then let it go. The class was already broken by groups. The board was composed of Dick, Tony, Jean, and Doug. The girls in the power clique were taking the role of students and the remaining twelve or so students were to be the parents. Of course, given the issue, these parents should have had the central role, but it did not happen that way. Sally, the leader of the power clique, was making eyes at Ralph, her boyfriend, and decided that the issue should be to get rid of the principal, played, of course, by Ralph. So she and her friends made up signs: "Stop the repression," "Get rid of Ralph," "Fire the principal," and so forth. They marched around and staged a mock protest. Dick, who was acting as Board President, recognized their petition and a lively discussion of the principal's tactics ensued. "He doesn't let us have any dances." "The food is terrible." "Why can't we smoke?" All this was going on between Sally, Ralph, a few of Sally's friends, and Dick, Tony, and Jean. As the principle participants, of course, Sally and Ralph were having a fine time.

Mr. Lilley came back and was sitting next to me. "This is not what they're supposed to be doing. I told the board members to work with the parents, the students have taken over, and Dick isn't doing anything with the parents. They're supposed to be the center—it's a lesson in communication."

My time in the school was almost up and I was starting to be more free with my observations, so I asked him, "You know why, don't you?"

"No, I don't."

"Because Sally is Ralph's girl. She's a big shot in that group of students, class officer, Student Council officer, well known and well liked, and so on. She turns the attention of her group to Ralph in order to make him the center of attention. Then she and her friends make Dick, who is also a friend and class leader, recognize them. Tony is also a big shot, president of the senior class, and he and Dick are friends. So it is no longer the issue you assigned that they are concerned with, it's the class big shots taking over and keeping control of things as you step back. I know what you're trying to do and that's why it's so hard."

He really did not believe it. "What about them?," meaning the group of students taking the role of parents who were supposed to be important. I pointed out they they simply had no status. Ben and his friends may be very pleasant and bright, but they had no friends among Dick, Sally and Tony. They were left out as soon as the prestige-based social system took over.

It was not that the students were completely wasting their time. They were discussing some shortcomings of the principal that I knew they felt about Vincent. "He makes his vice-principal do everything." "He stays in his office and never does anything." "He's a dictator." "He won't let us have any dances." In fact, it did not just fade as did many classes; they were getting serious about the issue of the school principal.

Then Mr. Lilley went up, interrupted, and pointed out that the parents were being slighted and that the principal was not the issue. When they resumed, the parents, with the teacher watching more closely, did more interacting with the board. However, Mr. Lilley still could not ignore the power clique and went out of his way to bring them into the role playing which he was now directing. Under his direction the class improved, but just as the process was getting good, the bell rang.

This incident seemed a good indication of something mentioned in an earlier summary. If the teacher expects to involve students to any significant degree, they may have to make in-class accommodations with those more prestigious students. This is not as simple as it sounds. Mr. Lilley, although quite a good instructor, was not attuned to student friendship and influence patterns, nor does it seem reasonable to ask him to be. In fact, although he liked and was well liked by his students, he explained the class as being composed of two groups: J.C. (Joe College) and studs. As he saw it, the senior class was beyond being separated into cliques and was by now "pretty well together."

"The studs wore long hair, hoody kids in the out-group. The J.C.'s were the sharper kids who ran things, got on the council, drama club—everything. It was a pretty clean break. Then something happened. Last year's variety show was all studs, or a large part studs, and proved to the J.C.'s that the studs were worthwhile. It was a thing that brought the groups together and showed each other that the other was human." As I said, Mr. Lilley was a good teacher, but his explanation of the class social structure was grossly oversimplified and inaccurate. But then, teachers were paid to teach, not to run sociological studies.

A few days later Mr. Lilley saw me and said, "I thought

about what you said, but it can't be Ralph. He couldn't have done that. He's stupid."

I told him that it was not a case of Ralph having done something by himself, and whether Ralph was smart or stupid was really not the point. It was a case of the student, social structure moving in to take up any lack of structure in the class. A structure exists in any social situation, and in that school if the structure were not carefully defined by the teacher, the deficiency would be taken over by the already formed student groups, with the more prestigious students taking command. When this happened, the other group-related individuals still had their group going, but the isolates were more isolated than ever.

This same type of phenomenon occurred a number of times. The humanities class was a good place to see it because the teachers were making an effort to utilize the students' sense of personal motivation. The trouble was that those who showed up best in those undefined situations were those who had already been defined as "prestige students." Thus, in a society which to start offered rewards, only a few were getting a share, not only from that part of the system we might call the formal or official, but from the student social system as well. At this point it has to be re-emphasized that when referring to the concept of "rewards," I am not speaking of the rewards of high grades, academic excellence, or college acceptance. It has already been stressed that students would work for, or fail to work for, achieve, or fail to achieve, those rewards as individuals, not as members of groups. Rather, I am speaking of the social rewards of recognition, participation, and leadership.

That only a few students could take over and receive the rewards in class was brutally evident. Once when the teacher opened the session up to a discussion of religion, there were twenty-two students in the class and only five participated. One was Tony, the senior class president; another was Jean, Honor Society vice-president and number one student; then there was Dick, a leader in almost everything; Mary, Student Council member and cheerleader; and finally Carol, the president of the Student Council. Although this sounds ridiculous enough, it appears even more so when we remember that four of those five were in a tight clique. The rest did not participate. One might say that they did not have any strong opinions, but I cannot accept that. At least some of those nineteen had some opinions, and suggestions about religion, but they kept them to themselves for the entire period while Dick, Mary, Jean, Carol, and Tony carried on.

On occasion students even excluded the teacher from the classes. Howard, a very able and well liked student, was leading a group-planning session on the issue of studying pollution. Although Howard did not appear to associate with any group, he and his best friend, Ed, a county champion wrestler, were very well liked. On this particular day he organized what I considered to be the most skillful student-organized study group I ever witnessed. He had his favorites. Bill came in late and was immediately recognized, "Ah, now we can start." But other students were being heard and encouraged also. He even managed to control Doug, who was trying to disrupt the session by making gross remarks. At one point in the discussion, Mr. Tomaso walked in and stated in a loud voice, "Now, listen. This fooling around is going to stop. You people, well not you, but too many are getting me into trouble. I had to lie twice this morning and I got caught. There are a lot of people in this school who would like to see this program scrapped. They think we're just fooling around, and they have a lot of power. If this wandering around the halls and skipping classes doesn't stop, the program will be dropped. So I'm warning you."

Out he went and the teacher who had been sitting in the rear added, "He's right. You know I have a saying, 'Superintendents come and superintendents go.' Now we have a superintendent that supports this program, but in a couple of years he may be gone, and we'll get someone who doesn't give a hoot. Therefore, if we want to keep the program, you people are going to have to cooperate."

He stopped. A moment of embarrassed silence passed, then Howard took right over. "Now, where were we?"

He went back to evoking suggestions. The teacher's input had been an obviously unpleasant interruption in what was a very skillfully organized class.

It is true that the teacher was talking about something different from the topic, but teachers changed the topic all the time. What Mr. Tomaso had done happened every day in that school. If a teacher wanted to say something to a group or an individual, he just broke in and said it, and, of course, he expected attention. Yet when the students are running the class, it is not quite so easy. If the students start to take over, teachers may have to be a little more respectful of a situation which they will no longer completely control.

Another point is that if the situation were unstructured by the teachers and the more prestigious students did not use their talents to do some organizing, no other student could. Howard, Jack, and about six others, Max included, were members of a panel which was assigned to do a project dealing with narcotics. It was going to be presented as their eight-weeks humanities project. Lou was the only one of the group who had experimented widely with narcotics and therefore was probably going to do most of the talking. In the planning sessions he wanted to get serious and make a good preparation, but Jack and Howard continually fooled around, fell on the floor, talked about girls and sports and led the group completely away from the task. Their only accommodation with the assignment was to agree that they should burn incense, turn on music in the background, and ask me if I would be sure to bring up some questions if the going got slow. I agreed and to Lou's disgust, that was the extent of their planning for a project that was supposed to take eight weeks. He kept shaking his head and saying, "Incense and music . . . eight weeks of planning and all we have is incense and music." The final production of Howard's group was actually quite good and well received due to both Howard's skillful handling of question and Lou's knowledge, but it would have been equally good with practically no planning time allowed.

In sum, there are some important points about the interaction of the group centered student society on official classroom activities. The first is that the group structure is potentially present in any classroom and if the teacher gives up his control of the class, it will emerge. As when Mr. C released his control of the geometry class in order to work with individual students, Jim and Greg carried on their interactions while a number of other boys watched. Or if no one gave Bill and his friends specific directions, they just carried on their group activity. Of course, this fragments the class into various groups.

The second point is that students such as Dick, Sally, and Jack, can, if the teacher releases his control in favor of student participation, simply take over and run the class. This may not sound bad, but when they do it, they may exclude all the nonallied, nonprestigious students from participation. That is, the class may become a setting where the "in-group" can carry on its activities. This, of course, will distort the teacher's purpose. In this case the teacher has to maintain his leadership of the class and simultaneously utilize the group structure for participation. He practically has to get them active and involved without allowing them to become actively involved with their close friends. For, if they do, they may easily slip into the group structure which was not organized for the purpose of completing some learning task. For the teacher such situations become extremely complex.

The third point is that if the teacher releases his control in favor of student participation and the more prestigious students elect not to become involved in the task, then they may immobilize the entire class. When Jim would not participate, neither Bob nor Sam nor the girls in the back could get the class going the way they and the teacher wanted it to go. When Howard and Jack elected not to get involved in planning the production, Lou, although he was the most knowledgeable student, could organize nothing. The unofficial student structure proved to be a very unpredictable entity. Sometimes it succeeded, sometimes it failed, depending, it seems, on the central individual. Howard was good by himself, with Jack he did nothing. Bob was supposed to be a class leader, but if Jim were present, he could do nothing.

There is an additional issue; that is, the teacher's personal involvement and control of the class. It was continually stressed that when the teacher controlled the class the students did not rebel or make overt attempts to wrest control from him. Only when his planning seemed weak and unstructured did the student groups take over and begin to carry on their own activities. Yet it also seemed that after the teacher allowed the groups to go their way, there was little he could do to influence them. He could either control them completely or leave them alone, but there seemed to be no middle ground.

One might suggest that the teacher "work with" the students, but at Horatio Gates that might mean developing a working arrangement with a social structure, the purpose of which was antithetical to the working arrangement. It is easier and probably much safer if the teachers keep their distance and therefore, their control of the class. Whether this is educationally sound is another matter which I shall reserve for the final chapter. Here I am attempting only to explain that the way the students behaved in their groups did effect the classroom environment. That teachers behaved as they did, doing most of the talking, keeping their distance from the students and ignoring non-task–oriented activity, was probably an attempt on their part to avoid the inevitable conflicts that arise when the student social structure emerges in the class situation.

Classmanship among the Seniors

An additional issue related to the interaction of the official structure and the groups is that of classmanship, or some common feeling of unity and belonging among the students. Mr. Rossi was fairly well liked by the students. Jim wrote once, "Mr. Rossi is to the school what penicillin is to the hospital." While a few, such as Marilyn disliked him for allying himself with the power clique, and a few, such as Jean, disliked him because his idea of education was more restricted than hers, most respected and obeyed him.

He had what I considered to be an impossible task, that was to somehow develop and utilize this consciousness of classmanship among the seniors and indeed among every other class. He recognized that a few ran things to the exclusion of most and really tried to help a larger number of students get a chance to participate in class activities. "I even changed the class meeting times to the school day instead of after school to make sure everyone would get a chance. But it didn't work. A few students still ran everything." I asked him how it happened. "Ah . . . They seem to be groomed for the job. Like Dick . . . he's been in on everything since seventh grade." But, although he seemed to accept it, he still tried to change it. Even in the middle of the fall term he decided to open up the Student Council by having each class elect ten at-large student representatives, but that did not work either. Among the seniors elected were Bob, Sally, Rick, Mary, and some others closely related to the already active in-groups.

His efforts to democratize the class in hope of making it more responsive to school issues were really futile. The only thing that seemed to be a common force was the student lounge and because the teachers were complaining about the noise and reputed sloppiness in there, he wanted to make it more attractive. Privately, he admitted that it was not all that bad, but, "The teachers are always after me, so I have to do something." He first tried to work through the class's elected representatives, but this did not work. Once when six of the athletes were about to leave the humanities class, Tony approached and told us, "Listen you guys, Rossi's pissed off about the pop bottles in the lounge and if we don't clean it up, he'll close it." Not one of the six even looked at him or gave any indication that he had heard. Jack, Jim, Greg, Bob, Rick, and Pete filed right past and out the door.

As far as I could see that was a good indication of the class president's influence. Since that did not work there was more complaining by teachers and the students got a little sloppier, so Mr. Rossi called a class meeting.

He started right off. "This class has 374 kids in it and unfortunately, a number of them are going to mess up the lounge for the rest. The other day I walked in and I didn't even know what to say. Someone had been eating an ice cream sandwich [student laughter] and he had dropped part of the ice cream sandwich on the floor [more laughter]. QUIET! And then someone else had come along and stepped in it [lots of laughter]. QUIET! And do you think, DO YOU THINK, that although all afternoon that ice cream stayed there, that one person would go to the lav and get towels and clean it up, just to keep their shoes clean if nothing else? [Laughter] QUIET! [The interruptions of laughter were getting to him a little, others were telling the laughing ones to be quiet.]

"Now, that lounge can go back to being a classroom as quickly as fifteen minutes, and if the cleanliness of it doesn't improve, it will go back. Now, I know that a lot of people care about it and clean it up. Those kids who stayed the other day, those same people who put up the Christmas decorations, most of which are home in somebody's drawers right now, I feel sorry for those kids because they do the work and someone else ruins it for everybody." He went on for a few minutes more about the lounge and how it has to be kept clean and concluded, "And starting after vacation, I think that something will have to be done about the noise. Now it isn't bad because next door there are no classes, or, maybe one class— yeah, the special ed class complained about the noise once [laughter at the mention of special ed]. But after Christmas the guidance offices are going to be in the big study hall next door, and then you're going to have to keep the noise down." Then he reiterated his point about keeping the lounge clean because he did not want to close it, but would if it did not improve.

He then called on three students to support his position. "You in the red sweater, I don't know your name. What's wrong with the lounge?"

She mumbled something and seemed unwilling to say anything except, "I don't go in there much."

"Why not?"

"I don't know."

He tried again. "You, over there, I don't know your name. What's wrong with the lounge?" He obviously wanted someone to tell him it was too dirty and that it must be cleaned.

"I . . . uhuhuh . . . know," said the boy.

Rossi retreated from that tactic. The students were making noise intermittently, too much noise. He had to keep saying, "QUIET! QUIET!"—something I had not seen him say often, usually his presence was enough to quiet them, but he was pushing his luck. It was already 10:45, he had been at it for twenty minutes.

"You, Doris, I know your name. What's wrong with the lounge?"

"NO GIRLS!" yelled Jim and got laughs from those around him. Rossi acted as if he had not heard.

"All right," said Rossi, changing his tactic since he was clearly getting nowhere. "There are plans for the lounge other than the key. I don't want to lock it; make some suggestions for improvements. If you could do what you wanted, what would you do with it?"

"Television," said one. "Radio." "GIRLS!" [Laughter, Jim was still at it.] "Beer," yelled another boy. Rossi continued to ignore the increasing number of wisecracks.

"QUIET!" said Rossi. "Shhhhhh," said a whole lot of students, but the undercurrent was getting stronger. "There's a pool table. It's already bought. It's in my cellar." (He laughed with them at that.)

"Now, if some clown takes his anger out on the pool table, recovering it will cost us 100 dollars, unless, of course, you want to play on adhesive tape and masking tape [laughter] and newspaper [more laughter]."

The mood of the class was getting lighter and more

out of hand. Then he told them if he got the table they would have to take care of it.

A boy said that it would take too much room. "I'll worry about that," said Rossi.

Others said they wanted a small one like they have in bars (laughter). Rossi said he did not "think it should cost three dollars each time a kid goes into the lounge" (more laughter, partly with him but not keeping quiet when he wanted it). Each time he or anybody said anything he had to ask for quiet. He was getting aggravated and nowhere. He dropped it at that, the lounge would stay open and they would get a pool table sometime. If they wanted a radio they could buy one. He did say they could have more furniture, but no television. Then he asked for quiet and, looking very serious, told them, "Now you seniors, anyone of you who thinks that he can come late or skip class or do what he wants will be out of school January first. No more!"

Then he said very seriously, "One more thing and then I'll turn the meeting over to Tony. [It was almost 11:00.] Some of you think that you don't need Gates anymore . . . or that Gates needs you. Now that you've been accepted in college . . . [crack]. Will the person who is cracking his knuckles please stop. [Crack] I said stop!" (CRACK) And then Rossi walked out, right out the door. There was absolute silence for the first time. Everyone's eyes followed him out.

"He's pissed off," said Greg.

"Sure," said Jack. "Those assholes don't know how to act."

The point was plain. When Rossi was trying to develop some class spirit around the lounge, he got nowhere. The meeting went on with Tony discussing the senior weekend, and when it ended, Mr. Rossi was outside the door talking to the girls from the power clique who were assuring him that they would look out for the maintenance of the lounge if only he would leave it open. So, when he failed to mobilize the class, he did the only thing he could do, he dealt with a group, and specifically with that group, which because of its place in the prestige structure was dependent on the school. With those girls, from both the music-drama group and power clique, he succeeded. They personally were very upset and began to take responsibility for the lounge. Lorraine was cleaning the place that afternoon and she told me, "They're going to close the lounge."

"For how long?"

"For the rest of the year."

"Who said?"

"Rossi. He came in here and there's ice cream on the floor and the furniture is all broken up and it's a mess and he said he was going to close it up on Monday."

Then Rossi came in, looked around disgustedly, shook his head, "Look at that."

"I know," said Lorraine. "But I didn't do it."

"Well, what you people have to do is work on keeping the place clean. You have to do the enforcing. Find the guy that did it and pop him. He won't do it again."

After he left Marilyn said, "He's not as mad as I thought."

A couple of the other girls found the school superintendent in the halls the next day and asked him to come see the lounge. He got the full story of how they would maintain the lounge if he would make sure it stayed open.

Rossi's attempt to evoke support from some feeling of "seniorship" or classmanship just did not work. Because of this failure, the vice-principal was forced to deal with the prestigious students in order to get results on any issue. This is what Marilyn referred to when she said, "He supports them and they support him and that's the way it is."

But what else could Mr. Rossi do? He tried to create cohesion but it did not work because the class members had relatively so little in common. What happened after he left the meeting that day was further proof of this. Tony got up and tried to deal with class business. First he turned it over to Dick who talked about the variety show. "Dick has a script which he and Jean wrote and said they would make it available to those who wished to try out." I was in back and at that there was some grumbling. "Who do they think they are having tryouts? Anyone who wants to be in it should have a chance."

"That's right. Tell him, Janet." But Janet did not, nor did anyone else dispute Dick's right to select the cast for the variety show.

Then he sat down and Tony got up again to consult with the class over the senior weekend. First he called on Marilyn to talk about naming the weekend. She offered the class three choices: "Cherish," "Tomorrow's Yesterday," or "Promises." By that time they had recovered from the shock of Rossi's leaving. There was a lot of talking in the auditorium and the students were getting their spirits up. "ATTABABY, MAR!" yelled Jim. "Com'on you guys, SHUT UP!" said Tony, but nobody paid attention. Marilyn was trying to get a vote. "WHAT SHALL WE CALL IT?" she yelled. "THE GOOD, THE BAD AND THE STUPID!" yelled Al, who was in school for the first time that month.

"YEAHHHHH, AL!" (Lots of cheering at that.) Al was a huge person about nineteen years old and developing into something of a local character, the kind that others tell stories about. Then amid a lot of laughing and talking the meeting just fell apart. No one was voting, so Marilyn got mad and sat down.

Then Bob got up and toyed with the microphone, and I think he was supposed to arrive at some consensus on the location of the dance. "All right, you guys, SHUT UP!" Of course, no one did except for some of those in front, the power clique girls, who were trying to pay attention and were trying to shush up the rest. "WHERE DO YOU WANT THE PROM?" yelled Bob.

"THELMA'S," yelled Jim, referring to a local sporting house.

"BURGER KING."

"MACDONALD'S!"

"MIKE'S BAR AND GRILL!"

At this everyone laughed and carried on and I asked Greg what Bob was doing. He did not know and neither did anyone else. Bob gave up and sat down and amid noise and talking the class waited for the bell to ring. Even

Marty got in the act. He got up, took the mike, and informed us that "The preceding has been brought to you courtesy of Sears Gas, located at the corner of Erie and Eighth, where you always get service with a smile." Marty smiled a big smile and sat down. Tony and Bob, the class leaders, were conferring about something in the corner.

One girl, Joan, who was a power clique leader, cheerleader, most popular girl, and so on, got up and screamed, "SIT DOWN! DON'T YOU KIDS KNOW HOW TO ACT? DO YOU WANT THE LOUNGE CLOSED?" She was really screaming and at that everyone cheered which, of course, made her madder. She sat down also and the bell rang.

So much for participatory democracy in the senior class at Horatio Gates. To me the lesson seemed clear. There was little to be done. Decide on a name, on a place, or hear from someone who was doing most of what there was to do himself. But nowhere was anyone asking the majority of class members for their participation and involvement in important class activities. There simply were no important class activities, and the class meeting, which was called with the implied assumption that there were, was a sham. The students consciously or unconsciously knew it. So, as usual, the majority refused to become involved, and what was done continued to be done by a few.

When Mr. Rossi said he "felt sorry" for those few who worked hard on the Christmas decorations, I am sure no one else did. They included Lorraine, a very pretty and popular cheerleader, power clique member; Mary, also pretty, popular, and she was Max's girl; Marilyn, the paper editor; and Pam, once referred to by Roger as one of "those really classy girls, Pam and them." The boys who helped them were Jack, Jim, and Bob, and all had been released from class to do it. Trying to evoke sympathy for those students by telling how hard they worked and how dedicated they were just made no sense. Certainly not to Sam, Andy, or Nick or indeed any of the 359 of the 374 members of the class whom Dick formerly termed "introverts."

Rossi, of course, knew that if the class had some unify-

ing spirit his job would be easier. He wanted certain individuals to have certain commonly understood roles to perform. For instance, he wanted the bigger, more prestigious
boys to police the lounge and act as school representatives when needed. He talked wistfully of the previous
year when the biggest boy in the class had acted as the
lounge's policeman and had thus made Rossi's tasks
easier. He wanted Jack to do it this year but he would not.
Nor would any others. Once when Jack, Jim, Bob, and Rick
were sitting in the lounge, a smallish student started running for the door followed by a larger boy. At the door the
big one caught the little one and started punching him.
"HEY, A FIGHT," said Jim. "KICK HIM IN THE NUTS,"
yelled Bob. "YEHHHH." They all got into position to
watch the big student try to demolish the little one. After
thirty seconds of very inept swinging, and no injuries, a
teacher came in and told both boys to go to the office.

"Let's go and see what happens," said Rick and they
followed down the hall. That seemed to demonstrate that
there was simply little use in trying to get those boys who
were the biggest and most respected to act as policemen
for the lounge or the class or anything else. They did not
see themselves in the class-defined role of policemen.

But Mr. Rossi seemed to have trouble understanding
the class. He admitted that it was broken into a series of
groups, but thought that the groups were more school-
centered than they were. For instance, in October we
were talking about the students and he said that although
the football players were a tight clique at that time, in
December basketball season would start and, "You'll see
all new groups form."

I watched, but it never happened. Groups did not realign around basketball players as he predicted they
would. The situation just was not that class oriented.

Actually, his inability to mobilize class consciousness,
while it disgusted and discouraged him, should not have
surprised him. He had admitted previously that, "High
school's really only two years long. After that it's a car, a
job, a girl, that takes up their life." And he also privately
admitted that he could understand why a large number of

students never even bothered to come to the senior prom. Still he harped at them for the condition of the lounge, about their general lack of spirit, and continued to threaten them with closing the lounge. But he never did close the lounge. In fact, the Monday after that meeting he added a ping-pong table. Personally, I think he would have been very loathe to close the lounge. The lesson of the cafeteria boycott was not lost on Mr. Rossi or Mr. Vincent.

While officially this business of class spirit and extracurricular activities were Mr. Rossi's responsibility, it seemed that much of it was beyond his control. It is not that the few planned to get all there was of the rewards, it was just that very few rewards were available. The example of the Honor Society member who thought only in terms of bake sales is typical. The whole extracurricular sector was permeated with a "bake sale mentality" and, as such, demanded little general activity and involvement.

It was always the same students who were involved. I asked Jean how many would be in the variety show and she replied, "As many as want to. We're always looking for new ideas." Yet that certainly was not the impression conveyed in the meeting when Dick was talking about "tryouts" for those who wished to participate.

This was the typical lack of communication that existed between the "ins" and the "outs." For instance, Debbie as an "out" said that she would never make the Honor Society because in addition to high marks, which she had, one had to receive the approval of those already in and they would not approve of her. On the other hand, Jean, when asked how one got in the Honor Society, said, "Oh, just hand back the essay."

"What's that?"

"We pass out a piece of paper to those that qualify and ask them to write an essay telling what they think should be the function of the Honor Society. If they hand in an essay on the subject, they're in." With this kind of misunderstanding between "ins" and "outs" there was little hope of developing the class into a cohesive unit.

The Student Body as a Unit

If the class was hard to develop into a unit, the school was even harder. One example of this is the Student Council. Council meetings were held once a month and were attended by about sixty to ninety student representatives from both the high school and the ninth grade school in Cowpens. Although the constitution written the previous year stated that the council was the "legislative and governing body of the school," there was little in the council that resembled either law or government.

The first meeting of the year was opened by Mr. Rossi who told the representatives it was their council and they could do what they wanted.

"How about a dance?" said a girl.

"We'll see," said Mr. Rossi.

"Can we have a pep rally?" asked Jack.

"Yeah," added Bob. "We finally have a team. Let's have a pep rally."

Rossi smiled, "We'll see about that, too. Maybe before the Georgetown game."

"You said we could have whatever we wanted."

Rossi called to Mr. Young, the council advisor, "Hey, Young, I gotta go, take care of these insurrectionists." He laughed and walked out.

Mr. Young ran the rest of the meeting during which the entire time was spent discussing the qualifications for officership. The second meeting in October was spent electing Carol, Jack, Sally, Bob, and Dick to office. Of course, they promised that they would get down to business. I concluded that their qualifications for election were their general popularity and "well known-ness," since not one indicated prior to election that he or she had any ideas or would do this or that. I already referred to the way Jack selected his position.

Carol was serious about her presidency. When she was first elected she told me, "I want to find some issue that will interest the kids in the council. Something that they feel needs to be worked on. Then make that our council issue and get the kids interested. Otherwise the council will just fade. In the past they've spent their time raising money, and that just isn't enough."

I asked what they did with the money. "Last year they paid for the whole junior weekend. That cost over $500 dollars and then they raised even more. So now we have no money problems at all. That's why we can do something more important."

Carol made her plea for support and involvement in the gym at the winter sports rally. She was introduced by Rossi as "The president of the entire student body," and then, with Rossi on one side of her and Vincent on the other, she made a very brief speech in which she asked the students to support the council and promised that the council would strive "to make the voices of the students heard." She also said some specific things about a computer dance (many oohs and ahhs at that) and then made her big pitch. "Now, as everyone knows, smoking is a problem in this school. Well, what we're going to do is try to get an area where the kids can smoke if they want to. This, we feel, will stop the smoking in the lavatories, make the lavs cleaner, make them better for kids who don't smoke, and stop the teachers from having to check for smokers all the time. This is something the Council can do which will benefit the whole school."

During the third meeting held in early December they tried again to get something going. Carol started the meeting and asked the treasurer for his report. He told us that the Council had a total of forty-one dollars and fifty cents in the treasury, not enough to do much of anything. No mention was made of the money which the previous class had earned. Therefore, this class was apparently going to have to devote its time and interests to making more money. Then Carol said that the reason she called the meeting was to find ways to raise some money for the computer dance that the Council was holding. (The decision to hold the computer dance had been made somewhere else.) She turned to Tony and Jean who were in charge of selling something. Apparently, despite what

Carol said about money, it was a foregone conclusion that they would attempt to raise some. Apparently, also, there are a number of businesses that get students to sell trinkets and sundries in schools and let the students have some of the profit. For example, the Council might buy nightshirts for three dollars each, sell them for three and a quarter each, and the Council keeps the twenty-five cents profit.

Then she and Jack passed around some leaflets advertising sweatshirts, pennants, T-shirts, and so forth. The leaders talked together quietly while passing these things around. The rest of the Council was sitting in the third and fourth row of the auditorium, not saying much to the leader, not saying much to each other. They seemed to be paying attention, proud to be a part of the Council, trying hard to do what Carol told them.

Tony suggested that they sell pennants, something they could buy for forty-two cents and sell for some unspecified price. That was brought to a vote after a little discussion between Carol, Jean, Tony and Dick. Jack asked for a vote, it passed so they set the price at seventy-five cents. Then a boy raised his hand to suggest that they have "slave days" in which a student council member is auctioned off to carry books and wait on his owner for a day. Carol sort of smiled, looked at Jack and that died. The boy stayed quiet for the rest of the meeting.

Tony passed out poster paper to the freshmen and were asked to draw a poster advertising the computer dance, while others were asked to sell tickets. Then Carol announced that Rossi had told her they could have the "Harriers" for a band and that he could get them for 200 dollars. She asked if everyone agreed and, of course, everyone did.

Then they talked about the matter of trimming the halls for Christmas. It was decided that Jack, as vice president, would be in charge, and at that the principal from the ninth grade class in Cowpens came in, announced that the buses were leaving, and his freshmen had to be on them. So, one-fourth of the governing body of the school got up and left, and the meeting was officially adjourned. That was a Student Council meeting. The discussion was limited to selling things and trimming the halls. It should be mentioned that Jack, when trimming the halls, took no other council members. Instead he chose Jim and Greg.

In all fairness it must be admitted that Carol was serious, so were Dick, Jean, Tony, and Jack, and they formed a political committee to deal with what they considered to be some serious issues of student power. They even forced Rossi to stop harassing a student who had been threatened with suspension for wearing a moustache. In itself that must have been quite a shock for Mr. Rossi. Jean told me, "He was really shook up. Seventeen times he told us it was none of our business. Seventeen times! 'Well, like I don't think that's any of your business.' And, 'Ah, I don't really think you should concern yourselves with it.' And, 'Well, what business is it of yours?' That's just the way he was. He was really shook up."

I asked Dick about other possible council issues. He said they were going to use smoking for the first one. "I'm chairman of the committee. Well, Jack, as vice-president, is supposed to be chairman of all committees, but I'm really chairman of it. We're going to send a letter to Rossi asking for either permission to smoke in an area outside or inside. Me, I'm president of the Drama Club; Carol's president of the Council; Jack, he's vice president of the council; Jean's vice president of the Honor Society; Tony's president of the senior class—all of us are going to sign the letter."

"Have you talked to Rossi?"

"No, we're going to do it formally with a letter."

It was a good letter. Mr. Rossi said he would take it to the board and work for the proposal's acceptance. While their political awareness and sense of power increased, it was still limited to a few students and these few could not understand why. "We'd like to get kids on the issue of the library. It's terrible. You can't talk or anything. And the study halls, one's rigid and the other's all fooling around. But we can't get anyone to do anything about it. And if we do, it's always the same ones."

What they failed to see, however, was that they were

doing what was to be done, not as school leaders, but as a clique. They were reacting only to each other, not to other students. According to them, of course, that other kids did not get interested was their own fault. In fact, Dick shared Mr. Lilley's simplistic view of the class. "What's it mean to be 'in,' Dick?" I asked.

"Well, it means the people who do things, who take an interest in activities, who go out and work for the school."

"Is it hard to get in?"

"No."

"What does it take?"

"If anyone makes an effort he can get in. You don't have to be in with a certain group. They respect talent. Take Larry, he came in last year and now he's one of the best liked kids in the clique."

"Do grades matter?"

"No. Nobody around here cares what your grades are. Like people think I get real high grades, they expect to see me on the honor roll. And I've got a terrible average."

"Does your clique exclude kids?"

"No. When we have an activity we try to get kids interested. We ask them and put it on the PA system."

Then I told him that when I go to meetings I hear only three or four kids talk. "Yeah, but don't you see me beg them to do things? Like, write for the talent show. I'm telling you, we open it up but only a few kids come in and do anything."

He thought for a minute and said, "In the first years of high school it seemed like the big shots were the dumber guys who are football players or drinkers or screwoffs, but in the last year, now, it seems that more intelligent ones come to the front. In freshman or sophomore year, if you made an intelligent statement in class, you were afraid they [the kids] would make fun of you but not now. Now they seem to respect brains."

I asked him if Jim was a leader in the earlier years.

"Yeah, and guys like him."

"What does it take to be in the lead clique?"

Dick thought. "I'd say personality, athletic ability,

brains, and looks, in that order. Personality is the most important. If you've got that and looks you don't need anything else."

I asked if the leading kids got more favors from the administration.

"They have to be good to us. We're their link to the rest of the student body."

"Are you really a link?"

"Well, we like to think we are. If some kid knows I'm on the council and he makes a suggestion, I'll definitely take it to the Council. He knows that."

I tried to tell Dick some of the impressions I had gathered at Student Council: that only a few leaders said anything, that anyone not in the "clique" was ignored, that there wasn't much happening. He was unconvinced. In fact, he repeated an earlier comment about students not choosing to be involved because they were introverted.

To me the issue was clear. On the matter of student power, just as on the matter of other activities, a few initiated the activity and did what there was to be done. Those few were members of the same clique that did everything else. The issue of class identity, just as the issue of school identity, was limited to a few; the rest of the class, even the rest of the student body, was excluded from participation.

While both Vincent and Rossi deplored this situation and attributed it to either the fact that the school was composed of two separate towns or to the obstinancy of the students, I attribute it to the fact that there was simply very little in which the majority could be involved. Therefore, that they separated into discrete groups, which, as opposed to the official structure, offered them real, personal involvement, was not surprising.

I have already considered at length the interaction of the group structure and the classroom. The class meeting and the student council meeting reinforced what was previously discussed. There was so little to do, so little activity actually going on that, as far as I could see, the whole student involvement issue was a sham. There was simply nothing going on that could possibly demand the active involvement of 354 students. There was barely enough to keep the fifteen busy. And so the rest just turned aside and continued to do what they always did. They involved themselves with their friends.

Summary and Discussion of Chapter 7

It is paradoxical that the school organization which allows and encourages students to spend their time maintaining a group-centered social structure should find itself frustrated by that same social structure. The structure affects the way the teachers behave, restricts the administrator's ability to deal with students as he wishes, structures the responses students give to both teachers and administrators, and even affects student attendance. For example, the existence of that structure means that teachers' ability to influence and direct students is more limited than it appears. That is, if one walked in the class and saw the teacher talking and gesticulating he might assume that the teacher is clearly in charge. But the social dynamics of that room are such that the teacher is in charge only in a very narrow sense. Should he fail to conduct himself with great care, he will no longer be in charge, and other forces will take over. Personally, I think that is why teachers talk all the time. If one keeps talking and doing everything there is to do, he won't have to worry about getting co-opted or even overruled and dominated by the student social structure. After all, there are few high school juniors and seniors who consistently make trouble, and those who do so get themselves either serially suspended or expelled. The great majority, even in tougher schools, make an effort to appear interested in what the teacher is saying, and will generally subdue their group interests and friendships if he wishes. Therefore, the teacher can be assured of a reasonably respectful audience.

If the teacher wants student participation and opens the class to group work or discussion, he will be opening his classroom to elements which he may not control, and therefore his centrality and authority will be threatened. If he happens to teach in a school where the principal believes in quiet, teacher-centered classrooms, he might just keep talking all the time to protect his financial and emotional security. Therefore, regardless of what we say about teachers in authority, there is that element of student dynamics in the classroom over which the teacher has no power.

This is reminiscent of a question one always hears in public education. "Why do all teachers teach the way they were taught instead of the way they were taught to teach?" While teacher colleges are constantly trying to come up with training programs which will turn out teachers with diverse techniques, few of those programs give any thought to the social dynamics of the student population and the way those dynamics restrict the teacher's behavior. In addition, I must mention that an isolated student might prefer a teacher-centered room because it gives them protection from their isolation. If the teacher maintains control he is addressing twenty-five individuals, not three groups, two dyads, and two isolates. At least it places the isolates and less popular students on an equal basis with the members of groups.

Administrators, too, are restricted. Rossi wanted the seniors' enthusiastic support for his efforts at maintaining a clean lounge. He wanted to develop a strong spirit of common purpose among the students, but he could never achieve it. The students were not emotionally involved with the school; there was so little with which one could become emotionally involved. Even at the pep rallies, it was the pretty and popular cheerleaders who stood out front, did their cheers, and then quickly ran back to huddle together for mutual reinforcement and support. The rest of the students stood and cheered as groups and when the cheering ended and they all went into the dance, it was the groups that were evident, not the individuals. Isolates didn't show up at the dances.

Administrators, whose concern is the entire organization, attempt to utilize value consensus or some degree of voluntary compliance among an organization's members. If the participants have a strong core of common beliefs binding them together, then they can get on to the task of doing what it is that the organization is designed to do. If there is no value consensus, a large part of the administrator's time and energy must be devoted to either (a) trying to build it, or (b) in its absence, trying to maintain the unity through the enforcement of rules and regulations. It seems that Rossi didn't have much hope of (a), so he concentrated his efforts on (b). Rossi wanted the students to value the cleanliness of the lounge and the Christmas decorations, but the only ones who cared were those few in the "in" group. The rest just sat and watched and gave every evidence of not caring. And indeed, why should they care? The decorations were put up by the same few who did everything else. Therefore, Rossi couldn't use the supposed "leaders" to generate or enforce compliance from the rest. So he did what he could—he accommodated the "leaders," or those who, because they got the rewards, gave the highest compliance, and threatened the rest with rules and regulations. It makes sense to behave as he did.

The example of the student council raises another issue. There is not an unlimited amount of power and responsibility in an organization and if the student council were to actually take some, then the administrators and teachers might be even more limited in their choice of options. For all Rossi's desire to have the students "involved" in school, he never intended them to become involved in questions of discipline. If one asks for involvement, he can't continually confine that involvement. He can't suddenly turn it off whenever he wishes. Actually, Rossi's and the teachers' jobs may have been easier because the groups drew off the students' interest and involvement and therefore allowed staff members to behave as they thought they should.

There is probably more to be said about the effects of the groups, but without a great deal of careful and extensive study, it is difficult to point out clearly defined, predictable relationships between those groups and other facets of the school. The point here is that the phenomenon of groupness was such an integral part of the whole organization that it effected and was effected by everything else.

CHAPTER 8

Conclusions

This book has attempted to describe the behavior carried on by a small number of students in a public high school. According to that description, which was taken from participation, observations, and interviews, there were some very definite patterns of activity that consistently emerged. The students at Horatio Gates formed themselves into strong, small-group associations with their peers. These associations were usually formed around neighborhood acquaintances, many having been in existence since early grade school, and were carried on not only in school, but out of school as well. Of course, by itself, this is not surprising. That high school students form strong friendships with their classmates is a commonly accepted phenomenon.

However, because a number of related facts emerged, the issue is not really that simple and should be further considered. The first of these is that the students who were studied, according to the observations and even by their own admission, spent most of their school time "hanging around together" in their small groups. Secondly, the patterns of activity that those groups carried on had little or nothing to do with the academic or productive sector of school and were only minimally related to the school's maintenance sector. That is, they did not speak of grades or learning, but they did recognize the necessity of adapting to the rules and regulations. And, finally, it was shown that those small group associations can and do strongly effect other aspects of the school organization, such as the teachers' classroom behavior, the extracurricular activities, the vice-principal's actions, and the behavior of other students. Therefore, rather than attributing the small group phenomenon to some adolescent "urge to merge," some attempt should be made to explain and perhaps better understand the issue as it effects the school, and, indeed, the whole educational process. At this point I will attempt to summarize my conclusions about the interaction of student groups and the organization.

To begin, there is a basic assumption about the nature of social reality; that is, the individuals involved in any situation will predicate their behavior on that situation. As Herbert Blumer points out:

> Any particular action is formed in the light of the situation in which it takes place. . . . action is formed or constructed by interpreting the situation. The acting unit necessarily has to identify the things which it has to take into account. . . . tasks, opportunities, obstacles, means, demands, discomforts, dangers, and the like; it has to assess them in some fashion and it has to make decisions on the basis of the assessment. Such interpretative behavior may take place in the individual guiding his own action, in a collectivity of individuals acting in concert, or in "agents" acting on behalf of a group or organization. Group life consists of acting units developing acts to meet the situations in which they are placed.[1]

Accepting this symbolic interactionist explanation of social reality means that instead of attributing the students' behavior to their social class, individual psychology, age, homelife, or parental relations, we should rather examine the environment in which that behavior took place. As was pointed out in Chapter 1, people will develop a reasonable way of constructing their behavior based on their perceptions of their situation. They will develop a consistent way of thinking and acting in that situation, and this combination of beliefs and actions is termed the perspective. Since the basic purpose of this work is to

[1] Herbert Blumer, "Society as Symbolic Interaction," in Arnold M. Rose, ed., *Human Behavior and Social Processes* (Boston: Houghton Mifflin, 1962), p. 187.

explain that student perspective, we might best start the explanation by examining the school environment to see if the actions and patterns of belief that those adolescents constructed were reasonable given their situation. Having started with the students behavior, we now work backward and try to determine the environmental patterns that lead to the behavior. This will, of course, leave the entire project open to the objection that we are creating ex post facto explanations which, according to some, constitute a lower order of explanatory research. However, in basic exploratory projects such as this, these are not necessarily bad. Rather, they should be carefully viewed and judged according to their individual worth.

Socio-cultural Characteristics of the School's Organization

The basic purpose of the institution is to articulate a specific body of knowledge, skills, and behavioral patterns in the form of a curriculum and then to pass this curriculum on to students. As such, the school has incorporated into it a number of social-cultural characteristics intended to support the process. Combined, these characteristics actually structure the school environment and have to be explained in detail if any understanding of the institution is to be reached.

The first of these characteristics is *subject matter speciality*, or perhaps one might call it *compartmentalization of knowledge*. The school is organized, and the teachers are hired to pass on particular specialties to the students. Second and most essential to the passing-on process is the characteristic of a *vertical organization* with the students in the position of subordinates and the teachers and administrators defined as superordinates. This characteristic facilitates the passing-on process by keeping the teachers and students in positions where one may "pass on," the other may effectively "receive" that which is passed on. These two characteristics, a vertical organization and subject matter specialization, are the basis for the school's productive subsystem. Supporting both of these is what

Stinchcombe refers to as the *"doctrine of adolescent inferiority,"* which is actually a third characteristic.[2] Although we live in a time of revolutionary rhetoric, it is still generally accepted that high school students should obey their elders in authority, both because they are elders and because they are in authority. Of course, the added implication is that as the adolescents increase in age and take on those things which the school is designed to teach, so they will become progressively less inferior.

These three characteristics support and are supported by yet a fourth, *downward communication*. That is, in high school communication, which is primarily verbal, usually flows one way, from teachers to students, superordinates to subordinates.

These four characteristics are not discrete entities. Rather, they depend on, reinforce, and take their identity from one another. Originally the teachers' authority was probably justified by both his speciality and the doctrine of adolescent inferiority. The communication flow naturally emanated from the view of the teacher as "speciality instructor." However, once events are in motion, they tend to reinforce the structure which originated them; they actually work to support their own survival. At that point they may no longer be thought of as a series of causes and effects, but become a cycle of mutually reinforcing events. In fact, if one questions the validity of any of these four characteristics, of necessity he would threaten the existence of the other three.

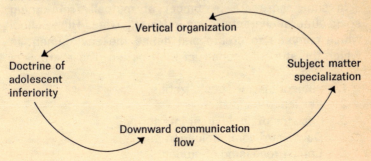

[2] See Arthur Stinchcombe, *Rebellion in a High School* (Chicago: Quadrangle Press, 1964).

Flowing from these is a fifth characteristic, *batch processing of students*, with a single teacher directing the activities of a large number of students at a sitting. Of course, this is a logical way to run a school if one has already decided that he needs subject matter specialization, teachers in authority, and that it is fitting for the communication to flow downward. Combined, these previously mentioned characteristics need yet another reinforcer in order to operate effectively. They need *routinization of activity* so that both teachers and students will know where to go and when to go there. This characteristic supports the passing-on and teacher specialization. Furthermore, to support that routinization, the school needs an extensive body of *rules and regulations* to insure that the students adhere to the routine. Carrying with it a number of sanctions, these rules and regulations provide the incentive needed to make the students stay in a subordinate position. After all, schools were never intended to offer present rewards. Rather, they are *future reward oriented*, which in itself is also a defining characteristic.

There is one additional characteristic. A brief glance at the school's floor plan in Chapter 2 will show the school's physical plant and even the room and furniture arrangement all work to support the idea of a teacher-expert passing on his speciality to batches of students. The *physical arrangements of the organization* should therefore be added to the list of characteristics.

In sum, there are a number of mutually reinforcing socio-cultural characteristics in Horatio Gates High School which combine to create and define the environment in which the students construct their action. These are:

1. Subject matter specialization
2. Vertical organization
3. Doctrine of adolescent inferiority
4. Downward communication flow
5. Batch processing of students
6. Routinization of activity
7. Dependence on rules and regulations

8. Future-reward orientation
9. Supporting physical structure

These characteristics are real, not only in Horatio Gates, but probably in most American high schools. Again, this is not a series of discrete entities nor could we even take a specific piece of student behavior and attribute it to one of these and exclude all the others. Rather this is a set of concepts which in total represents a cycle of continuous events. They are certainly not thought of as "bad." They are intended to further the aims of education by creating an environment wherein the students can listen, study, and learn in an orderly manner, and where the teachers will be free to pass on that which they are trained and hired to pass on. Nor is it my intent here to prove that the characteristics are "bad." Despite the increase in the amount of criticism leveled at the public schools, the great majority of American adolescents, at Horatio Gates and elsewhere, go to school, complete their requirements, and move into adulthood with a high school diploma. If some, or even many, do not have the substance of an education no one will ever know; they at least have the assumption of one.

Intended Effects of the Socio-cultural Characteristics

There are some additional points to be made about these characteristics. They are not inert, but continue to create a number of effects, some intended, some unintended, which must be explained. I would suggest that the first consciously intended effect of the sum total of these characteristics is that in Horatio Gates students are *denied freedom of activity*. They may not leave the building between 8:10 and 2:20 except for a school-approved activity, they must adhere to the routine and obey its supporting rules and regulations, and in their classes they have to obey the teacher's direction of the learning activity. They may do what they wish so long as it is what their superiors want or as long as it does not interfere with the teacher's intentions. A second effect is that the students are *massed*, and a third and closely related, reinforcing effect is that they are *undifferentiated.* The routine and the batch processing keep them constantly in the company of one another, and while there, the vertical organization, rules and regulations, and the doctrine of adolescent inferiority serve to have them all treated alike regardless of class, sequence, or academic rank.

This may appear to contradict what has already been said about the way the students construct their group activities, because in many cases it seemed that they were doing just what they wished and no more. The football players and the members of the music-drama clique did exercise control over their activities, and in doing so gained recognition from both other students and staff members. However, I am speaking of "intended effects." Those that were "unintended" will be discussed in the next section. My point is that there was no organizational provision for the attainment of individual recognition or student differentiation. Even Jean, the highest achieving member of the class, was treated exactly as were the other students. The organization made no provision for her to be free from the teacher's authority, the routine, the rules and regulations, or indeed anything else. She sat in class, faced the teacher, raised her hand, obeyed the time schedule. The fact that she had been at the top of her class for three years, the fact that she was a brilliant girl, bound for a prestige college, created no officially approved distinction between her and the other students. If a teacher wished to recognize her individual talent, that was his personal business. He could just as easily ignore her. The grades she received offered no real rewards in the school. Rather, they were symbolic of some undefined, future rewards. Indeed, nothing in the official organization provided behavioral recognition for academic achievement. Or we might consider Dick. His drama club responsibilities came about as a result of the trust placed in him by the music teacher, not because the organization made provisions for student-directed plays. When Jack, Jim, and Greg got away with some of their pranks, it was not because football and basketball players are officially allowed more latitude of action, but because they had better personal relations with the administrators. There were other excellent football players who got away with nothing. I am not saying that it is impossible for a student to gain some individual recognition, obviously some did, but I am saying that it happens in spite of a system which makes no provision for it, and in spite of some very definite, organizational characteristics which serve to deny it.

There seem to be three clear and fully intended effects of the school's socio-cultural characteristics. Students are (1) denied freedom of activity, (2) massed, and (3) undifferentiated. Again, it must be noted that these effects are generally approved and are thought to contribute to a smooth running organization, to teacher freedom to initiate and direct activity, and to student learning and orderliness.

Some Unintended Effects of the School's Socio-cultural Characteristics

In any chain of causal events, one must expect not only the directly intended, but also the unintended effects. As the descriptions of student activity show, there are a large number of behaviors in school which are not really organizationally approved or expected. It is these that now must be explained.

The first of these unintended effects is that there seems to be *little student-teacher interaction* in the school. The downward communication flow, the massing of students, and the specialized task of the teacher are simply not conducive to interaction. In fact, the rules, regulations, and routine actually serve to substitute for interaction. If one is aware of them, he does not need to ask or check with the teacher to be sure he is doing the correct thing and can actually go through many consecutive days in school without being selected for anything individually, or even talking to a teacher. He may experience interaction with his teacher only when he violates some rule. Of course, this is certainly not approved.

Teachers and administrators constantly deprecate the fact and appeal for more student interaction. But wishing for it makes little sense if, at the same time, one is maintaining characteristics such as batch processing and downward communication flow which combine to deny it.

A second unintended effect is that there appears to be *little student involvement in formal activities*, either in class or in the extracurricular sector. In class it is the student's duty to wait for the teacher to start, be patient when his request for recognition is denied, accept the material he is given, study it in a teacher-approved manner, and, in general, keep himself orderly and obedient. Indeed, most of what is done in class is done by the teacher. The moving about, directing, talking, responding, and participating are primarily teacher performed. The students sit, watch, wait and listen.

That a few students take over the extracurricular sector seems proof that there is little student involvement, because even those few involved do little more than collect money, sell things, or decorate the halls. There, too, both teachers and even the students deprecate the fact of noninvolvement, but there seems to be no way to avoid it since other than athletics, the extracurricular sector demands so little.

The third unintended effect is the *fragmentation of experience* for students. This is in part a result of the compartmentalization of knowledge and the corresponding routine demands that a new activity begin every forty or fifty minutes. It is also a result of the way classes are run. A student may be called on to ask a question, provide an answer, or make a point. Still the pattern of classroom activity is set up so that the teacher does the talking, explaining, outlining, and assigning, even often times answering his own questions to be sure that the correct sequence of events is maintained. It is the teacher who articulates the total learning experience, not the student. This is probably, at least in part, a result of the assumption that talking is teaching and learning is listening, and what is heard is learned. This probably deserves more consideration than I am willing to give at this point. I am only suggesting that the apparent lack of student involvement in class may be a result of the fragmented way that both the individual classroom experiences and the entire school day is structured.

A fourth unintended effect is that the students can do well in school even if they give only *minimal compliance* to the system. If one will equate "doing well" with graduating and perhaps becoming accepted in college, all but three of the students studied have graduated, and the members of the athletic group and the music-drama group, and Roger, of Bill's friends, are presently in college. After all, one did not have to learn, he had only to appear to pay attention, hand in his papers, his or in some cases someone else's. The teachers who kept the subject matter between themselves and their students really had no way of discerning whether a student was learning, or the magnitude of his learning or nonlearning experience. The organizational demands did not overtly deny learning, they simply made little provision for it. There was little to encourage either a teacher or a student to get beneath the requests for orderliness, attention, and compliance.

Closely related to the idea of minimal compliance is the impression that students seemed more concerned with the routine, rules, and regulations of the institution, which constitute the maintenance subsystem, than with the assimilation of knowledge. One must understand what he is to do, not to do; where he is to go, not to go; and when he is supposed to both do and go. If he understands these things and complies with them to a reasonable degree, he will have little trouble with school.

In sum, there are a number of intended and unintended effects flowing from the socio-cultural characteristics of the organization. These are:

I. Intended effects
    A. Students are denied freedom.
    B. Students are massed.

    C.   Students are undifferentiated.

II. Unintended effects
    A.   Little student-teacher interaction
    B.   Little student involvement in formal activities
    C.   Fragmentation of educational experience
    D.   Minimal compliance on the part of students
    E.   Student concern for the maintenance subsystem

Conclusion

At this point, some attempt must be made to explain the total phenomenon. I would suggest that the students continue their out-of-school group affiliations in school simply because those affiliations can and do provide so much of what the organization denies. Whereas the school denies students freedom, masses and fails to differentiate them, keeps them powerless and in a state of spectatorship, provides little human interaction, and gives them primarily future-oriented and symbolic rewards, the groups themselves are rigidly segregated with little cross-communication, give students a degree of independence and power over their activity, and give them the immediate pleasure of participating in human interaction. This is not particularly revealing until the second part is added; that is, that the school, with its emphasis on teacher-initiated action, its routine, batch processing, and reliance on maintenance procedures, provides an enormous amount of time when students are actually required to do little other than be in attendance and minimally compliant. It is this that provides them with the time to carry on their group activity, and their group activity seems to consume over half the school day.

As consistently noted, these group activities are carried on in such a way that they do not interfere with the formal school processes. An individual student, therefore, is free to gain the future and symbolic rewards of grades and graduation promised by school, and the present rewards of participation and activity provided by group membership. To do that the students in their groups seem to have developed a perspective of noninvolvement with the general productive structure of the organization.

Of course, this was purposeful. It enabled the members to maintain their friendships in spite of differences in grades, amount of work done in class, and opinion of teachers, and in effect prevented the rupture of the group.

A second part of the students' perspective concerns the school's maintenance structure. Both individuals and groups give at least minimal compliance to that structure with its rules and regulations because doing so enables them to continue their activities without overt interference from the school. As long as the students are at least minimally complaint, there is no interference into private group activities by teachers and administrators. Of course, if an individual member is expelled or suspended from school, he would be excluded from the group.

The teachers at Horatio Gates recognize that the students associate with one another but do not seem to be aware that this consumes a major part of their day, and while they probably worry about the lack of student involvement, they do not seem to be aware that the school is simply unable to deal with or reward student involvement as effectively as do the groups. This serves to reinforce the process. When the students fail to get involved, the teachers make more of an effort to direct, take command, articulate, and structure the classes, which reinforces the organizational effects mentioned as being partly responsible for student noninvolvement.

These same socio-cultural characteristics of subject specialization, doctrine of adolescent inferiority, and so forth, which prevent student interaction with teachers also prevent the teachers from extensive interactions with students. They severely limit the teacher's range of possible behavior just as they do the students. As demonstrated, the teachers simply have no effective way to deal with individuals such as Joe, Red, or Roger, or even to assist friendless and isolated students such as Nick, Andy, or Marian.

I have observed and examined the phenomenon of student groupness and some of its effects on a single school. The conclusion is that this groupness, because it seemed to emerge from the observations and interviews so consistently, is not some temporary aberration from normal, student behavior. Rather, because people will develop a reasonable way of behaving and believing in any environment, there must be some basic reasons for the continued existence of it in that situation. After examining the school, I am suggesting that the tendency of the students at Horatio Gates to maintain tight, in-school groups was a natural, but unrecognized, consequence of the school's basic organizational structure. As long as the supporting structure exists, the students will probably continue to form groups and behave as the data indicated they did.

One additional point should be made. In a very real sense, the student groups were serving a maintenance function in the organization and thus were perpetuating that structure which fostered their existence. That is, they provided a socially acceptable outlet for the interest, enthusiasm, and involvement of the students and prevented the official structure from having to deal with those things. If the students had ever become excited and involved about learning as they were excited and involved with their in-group activities, the organization would have had to change its basic pattern. Therefore, the successful diffusion of student enthusiasm and energy into group interests and activities actually served to preserve the school's standard operating procedure.

Implications of the Findings

There are a number of reasons why I would prefer to be as careful as possible with implications. First of all, the project was based only on the senior class of one high school, and within that class I had direct contact with only about sixty students. While I watched or was told about many of the others, there were a large number whom I probably never saw.

There is also the question of whether the behavior of those seniors was similar to the behavior of the 726 sophomores and juniors in the school. I tried to get some indication of this by asking informants, "Did you behave

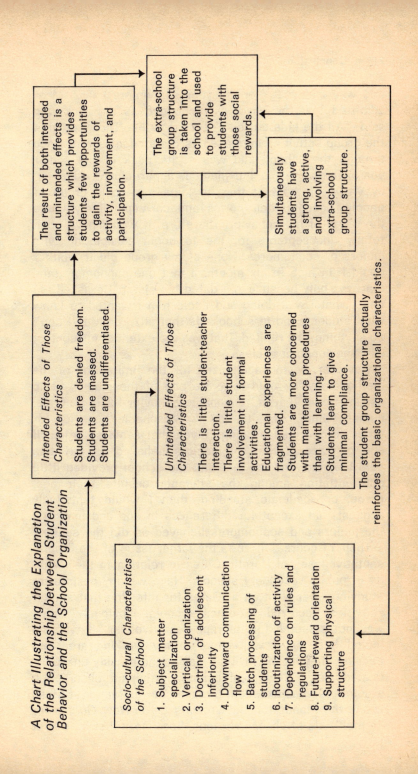

A Chart Illustrating the Explanation of the Relationship between Student Behavior and the School Organization

Socio-cultural Characteristics of the School

1. Subject matter specialization
2. Vertical organization
3. Doctrine of adolescent inferiority
4. Downward communication flow
5. Batch processing of students
6. Routinization of activity
7. Dependence on rules and regulations
8. Future-reward orientation
9. Supporting physical structure

Intended Effects of Those Characteristics

Students are denied freedom.
Students are massed.
Students are undifferentiated.

Unintended Effects of Those Characteristics

There is little student-teacher interaction.
There is little student involvement in formal activities.
Educational experiences are fragmented.
Students are more concerned with maintenance procedures than with learning.
Students learn to give minimal compliance.

The result of both intended and unintended effects is a structure which provides students few opportunities to gain the rewards of activity, involvement, and participation.

The extra-school group structure is taken into the school and used to provide students with those social rewards.

Simultaneously students have a strong, active, and involving extra-school group structure.

The student group structure actually reinforces the basic organizational characteristics.

this way last year," or "in your sophomore year." Most admitted that they had, or responded as did Jack who said, "All the kids do this." But a few like Dick said that the group activities increased as the students progressed through the school, and was at its peak in the senior year. Of course, as I explained, a participant observer, by virtue of the fact that he joins a specific group of people, accepts their norms and correspondingly limits the range of his behavior. Therefore, it would have been totally unacceptable for me to begin associating with juniors or sophomores. None of my group did it, neither could I. In fact, in six months I met one sophomore, and that was only because Jim dated his sister. He asked me once what I was doing and I told him I wanted to know what students did in school. "Is that all? . . . Me? I don't do anything," he replied. That was the extent of my contact with the sophomore class.

However, having apologized for the limitations of the methodology, I would reiterate one of the study's basic assumptions. That is, reasonable behavior for one normal human being in a situation is reasonable behavior for other normal human beings given that same situation. If one can accept that the seniors behaved as the data said they did, and the fact that the school provided little differentiation among the students despite their age, grade, or academic standing, then I would tentatively suggest that except for differences in age and maturity, the juniors and sophomores behaved as did the seniors.

Then, of course, there is the larger issue of the "representativeness" of Horatio Gates in relation to the majority of public secondary schools. Have we any basis after studying what went on at Gates for inferring that similar activities occurred in other schools. Obviously Gates was not selected for its representativeness, it was selected because it was close to my working area and because they let me in. That may sound grossly unsophisticated, but it is typical among participant observation studies. Even as excellent a researcher as Margaret Mead chose the Manus for her *Growing Up in New Guinea* for "a multitude of chance reasons, because a district officer recommended them as easy to deal with, because a missionary had published some texts in their language and because we were able to get a schoolboy in Rabaul to act as an interpreter in the beginning."[3]

However, based on my own experience as well as the literature of the field, I personally feel that Gates is not unlike most secondary schools simply because the characteristics which defined the Gates' environment, from compartmentalization of knowledge to the physical arrangement of the classrooms, are present in most other schools. However, for the purposes of this study, I feel neither obligated nor qualified to defend that feeling. It is only a tentative suggestion, and I would leave it up to an individual reader to determine whether or not his school is similar to Horatio Gates.

There is an additional reason why I wish to be careful. If upon reading this one concludes that students seemed to prefer peer-involvement to academic activities, the study might seem to support the wave of criticism leveled at the public schools. I would prefer to avoid this. While much of the criticism is at least partially justified, the purpose of this book remains to describe and explain, not to suggest remedies to help school people solve national social problems which show up so pointedly in public school settings.

My third reason for caution is that there are two very different ways in which these findings might be viewed. The first is that Horatio Gates is in general doing what it is supposed to do. That is, as a transmitter of our society's culture, it is really quite successful. Those who would defend this position, upon hearing the results of this study, might say "So kids hang around together. So what? We did the same thing and it didn't hurt us any. They'll do all right." It is true that if it were asked, "Were the students hurt by their patterns of inschool behavior?" one would have a hard time proving that they were. A year after graduation, Jim, Greg, Pete, Max, Dick,

[3] Margaret Mead, *Growing Up in New Guinea* (New York: Dell, 1968), p. 212.

Tony, Roger, Marilyn, Joan, Sally, and Kathy are all attending college. Ralph, Jack, Bob, and Bill are in the Armed Forces. Some of the others are working and/or married and two or three, such as Joe and Kim, I lost track of. So far they appear to have gone on in various sectors of society and will, in all likelihood, live out their lives in the American mainstream. Based on this we could conclude that their experience at Horatio Gates was reasonably successful.

Now, if one can accept this, then it is tantamount to regarding school primarily as a maintenance subsystem of the larger society. The primary duties of the maintenance subsystem in any organization are to (1) socialize new members, (2) teach and enforce society's reward structure, (3) give the society permanence, and (4) insure that the mechanisms designed to implement the productive structure of society are carried out smoothly and their disruption prevented.[4]

If we ask "Did Horatio Gates do these things?" I think that the answer would have to be "Yes." It did what it was supposed to do. It taught its students how to get along in an organizational society and to be the kind of people that organizations need. Those students who adjusted so well and with so much sophistication to Horatio Gates will have little difficulty adjusting equally well and with an equally acceptable degree of compliance to their jobs at General Motors, Sears, the U. S. Army, the New York State Electric and Gas Corporation, the A & P Company, Bell Telephone, or any of the large, impersonal, bureaucratic, future-reward–oriented organizations that make up the bulk of America's economic and social life. Horatio Gates, like those other organizations, demanded only a part of the whole person. Specifically, it demanded that students (1) accept a limited role, which required only part of their faculties for a set number of hours each day, (2) promised them future-oriented rewards in return, and (3) provided a not-unpleasant environment where they were free to exercise other faculties in search of other rewards as long as that activity did not interfere with the organization. They will be similarly free to do the same at work, and those who adjust well to the school-defined role of "student" will have little trouble adjusting to the factory-defined role of "worker," or the store-defined role of "salesman" or "consumer," or the state defined-role of taxpayer, voter, and law abiding citizen. Would the skills of acceptance and adjustment to organizational life be as effectively learned if the student stayed home with his parents, or if he accompanied his parents to work and emulated their activities? Probably not. Therefore, Horatio Gates did what it was supposed to do. That it contained a number of factory-like and bureaucratic-type characteristics, even including its shopping-center architecture, is no sheer accident. It emulated the society for which it prepared its students.

One can extend this line of thought even to the point of saying that a few students received the top rewards in Gates, just as a few will receive them in any organization. Dick, Tony, Jean, and Jack excelled at getting what there was to get at Gates, and blamed others for not sharing their enthusiasm. Is this significantly different from any organization where the top executives, secure in privileges and position, wonder why the "workers" do not identify strongly with the organization's goals, or do not give their all to the United Fund Drive?

I would say, "No, it is not significantly different." And I would conclude by suggesting that one might, after reading this book, infer that Horatio Gates, serving as a maintenance subsystem of the larger society, was an extremely successful educational enterprise. And if one might ask, "What about Nick?" I would only point out that nowhere in our society have we devised a solution to the problem of lonely and disaffected individuals.

There is a second and different set of conclusions that could be drawn from the findings. That is, to conclude that Horatio Gates, at least to some degree, has failed in its responsibility to its students. It has not accepted them as active participants in their own education;

rather it has systematically denied their involvement in basic, educational processes and relegated them to the position of watchers, waiters, order-followers, and passive receptacles for the depositing of disconnected bits of information. They, in turn, have responded by paying only a minimal amount of forced attention to "formal" educational processes and simultaneously channeled their energy and enthusiasm into their groups wherein lie the more immediate rewards of activity, interest, and involvement.

I expect that this would be a more acceptable set of inferences than was presented previously. There are a number of obvious reasons. First of all, the latter demands action, involvement, and commitment, and there are a tremendous number of people being paid good salaries to be active, involved, and committed to improving public schools. To tell these people that Horatio Gates is all right the way it is would be tantamount to telling the military that the country is secure.

However, they have a legitimate issue. As John Dewey pointed out:

> There is I think no point in the philosophy of progressive education which is sounder than its emphasis upon the importance of the participation of the learner in the formation of the purposes which direct his activities in the learning process.[5]

Dewey would have the learner assist in setting the purpose and no doubt in setting the means of the pursuit of the purpose, but it did not happen at Horatio Gates, not to any discernible degree, and that seems justification for examining the school to see how it perhaps might be changed. Those who support this view see sixteen to eighteen year olds being forced to sit in rows, denied the right to express themselves except with teacher approval, being made to wait for hall and lavatory passes, and being unable to leave the building for any other than

[5] John Dewey, *Experience and Education* (New York: Macmillan, 1956), p. 67.

a teacher accompanied activity. They probably think of Horatio Gates the way Friedenburg thought of Milgrim High, which he described as being enveloped in an atmosphere wherein "the fundamental pattern is still one of control, distrust and punishment."[6] Having deprecated the environment and the way that the Gates' students are behaving and having simultaneously accepted the functionalist explanation that the structure of the school is responsible for that behavior, then one must become specific in terms of what to change. Unfortunately, the critics are no better equipped to deal with this question than are the professional school people who are the presumed perpetrators of foul deeds.

However, there are changes already taking place in public high schools. Over the last two years many have ceased feeling responsible for students' hair and have totally given up the idea of dress codes, are seriously questioning and will probably drop their pass systems, are working hard to provide student areas where all students will be free to go, and if they persist in having study halls, are providing both "noisy" and "quiet" atmospheres.

A second level of change that is also occurring in many public high schools is a move toward a more variable scheduling pattern designed to provide more latitude in the length, size, number, and spacing of classes according to the "nature of the subject, the type of instruction and the level of ability and interest of pupils."[7] This was basically what Mr. Summers had in mind in his humanities class, an innovation which is also currently being adopted by many other high schools. Implicit in this change is the idea that the range of possible behaviors open to the teacher must be expanded if students are to be provided more opportunities for learning.

Added to these changes in the school's curriculum are

[6] Edgar Friedenburg, *Coming of Age in America* (New York: Random House, Vintage Books, 1965), p. 36.

[7] Robert Bush and Dwight Allen, *A New Design for High School Education* (New York: MacGraw-Hill, 1964), p. 8.

staff changes. Schools are presently adding a greater variety of audio-visual aids, teacher assistants, and some sort of differentiated teaching staff which hopefully will provide the students with more opportunities for teacher interaction, individualized attention, and a wider range of adults with whom the students may interact. In addition, a number of schools have implemented or are seriously considering the possibility of college-type class selection with the students being allowed to enroll for courses as they wish, with an increased effort on the teacher's part to make their offerings more palatable.

But the task here is not to enumerate specific changes or even to become an advocate of one type of change. Rather, the issue is to ask the question: "Can any of these changes make a behavioral difference in the students at Gates?" Will Jim and Greg behave any differently in a school with a flexible-modular schedule? Will Bill and his friends continue to spend their school time discussing their hubcap stealing if there is more A.V. equipment and a differentiated staff? Will Nick receive more recognition from his classmates or will Sam be allowed to freely participate in a school with open class selection procedures? All of these questions, I would answer with a qualified "No." The country's public education system is not in a state of imminent demise, and it is highly unlikely that, except for a few isolated experiments, secondary schools will be disestablished. For the foreseeable future we will continue to have a secondary education system consisting of large schools where the characteristics of teacher specialization, doctrine of adolescent inferiority, and future-reward orientation will continue, even while under attack, if for no other reason than combined, they provide a basis for orderly processes in our complex and dependent-on-order society. As long as that situation exists, the students will be in a position to seek and discover activity, involvement, and participation from one another in any setting and there will be little that the school can do to either discourage that phenomenon or channel it into the pursuit of more formal educational goals. Is that bad? I do not think so. While some of it may appear to be inconsistent with our stated ideals, it seems to me that the best and worst of any society can be seen most clearly in those formal processes by which it transmits itself to succeeding generations. As conflicts, inconsistencies, and even hypocrisies are evident in our public schools, so they are probably endemic to us and our civilization.

Summary and Discussion of Chapter 8

Finally, there are three questions which I would like to raise, discuss briefly, and suggest answers to for those who work in or plan to work in public schools. Number one is: "Can we expect a reasonable resolution to the conflict between those who see schools as maintainers of society and those who see schools as changers or perhaps producers of a new society?" I would say "No." Schools really are set up to maintain society. They are supposed to keep the present world before them as a model and train their young charges to take respectable places in that world. But, on the other hand, society never stands still and, because they deal with the young, schools are integrally bound up in the processes of change. Therefore, perhaps schools should be more free, more open, more liberal in the hope of preparing the young not for the fleeting present, but for a future in which they will have to work out their own lives, not the lives envisaged for them by the maintainers of the present society. The conflict between the two views is endemic to civilization. We set up schools in the hope that through institutionalization the processes of growth and change can be made procedural and orderly. But pain and conflict are inevitable accompaniers of change, and cannot be alleviated through rational organizations. There is simply no solution to the conflict, and teachers and administrators, regardless of their personal views on the matter, will continue to face that conflict every day of their professional careers.

The second question is: "How can a teacher best conduct himself in relation to informal student associations?" Personally, I think the best teaching takes place when the teacher accepts his role as subject matter specialist, accepts the difference between himself and the students, and utilizes his status advantage to concentrate his efforts on instruction. That sounds simple, but I find few teachers who do it. Many confuse their instructional role with attempts to be a friend, personal adviser, confidant, or critic of students' personal behavior. Then instead of keeping the subject before them, they spend their time watching the students to see what they want, trying to utilize the student groups to attain their own ends, or moralizing about students' personal behavior and associations which are none of their business. I think those who succeed best in public schools are those who are perhaps the most conservative in their view of their role, the most liberal in their acceptance of students.

The third question is: "How can we change the role of the teacher—or perhaps, even the school?" First, I want to point out that I didn't say, nor am I sure, that it has to be changed. I ask this question to give cognizance to my friends who keep using that word, not to advance a position. The answer for those who want one is, one has to deal with the basic structure of the organization. Personal counseling, teacher training and retraining, even group sensitivity sessions won't change the school. The factors listed as "organizational characteristics" have to be considered and dealt with as they constitute an entire system. When considering them, remember they reinforce each other, so changing one without changing the others will not result in a difference.

I think teachers should (1) be prepared to accept the school as a place where conflict is inevitable, (2) keep their instructional role primary and avoid confusing it with maintenance details or personal issues, and (3) if one doesn't like the way schools are and wants to change them, he should start with the basic structure and be prepared to give up some of the traditional power and privileges of the teacher.

Appendix
on the Methodology

The methodology used in any research should be intrinsically related to the basic assumptions about the nature of the phenomena to be studied. Accordingly, an explanation of the methodology used in this work should begin with a brief discussion of the theory of symbolic interaction.

According to Herbert Blumer:

> The term "symbolic interaction" refers, of course, to the peculiar and distinctive character of interaction as it takes place between human beings. The peculiarity consists in the fact that human beings interpret or "define" each others' actions instead of merely reacting to each others' actions. Their "response" is not made directly to the actions of one another but instead is based on the meaning which they attach to such actions. Thus, human interaction is mediated by the use of symbols, by interpretation, or by ascertaining the meaning of one another's actions.[1]

An individual is conceived of as an acting unit engaged in the longitudinal process of constructing his action through constant interaction with his environment. Extended to a number of individuals, collective action takes place as those individuals, seeking social rewards such as esteem, status, and recognition, ascertain the directions of others' acts and then fit their lines of action together. A collectivity, then, is an acting unit made up of individ-

[1] Herbert Blumer, "Society as Symbolic Interaction," in Arnold Rose, ed., *Human Behavior and Social Processes* (Boston: Houghton Mifflin, 1962), p. 180.

uals who are themselves acting units. Just as an individual guides his actions according to his interpretation of his surroundings, so collectivities as acting units guide themselves according to the members' perceived, shared understandings of the environment. Collectivities such as groups also engage in the process of constructing their action within their environment.

As Becker *et al.* explained, the members of a collectivity will create a perspective. They will:

> develop ideas that, because they are held in common, create a universe of discourse, a common frame of reference in which communication may take place. Similarly, they develop, as they interact in a variety of institutional settings and specific situations, patterns of individual and collective activity. The activities grow out of the ideas being their logical extensions in actions. They also give weight and meaning to the ideas by creating patterns of everyday experience that made the ideas seem reasonable and appropriate to the situations they are applied to. In this sense, the ideas grow out of the activities.[2]

Analytically, the group perspective may be broken into (a) a description of the environment within which the group exists, (b) the rewards that the members of the group may strive for in the environment, (c) the proper modes of individual behavior in the group and in the environment, and (d) criteria against which group members and others may be judged. Of course, as the situation changes, it is likely that parts of the perspective will also change. Thus, in this case the individual students and the groups developed a number of situationally specific perspectives for dealing with various facets of the school as well as for dealing with each other.

The original questions asked in this study were, "What do the adolescents do in school?" "How do they perceive and react to each other, and the various facets of the school environment?" "How do they view themselves as

---

[2] Howard S. Becker, Blanche Greer, and Everett Hughes, *Making the Grade* (New York: Wiley, 1968), p. 28.

students?," or, in short, what are the perspectives they use to deal with what they perceive to be the social reality of the school environment?

These questions, of course, lead directly to the methodology. Again, according to Blumer, the procedure suitable for studying a dynamic, social situation is "to approach the study of group activity through the eyes and experience of people who have developed the activity. Hence, it necessarily requires an intimate familiarity with this experience and with the scenes of its operation."[3] He goes on to say: "The study of action would have to be made from the position of the actor. Such action is forged by the actor out of what he perceives, interprets and judges; one would have to see the operating situation as the actor sees it. You have to define and interpret the objects as the actor interprets them."[4] Having accepted the perspective and even the social reality, not as a static entity but as a creative process, it is the task of the researcher to actually take part in the process of creation. He simply cannot stand outside and make judgments about it. Again, according to Blumer:

> The objective approach holds the danger of the observer substituting his view of the field of action for the view held by the actor. It is unnecessary to add that the actor acts toward his world on the basis of how he sees it and not of the basis of how that world appears to the outside observer.[5]

The research methodology which enables the researcher to get closest to the social situation from the actor's point of view is participant observation.

A participant observer in the field is at once reporter, interviewer, and scientist. On the scene he gets the

[3] Herbert Blumer, "Sociological Analysis and the Variable," *American Sociological Review*, Vol. 21 (Dec. 1966), p. 689.

[4] Herbert Blumer, "Sociological Implications of the Thought of George Herbert Mead," *American Journal of Sociology,* Vol. 71 (March 1966), p. 542.

[5] Blumer, "Sociological Implications of the Thought of George Herbert Mead," p. 542.

story of an event by questioning participants about what is happening and why. He fills out the story by asking people about their relation to the event, their reactions, opinions, and evaluation of its significance. As an interviewer, he encourages an informant to tell his story, or supply an expert account of an organization or group. As scientist he seeks answers to questions, setting up hypotheses and collecting data with which to test them.[6]

The methodology works at two levels—(1) Description: the researcher on the scene describes what he reads, sees, and hears and then expands his descriptions from accounts of the situation by his subjects, and (2) Explanation: the researcher attempts to make sense of his subjects' observations, and by further searching and questioning of informants, he obtains the explanation of the situation from the actors. Participant observation then, (1) describes a social situation through the senses of the researcher and his subjects, and (2) explains the situation from the point of view of both the researcher and his subjects. Since the researcher is in part a principal, in him these two levels are combined.

As a researcher immerses himself in the situation, he simultaneously formulates tentative or working hypotheses, and as he continues his field work so he attempts to gather data which will either substantiate or contradict those hypotheses. Thus he is in the constant process of refining his hypotheses. The question always arises, "When may one safely withdraw from the situation with the assurance that his description and his explanation is adequate to answer his basic questions?" There is no single rule which will apply to all situations, but when the researcher finds that his continually refined hypotheses seem to explain the phenomenon, then he may withdraw.

In this work I began in September to think that the in-group relations were the main topic of conversation with my subjects, but I was fearful that their conversations were a result of my presence at least to some degree. However, by the end of November they had still not

[6] Blanche Greer, "First Days in the Field," in Phillip E. Hammond, ed., *Sociologist at Work* (New York: Doubleday, 1964), p. 383.

mentioned anything academic, and I began to conclude that it was simply the way they chose to behave. I could not believe that they had been putting on a show for me over a three month period, not when the total accumulation of data so consistently pointed to the fact that none of the groups dealt directly with the academic sector of the school.

It may be unnecessary to mention the fact that participant observation is not meant to determine the final answer to any social phenomenon, rather it is purely exploratory and is to be used in cases where little work has been done. The final product of the study is the tentative explanation of social behavior which may be used to generate hypotheses for further testing. The end of the participant observer's work is the beginning of someone else's.

There are two standard objections to participant observation studies. One is that participant observation studies, dealing with a limited and perhaps unique sample, may be ungeneralizable. The reply is that while an instance of social phenomena may be unique, that need not prevent one from learning about and from it by intelligent study. That is, one should not have to duplicate or recreate the Battle of Saratoga to understand the lessons therein. While a situation may be unique, human reaction to it may be quite common. A basic humanness transcends social settings and enables one living in New Jersey to understand and appreciate both Greek drama and Etruscan art. The uniqueness, therefore, lies in the social setting and not in the human reaction, and a good description of a social phenomenon, however unique, may be quite intelligible to one who never participated.

A second oft-repeated objection has to do with the absence of standardized tests of validity and reliability. This involves some explanation. Some researchers assume that social reality is objective and can be perceived by someone living close to and observing it. Others adhere to symbolic interaction and assume that participants actually create their own social reality, and, in order to understand it, should actually take part in that creation.

I believe more strongly in the latter, but either way the strength of the methodology comes out. As one lives close to a situation, his description and explanation of it have a first-person quality which other methodologies lack. As he continues to live close to and moves deeper into that situation his perceptions have a validity that is simply unapproachable by any so-called standardized method. Likewise, as his validity becomes better, so his reliability, which is an extension of his validity, becomes better. As the researcher is the actual instrument, as he becomes more aware, more valid, so he must of necessity become more reliable.

To produce a worthwhile study a researcher should endeavor to tailor his work to the six indices of subjective adequacy stated by Homans. (1) Time: the more time an individual spends with a group the more likely it is that he will obtain an accurate perception of the social meaning its members live by. (2) Place: the closer the researcher works geographically to the people he studies, the more accurate should be his interpretations. (3) Social circumstances: the number and variety of social circumstances which the observer encounters within the social structure of the community increase his accuracy. (4) Language: the researcher and his subjects should share a common language. (5) Intimacy: the greater degree of intimacy the researcher achieves, the greater his accuracy. (6) Consensus: confirmation that the meanings interpreted by the observer are correct.[7] With these six indices in mind, the researcher who undertakes a participant observation study would have some assurance that his findings reach an acceptable degree of validity.

The real proof, however, is in the presentation of the data. For that reason one reporting such a study must present his findings in extensive narrative form. It is especially important to avoid over-inferring in the data chapter. The writer must allow the reader to draw his

[7] See Severyn T. Bruyn, *The Human Perspective in Sociology: The Methodology of Participant Observation* (Englewood Cliffs, N. J.: Prentice-Hall, 1966), p. 181.

own conclusions from the data as he presents that data in as realistic and complete a manner as possible. In fact, this is a major test of validity. If as others who are engaged in similar situations upon reading the data agree that "that is the way it is," so the researcher's findings demonstrate a higher degree of validity.

Under the heading of participant observation are a number of variations, best stated by Lutz and Iannaccone who explained that "a researcher who undertakes a participant observation study may assume one of three roles:

1. "The participant as an observer": In this case the researcher already has his group membership before he undertakes a study and therefore his role as observer or researcher would be unknown to his subjects.
2. "The observer as a limited participant": The observer would join a group for the expressed purpose of studying it. The members would, perhaps more than likely, know of the researcher's intent in joining the group.
3. "The observer as a non-participant": That is, without group membership. Here the presence of the observer may not even be known to the group and if it were known, he would still be outside the group.[8]

In this project I used primarily the second role. My entrance into the group was explained on the basis of my role as an observer, so there was no question of my intent or function. However, as I gained increasing empathy with the group, I approached role number one; that is, I was accepted more as a member than as a researcher.

By way of preparing myself to carry on such a project and to test my ability, I undertook a one month's study

[8] See Frank W. Lutz and Laurence Iannaccone, *Understanding Educational Organizations: A Field Study Approach* (Columbus, Oh.: Merrill, 1969), p. 108.

in a Catholic high school in the same area. Permission was granted by the superintendent and the principal who suggested that I concentrate on a particular lower-academic track of students that spent most of their day in the same classes. They described the students as "interesting" and some of them as "very intelligent, but without motivation." They hoped that I "could find something about them that would help the principal relate to them better." I was then introduced to six students, three boys and three girls, from the track. I explained that I was from the university, wanted to find out what they did in school, and asked their permission to follow them through their day for a period of a month.

"You want to follow us?"

"To see what we do?"

"We don't do anything." (With laughter)

"O.K., sure, come on."

Throughout the month I arrived at the school at 8:20 a.m. each day, Monday through Friday, attended classes in English, history, math, language, the study halls, and ate in the cafeteria with them. I even participated in gym class. In the first few days it became evident that two of these boys, to whom I was originally introduced, were part of a group which stayed together most of the day. They passed to classes together, ate together, took their study hall together in a non-work study hall, obtained the same general level of marks, from high sixties to high seventies, and associated with one another outside school. I stayed with that same group for the entire period of the study and was actually accepted much more quickly than at Gates. It was only a week before I was asked to go into the john for a forbidden smoke and invited to the Sunday afternoon beer picnic. The results are not the subject of this paper, but when the study under consideration was begun, I had already had a similar experience and was in a position to have some knowledge of what to expect, how to act, and what to do.

This project began officially on September 10. I had been in contact with the school district superintendent who agreed it would be a worthwhile study and said that

I should talk to the principal. With that assurance, I sought and obtained an interview with Mr. Vincent who was also amenable to the idea. Both men readily understood my wishes to be with the students as they carried on their daily activities and neither displayed the least bit of nervousness about my intent to penetrate the student subculture. Both understood that the focus was to be on the students and their perceptions of the school. The principal then invited me to come into the school "in a week or so after we start . . . to give us time to get settled." He also agreed to notify the teachers that the study would be done.

Thus far, with neither the principal nor with the superintendent had I discussed the students on which I would concentrate. Certainly in a school of 1100 students one could never establish a relationship with all of them. When the vice-principal suggested that the study be done on the senior class because of two interesting innovations, the humanities program and the impact of the new student lounge, I agreed. He added that "It was a good class, one with a lot of spirit."

Having made the decision to study the senior class of the school and having obtained permission of the administrators and teachers to do so, my next step was to approach the students. The vice-principal suggested I introduce myself during the September class meeting. Therefore, on September 15, first period, I went into the auditorium where the class was assembled and after other business was taken care of, I got up and explained briefly that I was from the university and doing a study on the way the students react in school. I made a few comments on going to school for a while and on the questions I would be asking.

I finished, and the president returned, recapped the meeting with an account of the new committee, and the bell rang. When I got up to leave with the crowd, no one even looked at me. Outside everyone seemed to go his way, and I went back to the vice-principal. Not knowing what to do next, I asked him to introduce me to some specific students. He took me to Mr. Summers, head of the English department. More explanations followed—to him, to the head of the social studies department, to a student teacher, to a music and drama teacher. I took pains to assure them that I was focusing on the students, not on teachers, and that I would cooperate with them to the extent of telling them what was important for them to know. I had expected to find them somewhat threatened about my wanting to sit in their classes, but was frankly surprised at their openness and lack of concern for some hidden motive. In fact, at no time during the entire study did any teacher refuse me permission to come into his classes. Three times I got replies that there was not much going on for a while and an invitation to come back when something exciting was occurring; but when I told them that I was not concerned about them but about what the students were doing in classes, they readily agreed to let me in.

Mr. Summers, after discussing my particular need for some senior boys to associate with, asked Mr. Tomaso or, "How about Jim, Greg and maybe Rick? That's a good group. Jim's sort of a leader."

Tomaso said, "Yeah, but all he'd meet would be the football players."

"Well, he has to start somewhere."

Mr. Summers told me to wait in his office until after fourth period started. He would send in Jim, Greg, and Rick, and I could tell them what I wanted.

Soon Jim, Greg, and Rick walked in and introduced themselves. "Mr. Summers sent us in, said you wanted to talk to us."

I explained that I wanted to follow them for a period of time to see what they did in school and they had been recommended as those who knew their way around. They nodded. I asked them if I could start the following morning; they agreed to this also. I asked what classes they had. As it turned out they all started the day with a different class; I was disappointed but realized this was bound to occur and elected to go to the ceramics class with Jim the first period, the language class with Greg second period, and the match class with both for the third

from the top, that is, with the approval and consent of the superintendent, principal, teachers, and high status students, I feel I was granted access that an entering student would never have gained. At the same time that I came, a boy transferred in from another school. To all appearances he was a pleasant, well-dressed, intelligent person, but it was not until January that I saw him begin to interact regularly with a number of other students. If I had attempted to disguise myself as a student, it may have taken me much longer to gain access into a group, and I may have never gained access into a group as prestigious as the "athletes."

In general while in the school, my field work used six major approaches. (1) Attendance at classes: I made it a point to attend the classes that those students whom I knew attended. This ran from calculus to ceramics to automechanics to humanities. (2) Attendance at meetings such as student council, prom committee, drama club, ski club, yearbook, and newspaper meetings. (3) Informal interviewing: As I moved through the halls, the lounge, the classes, the cafeteria, I would talk to various students about what they were doing or where they were going. (4) Formal interviewing: Toward the end of the study I interviewed twenty-two students and teachers to test my general perceptions. (5) Use of records, such as honor roll, activity lists, club membership lists, past yearbooks, and old newspapers. These were used as background material. And, of course, (6) observation.[9] There is no substitute for being on the scene. At the end of each days field work, I would sit down and type everything that occurred that day. Needless to say, it was a long and painful process before I became reasonably accomplished at the art of remembering and recording events and conversations.

All these notes were compiled into 550 pages in addition to all the records, papers, and so forth collected during the time. The notes, as Becker suggests, were

---

[9] These six approaches are similar to those suggested by Herbert Gans, *The Urban Villagers* (New York: Free Press, 1962), p. 338.

classified and coded according to the event, participants, physical setting, time of occurrences, and reaction of the participants.[10] The events and statements of belief which occurred with greatest frequency were combined into tentative perspectives concerning particular situations. Subsequently each tentative perspective was checked by directly asking the group members or others about its applicability to a particular situation. The perspectives that were verified by the subjects were considered to be a part of the total set of perspectives.

Learning how to behave as a student was a difficult but valuable experience. Although a secondary school teacher for several years, I really didn't understand the student perspective. I thought I did—most teachers think they do —but I didn't and neither do they. The problem is that teachers get locked in their role and spend their school time living up to their own, their colleagues', or the students' expectations, and there is simply no opportunity for them to cast off their images and drift into the students world. It is too bad, really. I, personally, found it to be of tremendous value and I know that what I learned while on the student's side of the desk made me a better teacher.

[10] Becker, Geer, and Hughes, *Making the Grade*, p. 67.

Bibliography

Becker, Howard S., Geer, Blanche, and Hughes, Everett, 1968, *Making the Grade.* New Work: John Wiley & Sons.

Blumer, Herbert, 1962, "Society as Symbolic Interaction," in Arnold M. Rose, ed., *Human Behavior and Social Processes.* Boston: Houghton Mifflin Company.

———, 1966, "Sociological Analysis and the Variable." *American Sociological Review,* Vol. 21 (December), pp. 683–690.

———, 1966, "Sociological Implications of the Thought of George Herbert Mead." *American Journal of Sociology,* Vol. 71 (March), pp. 535–544.

Bruyn, Severry T., 1966, *The Human Perspective in Sociology: The Methodology of Participant Observation.* Englewood Cliffs, N.J.: Prentice-Hall.

Bush, Robert, and Allen, Dwight, 1964, *A New Design for High School Education.* New York: McGraw-Hill.

Coleman, James, 1962, *The Adolescent Society.* New York: The Free Press.

Deyoung, Chris A., 1955, *Introduction to American Public Education,* 3d ed. New York: McGraw-Hill.

Dewey, John, 1956, *Experience and Education.* New York: The Macmillan Company.

———, 1916, *Democracy and Education.* New York: The Macmillan Company.

Friedenberg, Edgar, 1965, *Coming of Age in America.* New York: Random House, Vintage Books.

Gans, Herbert, 1962, *The Urban Villagers.* New York: The Free Press.

———, 1969, *Levittowners.* New York: Random House, Vintage Books.

Geer, Blanche, 1964, "First Days in the Field," in Phillip E. Hammond, ed., *Sociologist at Work.* New York: Doubleday & Company.

Gordon, C. W., 1957, *The Social System of the High School.* New York: The Free Press.

Hollingshead, August B., 1949, *Elmtown's Youth.* New York: John Wiley & Sons.

Katz, Daniel, and Kahn, Robert, 1967, *The Social Psychology of Organizations.* New York: John Wiley & Sons.

Liewbow, Elliot, 1967, *Tally's Corner.* Boston: Little, Brown & Company.

Lutz, Frank W., and Iannaccone, Laurence, 1969, *Understanding Educational Organizations: A Field Study Approach.* Columbus, Oh.: Charles E. Merrill Books.

Mead, George H., 1934, *Mind, Self, & Society: From the Standpoint of a Social Behaviorist.* Chicago: University of Chicago Press.

Mead, Margaret, 1968, *Growing Up in New Guinea.* New York: Dell Publishing Company.

Shibutani, Tamotsu, 1967, "Reference Groups as Perspectives," in Jerome G. Manis and Bernard N. Meltzer, eds., *Symbolic Interaction.* Boston: Allyn and Bacon.

Stinchcombe, Arthur, 1964, *Rebellion in a High School.* Chicago: Quadrangle Books.

Whyte, William F., 1967, *Street Corner Society.* Chicago: University of Chicago Press.

Nick, 67, 164–167

Organization, assumptions
about, 13–14
characteristics of, 56
effects of, 209–213, 217
structure of, 13–14
subsystems of, 18–19

Participation observation. *See*
Appendix
Perspective, defined, 2–3
explained, 214–215
Pete, background of, 82
friends of, 66
Power clique, 153–156
according to Marilyn, 68–70
vice-principal and, 70
Principal, 20
cafeteria boycott and, 63–64
Greg and, 103
humanities program and, 32
Jim and, 103
school organization and, 22
smoking and, 20
students and, 36
teachers and, 20–25, 31–32
Productive subsystem, 18–19
Psychology class, 61–62

Ralph, 82
Rick, background of, 81
Jack and, 87
Roger, 53
background of, 124
groups and, 140–141

Sam, 168–169
Shibutani, Tamotsu, 2
Smoking, 20, 25, 197
Steve, background of, 125
Stinchcombe, Arthur, 207
Student Council, 73
meeting of, 194–197
Student group interactions,
157–162, 177–180

Students, general background
and behavior of, 41–49
maintenance details and,
61–63
Symbolic interaction, 205
defined, 227
Teachers, and administrators,
20–25
classroom behavior of, 25–
30
community and, 33–34
role of, 35–38
student groups and, 183–
184, 200–203, 159–161
student lounge and, 185
students and, 29–31, 49–56

Testing, 16–17
of students, 63
Time schedule, 17, 48–49
students and, 42–44
Tom, background of, 125
Tony, athletes and, 185–186
background of, 145
class meeting and, 189–191
as class president, 72

Valedictorian, 15
See also Jean
Vice-principal, athletes and,
101–102
athletes' academic ability
and, 81
cafeteria boycott and, 63–64
class leaders and, 185
class meeting and, 186–189
discipline and, 24
humanities program and, 32
Mrs. J. and, 34, 37
lounge and, 24
power clique and, 70
smoking and, 25
students and, 25, 37
teachers and, 23, 31–32

Whyte, William F., quoted, 7
Winnsboro, described, 8–9